From a Mount

A Monk's Journey

LAMA YESHE LOSAL RINPOCHE

PENGUIN LIFE

AN IMPRINT OF

PENGUIN BOOKS

PENGUIN LIFE

UK | USA | Canada | Ireland | Australia
India | New Zealand | South Africa

Penguin Life is part of the Penguin Random House group of companies
whose addresses can be found at global.penguinrandomhouse.com.

First published 2020
001

Copyright © Lama Yeshe Losal Rinpoche, 2020

The moral right of the author has been asserted

Set in 12/14.75pt Dante MT Std
Typeset by Jouve (UK), Milton Keynes
Printed and bound in Great Britain by Clays Ltd, Elcograf S.p.A.

A CIP catalogue record for this book is available from the British Library

ISBN: 978-0-241-43927-2

This book is dedicated to my root *guru* His Holiness the Sixteenth Karmapa and to my brother Chöje Akong Tulku Rinpoche. It is thanks to their wisdom, compassion and tolerance that I became the person I am now. If you find anything in this story useful, it is down to them. The proceeds from the book will be equally divided between the offices of His Holiness the Seventeenth Karmapa and the third Akong *tulku*, once he is found and recognized.

Contents

Introduction   ix

1. A child of Tibet   1
2. Ritual and resistance   18
3. Return to the monastery   28
4. Escape   48
5. Crisis   69
6. Refugee   85
7. Outsider   103
8. Rebel   121
9. Wild days in the USA   139
10. Transformation   157
11. Teacher   179
12. Mystic   198
13. Rinpoche   218
14. The great test   228
15. More work to do . . .   238

Glossary   250
Reading list   255
Acknowledgements   257

Introduction

I was born in a place where there were no roads or motor vehicles to travel on them; no electricity, no radios to bring us the news; no shops or schools. My village was home to twelve families and the animals we tended. I was born as the tide of the Second World War was turning in favour of the Allies, and the Chinese civil war that would lead to victory for the Communists was resuming. As a child I knew nothing of the tumultuous times that were encroaching on my idyllic world. I didn't see a car until I was fifteen years old, and when I did it appeared to me as an inexplicable marvel. It was being driven by a Chinese soldier.

Since then I have lived in the monastery where my brother was abbot, high on the freezing desert plains of eastern Tibet. I have lived in a refugee camp on the border between Tibet and India, then in a cramped flat in 1960s Delhi, in a draughty Victorian hunting lodge when I arrived in the UK, and in swanky private houses in London and New York. I have spent years living in a bare cell in solitary retreat, and many more years in the Buddhist monastic community of Samye Ling that my brother co-founded in the late 1960s.

Now I am an old man of seventy-seven and I still live at Samye Ling, which has been my home for most of my life. The view from my window is of green rolling hills, as it was when I was a child, but now I live near Lockerbie in Scotland and the Tibet of my childhood is no more.

My life has been far longer than I ever expected, and I am

content when I survey its contours. Every turn, however challenging or unexpected, has brought me to this place where I am able to offer reassurance and guidance to anyone who is seeking peace. This is my most deeply held wish: that more and more people will begin to tame their unquiet minds so that they may be able to live joyfully and to offer compassion to every living being on this Earth.

During my time as a teacher, many people have come to me with stories of hopelessness. They are so disheartened that they genuinely believe they have no chance of freeing themselves from their issues. They feel too much has already gone wrong in their lives. They tell me about the traumas they are carrying – the difficult childhood, the parent who was not there for them, the youthful transgressions, abusive or failed relationships, the addiction or bereavement – all the messy things of life that have left them feeling like a failure, or irredeemably hurt and lost.

I reply that their stories may appear to them to represent reality but that I see things, and see *them*, quite differently. I insist that change is possible for every single one of us, however broken or exhausted we may feel. It's not easy, I know, but each difficult experience we have struggled with, every challenge we face, is the raw material for our transformation. All our sorrow, suffering and confusion can be the basis for our unique process of change. Nobody is beyond hope.

Sometimes the person's response is that this may be true for someone like me – a *lama*, a holy man, born into a culture in which Buddhism was part of everyday life – but it doesn't apply to *them*. They say to me, 'Lama Yeshe, you are not like me; I am not like you.' The implication always seems to be that they are destined to remain stuck, while I was born with some mystical faculty for evading suffering which they themselves lack.

This is not the case. I'm not that different and am certainly not special. Not at all.

It is true that I was born into a religious feudal system, and that I fled my homeland at the age of fifteen when it was invaded by the Chinese military. I was one of a party of around 300 people that left our country to escape over the Himalayas, and one of a group of only thirteen who reached the safety of the border with India, many months later. Those experiences, I will admit, are unusual.

But, then again, I have been a refugee, an immigrant, an Asian man living in a small town where there were few other Asians. Those experiences are not so unusual. Millions of people have lived them. And I have felt deep frustration and resentment, have been a disappointment to my immediate family and myself, a layabout without sense of purpose, a man desperately searching for peace. I have been selfish, self-indulgent, a failure. I have lost the person I loved most in the world. All that, I suggest to anyone who tries to tell me why I am so different, makes me just like them.

Perhaps the only thing that does distinguish me from many of those people I speak to (mainly Westerners) is that I have spent many years purifying my mind to enable it to settle easily into positivity rather than cling to negativity. It has not been an easy task, but I never thought it was impossible, because I have faith in the essentially positive nature of the mind. In Buddhism, mind is king. If we can change our mental orientation then everything else will follow.

This understanding is the opposite of what I've come to think of as the typical Western mindset. I've never forgotten the man who described himself to me as 'damaged goods'. I could see the powerful hold that this idea of his own flawed nature had on him and it shocked me, because it was so alien to the way I view myself, other people and the world. In Buddhism we start from the understanding that there is always a part of us that is perfect and perfectly at peace. At the core of every human being is not sin or some sort of void but an innate goodness and intelligence. We call this Buddha Nature.

It has been my life's work to find that part of myself in order that I might demonstrate to others that they too have the potential to find their own, and so bring about personal transformation. When such change is sought sincerely, for the express purpose of bringing more peace and happiness into the wider world, it will always come to pass. May this book offer hope and guidance to all who seek them.

1. A child of Tibet

My earliest memory is of playing with my friends. Our game was killing birds.

I don't recall whose idea it was or whether we were competing to see whose hunting skills were the best. Probably we were bored and looking for something to do, full of the restless excitement typical of children all over the world. We had no toys, which were unknown in our society, and no schoolteachers to direct our energies. Our parents were hard at work in the fields and we had nothing to do but go in search of amusement. I do remember the feel of the catapult in my hand and my pride in my skill when the small stone struck a bird and it fell to the ground.

We all knew it was wrong. Of course we did. 'Do not kill' is one of the Five Precepts that every Buddhist person is enjoined to uphold. Those precepts – to abstain from killing any living being, from stealing, sexual misconduct, lying and intoxication – were a fact of life. No adult in my village would kill any creature, even for meat. So part of our excitement was about transgression. We had taken ourselves off to the edge of the village, to the banks of the river, where we would not be detected. One of us swiped at the reeds to send the birds flying up in panic and another aimed his catapult to bring down his prey. All of us shouted in glee when somebody hit a strike. I don't think we were considering, even for a second, how the birds felt. I know I wasn't. I don't remember feeling any remorse, either at the time or later. If we had ever been discovered we would have been punished, but nobody ever found out.

It is not comfortable, this memory. Neither is the fact that it was not the last time I would break the commandment not to kill. But I acknowledge that I have not lived a life free of error. Far from it. This, I believe, is what makes my life potentially instructive.

I was born and grew up in a tiny mountain village named Darak. It lay at the junction of two of the biggest rivers in Tibet, the Ngom-chu and the Dza-chu, which go on to become the Mekong. Our province was called Kham, in eastern Tibet. As a child I knew that Chamdo, the province's principal town, was a day's ride away and that the monastery of Dolma Lhakang lay some three days travel by horse to the west. Beyond that, at a vast distance, was Lhasa, the capital city. Neither I nor my immediate family had ever been there, but we received news from the merchants who arrived to sell their goods and from the occasional lama, or priest, passing through on his way to or from his monastery. It was hard for me to imagine the Dalai Lama's great palace or the splendid temples, because in my village there were scarcely more than a dozen houses, scattered up and down the green hills, connected by paths worn by our feet and the feet of our animals. There was no central village hall, no religious or institutional building of any kind. Lhasa felt as remote as the moon, and almost as mysterious.

My birth name was Jampal Drakpa or Jamdrak for short, and I grew up lacking for nothing, surrounded by an abundance of love, support and devotion. I was born in the year of the Water Sheep, which was 1943 in the Western calendar, and I believe I was born in September. I don't know exactly, because we had neither clocks nor calendars in our village. We didn't need them. The only time that mattered was the turning of the seasons, which governed when to plant, when to take the animals to the high pastures and when to harvest. The precise day on which a person was born mattered very little to us, because we did not count the days. For us, you were young until you were old.

I was the youngest of four surviving brothers (there had been another boy born before me but he died before receiving a name) – Jamyang Chogyal, Palden Drakpa and Karma Shetrup Chochi Nyima – and I had two younger sisters, Yangchen Lhamo and Zimey. I lived with my mother, father, an older cousin whom I knew as Auntie and my two sisters. My mother was endlessly loving, a large woman whose embrace seemed to wrap me up completely. Since I was the smallest boy, she, along with everyone else, indulged me in everything.

All the family units in my village were related by marriage if not blood. Everyone was an aunt or uncle, a cousin or a kinsman. Every adult I knew would clip me on the side of the head if I was slow to come when called, feed me if I was hungry or embrace me if I was crying at some minor childhood mishap. My world was contained by the familiar landscape we children roamed through as we played, and by the care of the adults who had known me since the day I was born.

The mountains in Kham form jagged peaks that soar to 18,000 feet (about 5.4 kilometres), and when I was a child they still housed mystics in caves, meditating for months in hermitages with eagle-eye views. Kham had been the centre of a great military power in pre-Buddhist Tibet, had been fought over for centuries by Mongols and Chinese, and was always politically and economically powerful. It is one of the highest inhabited places in the world and even now is dauntingly remote, but its valleys are fertile and abundant in comparison with its barren highlands. It was a pristine wilderness that gave us everything we needed but required our respect.

Western people are sometimes surprised to discover that Tibet is not a completely snow-bound country, despite its high altitude. It is usually too dry for snow, since most of the rain is blocked by the Himalaya mountains. During the winter months the cold catches in the throat, despite the fierce glare of the ever-present sun – you can suffer frostbite and sunstroke on the same day!

In Kham, settled people such as my family lived close by nomads who lived in tents made of yak skins. All of us *Khampas* (locals from the Kham region), whether settled or nomad, had a place within a spiritual order that was governed by a monastic culture of monks, nuns, lamas and *tulkus*, the reincarnate lamas, who were given the honorific title 'Rinpoche', or 'Precious One', and were the heads of the monasteries. We revered the tulkus and observed the distinctions of a deeply hierarchical culture, but we received far more from the religious authorities than we ever paid them, either in money or in devotion. Buddhism is based on searching for the wisdom and goodness that is within every single one of us. The teachings of the Buddha, which have been handed from generation to generation, are our guide to finding this wisdom and goodness within ourselves. We speak of Three Jewels in Buddhism: the Buddha, the *Dharma* (the teachings) and the *Sangha* (the monastic community who embody and transmit the Dharma). In the Tibet of my childhood none of us questioned any of this. It was the backdrop to our lives, so ingrained as to pass almost unnoticed, and the object of our absolute devotion.

The character of our Tibetan Buddhist culture has sometimes been described by the West as magical and mystical, and now that I live in the West I can see why. But for us the acts of clairvoyance and dream prophecy that were, for example, deployed to identify the latest incarnation of a particular lineage of tulkus were no more magical or mystical than the electricity I now flick on with a switch when I enter my bathroom. Our ways of being in the world and relating to one another and to every living creature were governed by a particular understanding of reality, and of the powers of the mind. Central to our worldview was the religious culture that had created the exquisitely decorated temples, with their delicate pastel-coloured murals of the lives of the saints and their gilded shrine rooms. Each one of us, whether we were a monk, a tulku, a highly realized meditator dwelling in a cave, a mother of ten children living in a yak-skin tent, or indeed a small, spoiled and unruly boy, was part of an interconnected world.

Not that any of that mattered to me when I was a young child; nor did I feel any particular spiritual resonance from my everyday life. Buddhism was as present as the air that I breathed, as the water of the stream, as the yak turd I slipped in when I fell while playing hide-and-seek.

My immediate family's life had been shaped by the religious order, but then so had everyone's. My oldest brother, Jamyang Chogyal, was a monk at Riwoche, a very beautiful monastery quite close to our home in one of the loveliest parts of Kham. He was seven years older than me, had left for the monastery before I was born, and consequently I didn't know him. That was quite typical. From every family a boy or girl, usually the eldest, would enter a monastery as a monk or a nun.

I didn't know my second brother, Palden Drakpa, either. When he was born my mother didn't have enough milk for him, and in order for him to survive he was taken to my mother's sister in another village so that my aunt could feed him. I didn't meet him until many years later, just before I left our village, and then I knew him only briefly. My parents had picked him to succeed them in taking care of the immediate family. He would be the one to inherit our house and look after our parents in their old age.

Again, that was customary. Tibet was not only a monastic but a patriarchal culture. The head of the household was a man, and a son must be lined up to succeed his father in running the family's affairs. Women were powerful within the domestic context and were revered as mothers, but they led more circumscribed lives. Many women were nuns, for example, but they were unable to take the highest level of ordination, which was only available to men.

It was my third brother, whom I knew my whole life as Akong, born in 1940, the year of the Iron Dragon, who was the unusual one. His birth name was Karma Shetrup Chochi Nyima, but he had been recognized as the second incarnation of the Akong lineage of tulkus when he was just two years old and taken at the age of four to his monastery, Dolma Lhakang, where he was destined to become abbot.

Tulkus are a unique feature of Tibetan Buddhism. We believe that enlightened spiritual teachers can intentionally reincarnate in order to carry on their good works in the next life. When this happens, living high lamas ('lama' can be roughly translated as 'high priest') and spiritual teachers will detect their presence through dreams and divinations, consult the sacred texts and then set out to locate the child. When they find him, the child is put through a series of tests to determine whether or not he is authentic. It is a great joy when a past spiritual master is recognized, because now he can resume his work in this life. For Tibetan families, having one of their children recognized as a tulku is a huge honour, so they willingly relinquish their child. Historically the vast majority of tulkus have been boys and

men, though there are exceptions. The Samding Dorje Phagmo
tulkus, for example, who have their seat at Samding monastery,
are female. The first incarnation lived in the fifteenth century
and the current incarnation, the twelfth, still lives in Lhasa.

I was born not long after Akong's departure for his monastery so, as with my other brothers, I didn't know him. What I
did know, from as young as I can remember, was that I was
expected to join him when I was roughly twelve years old, to
serve under him as his assistant.

Ours was the only family in the village that had a child
who had been recognized as a tulku. In fact, Akong's case was
even more exceptional, because the place of his birth had been
divined by His Holiness the Gyalwa Karmapa himself, the
head of the *Kagyu* spiritual lineage to which our family paid
allegiance.

There are four schools, or lineages, of Tibetan Buddhism.
The Nyingma is the oldest, then there are the Kagyu, Sakya
and Gelug schools. Each one has its own leaders and monastic
institutions, and every Tibetan person will practise within a
particular school. The line of tulkus known as the Karmapas
are the ultimate leaders of the Kagyu school, which traces its
origins back to the eleventh-century Indian teachers Tilopa
and Naropa. It was Naropa's pupil, Marpa, who established the
Kagyu lineage in Tibet.

For more than a thousand years there has been a certain
amount of jostling between the four schools, but since the
seventeenth century the Dalai Lama tulkus, who are the
heads of the newest school, the Gelug, have been the overall
leaders of Tibetan Buddhism. Until China assumed full control in 1959, they were also the temporal leaders of the country
of Tibet. There is a clearly defined hierarchy among the
heads of the schools and other high lamas. His Holiness the

Dalai Lama is at the pinnacle of this hierarchy, the Karmapas one step below. The Kagyu lineage and the institution of the Karmapas who lead it was the focus for devotion among my family and at my brother's monastery. We recognized His Holiness the Dalai Lama as our ultimate spiritual leader, but it was a less emotive and devoted relationship than the one we had with the Karmapa. For us, His Holiness the Sixteenth Karmapa was something like a spiritual king. He was also a man of exceptional brilliance and mystical power, as I would come to discover.

Akong's qualities made him a person of huge importance in our society, but all of that tulku business felt remote to me. I gave no thought to the moment when I would travel to far-off Dolma Lhakang and I wasted little time wondering about Akong. I was busy leading a charmed life as, in effect, the only son of the family.

During the warmer months of the year my village was lush and green and we grew crops of wheat and barley in the fields closest to our houses. Every spring, as wild flowers exploded into drifts of colour and scent, one of the elders would call a meeting of all householders, where he drew up a written plan of who was going to plant what, when and where. All the animals had to be moved up the mountainside to their summer pastures to make way for the crops. This was the responsibility of the slightly older children. There was no such thing as school to go to and during my early childhood I did nothing but play; however, once I reached the age of eight I was expected to join the other children in driving our animals up the mountainside to pasture.

My parents had plenty of land and a sizeable herd of yaks and goats. In early spring we moved them up to the tree line, which wasn't far from home. Then, as the ground thawed fully and the animals needed more to eat, we moved even higher up, where we had a tepee-style tent made from yak hair called a *baa*. It was supported by a huge pine log that was left there year round. Inside was a proper fireplace and room for all of us to sleep. We made soft beds by cutting branches from a small aniseed-scented bush that grew wild in the area. Outside the tent was a large enclosure where all the animals slept, aside from the babies, which we brought into the tent with us at night for safekeeping. We curled up close enough to kick each other as we joked sleepily, our bellies full of *tsampa* and *dri* milk.

We would spend days at a time camped out on the mountainside with Auntie (my older cousin) nominally in charge. In the mornings and evenings she would milk the goats and the dri, the female yaks, leaving just enough for the animals' young. She then made yogurt and fresh cheese and churned the cream into butter, which was packed into wooden boxes. We would each be given a fistful of freshly churned butter each day to eat with our tsampa, and it was so good. We also ate the yogurt and cheese, and could have as much milk as we could drink. My father came every day to bring us further supplies. He collected the milk and butter Auntie had packed into the boxes, and took them back down the mountain to the village.

We spent about a month up in the high pastures and, though I missed my mother, I loved being up there. The landscape was awe-inspiring even for a young boy whose mind was (I'm embarrassed to admit) mostly on his catapult. I just couldn't resist aiming at moving targets. On one occasion I broke the leg of our neighbour's *dzomo* (a yak–cow crossbreed) when I hit it with a rock. My parents were furious with me. My punishment was to be responsible for feeding the dzomo all winter long. But nothing could put me off hunting with my friends. Once we'd moved the animals in the morning we had nothing to do until evening, when we had to fetch them back. There was a rhythm as natural as breathing, as we flowed up and down the mountainside twice a day. When it came to the end of the summer we all trooped back down to the village in the valley and I would be reunited with my mother and her familiar embrace.

Besides the yaks and goats there were also mules, horses, a few cattle, and many *dzo* and dzomo in and around our village. The female crossbreed, the dzomo, yielded more milk than a purebred dri (female yak), and the males, the dzo, were stronger, so they were put to plough in the fields. But these beasts were less hardy and agile at altitude than the yaks, which were the power source of our working lives. Yaks pulled carts loaded with wheat and barley. They carried piles of goods for trading lashed to their backs over mountain passes. We depended on them totally since we also wove their long hair into tents, turned their hides into shoes and bags and used the butter we made from their milk as fuel for lamps. Not to mention eating their meat and turning their milk into yogurt and cheese.

Horses were our only means of transport and every Tibetan child learned to ride as naturally as they learned to walk. Men took particular pride in their horsemanship. They would groom their horses and adorn them with tassels ready for races and demonstrations of skill. Tibetan men feel about their horses as many Western men seem to feel about their cars. When I came to the West I quickly developed a thing for cars myself!

There was definitely a joy in the bond between a man and his horse and we respected animals as an integral part of the smooth running of our world, but I don't recall much sentimentality about them. Some people did keep a house dog for companionship and every household kept a *drog-khyi*, or nomad dog, which is known in the West as a Tibetan mastiff. They were huge creatures with long, dense coats and were said to be strong enough to kill a bear. The dog would be tied up in front of the house during the day and left free at night to protect livestock. Ours was black and white, a magnificent animal who wore a red tassel round his neck.

The winter months were bitterly cold even during the day. I was in and out of all the houses in the village, just one component of a rolling ball of small boys, dashing from one warm house to another. We played like wild puppies in the space on the ground floor of our large stone-built houses, where our herds of yaks and goats were stabled for the winter. I recall playing hide-and-seek, burrowing through straw, dodging yaks as they munched and trying not to slip in their turds as I searched for my companions. Inevitably we would mistime our leaps and land with a splat in a yak turd, but that was all part of the fun.

One of the adults' duties was to shovel the animals' soiled bedding outside, where it would dry into huge piles to be used as fertilizer in the springtime. Those dung heaps were another irresistible hiding place since they were always cosy and dry. We must have been grubby little creatures, with straw in our hair and dried dung on our legs, but the air was so cold and dry that I don't recall any smell and we didn't feel filthy, only carefree. There was no sanitation, of course, no running water. In the corner of the house was a long drop latrine that fed into a deep hole in the ground. We washed using tubs of water in front of the fire.

On the top floor of the house was a large haymow for storage where we kept the dry crops, mostly barley, to make a winter's worth of food. The middle floor was divided into different rooms for sleeping, living, cooking, and storage of clothing and adults' belongings, which were packed away in chests. There was a special guest room for visiting lamas that was kept very nicely, with soft furnishings and decoration on the walls. In most of the house, smoke from the fire would darken the walls no matter what you did, so they were just left as plain wood. The guest room was the only one where walls were plastered and painted, and the window was covered with thin paper to let some light through but keep out the worst of the cold. I used to sneak in sometimes just to look at the bright yellow and blue of the painted walls and the pink, green and blue swirls of the hand-woven rugs.

Next to the guest room was our family's shrine room, where we all gathered for prayers and meditation on special occasions. We children slept in one bedroom and my parents had their own room, next door. In practice, though, we all tended to drag our respective sleeping mat to the spot most appropriate for the season. Sometimes, in the summer, my sisters and I would take a blanket and go to sleep on the verandah that opened out from the kitchen. I loved to look at the stars and feel the breeze on my skin.

The three of us would chat as we were nodding off. Yangchen Lhamo and Zimey were younger than me and I played more with the other four boys of the village than with them, but one game I loved to share with my sisters was floating flowers down the stream. As we grew older they spent more of their time on chores inside the house than I did, so we often spent our days apart. This was the way of things in Tibet at that time. It was a traditional pre-industrial society. I never felt that men were seen as superior to women and I never saw any abuse of women, but the sexes did have very distinct roles.

Our kitchen area had shelves piled with cooking implements and numerous pots full of drinking water. It was the women of the family who had the job of fetching water from the river every day. There was a huge central fire for cooking where my mother, Auntie and sisters would prepare food. The fireplace was enormous, whole logs could be fed into it. Its fire burned so hot that everything cooked quickly. There were niches built into the chimney for baking bread. We also had a separate dining room, although mostly we ate informally around the fire. At lunchtime we ate tsampa, the staple foodstuff for Tibetans, a mix of roasted wheat or barley flour and salty butter tea, rolled up into balls. We ate it with more butter, cheese, yogurt and vegetables, sometimes with meat, though that was not a daily occurrence. And that was pretty much our entire diet. We had no rice until the Chinese came, no potatoes, no fruit. We had nothing sweet.

Some people are surprised that we Tibetans eat meat at all. Buddhists are forbidden to kill any sentient being, and in many countries where Buddhism is practised Buddhists are vegetarians. In most of Tibet, though, the conditions do not support a lot of arable agriculture and we depended on meat, and even more so on dairy, for our nutrition. We also depended on the butchers who arrived every autumn to kill our animals for us. They were Muslims and made their living travelling from one village to another to slaughter and butcher sheep, goats and yak.

In the evenings we ate hot soup with more tsampa and afterwards everyone would recite the twenty-one praises to Green Tara. We all knew these praises off by heart. Green Tara is a very important and popular deity within the Tibetan Buddhist tradition as she is viewed as a protectress who rapidly comes to our aid when we are dealing with obstacles and our fear. Tara is a female *Bodhisattva* and strongly associated with compassion, healing and protection. She has twenty-one manifestations, each of which is linked with particular qualities and activities. Each one also has its own colour. White Tara, for example, is also very popular and is associated with healing and longevity.

During the winter we all usually slept by the fire. I remember more than once drifting off as I watched my mother and Auntie dressing each other's hair with yak butter to keep it shiny, the firelight flickering on their faces as their hands twisted the hair into plaits and swirls that they pinned to their heads. They didn't talk as they worked, and the motion of their fingers and the shadows on their faces lulled me to sleep.

If this sounds like a rather primitive world, then I suppose in some ways it was. It was a subsistence economy where we ate what we grew, used firewood as fuel and made our own clothes and blankets out of animal hair and skins. Small surpluses were traded for goods such as cooking pots and shoes. It was not purely a barter economy since we did use money to purchase more valuable objects such as finer clothes, devotional objects for our shrine room and wall hangings for the guest room. But it was a world of such material simplicity that it can be hard for people who have grown up with supermarkets and offices, credit cards and salaries, to grasp what it must have felt like. Our obligations came from being mutually dependent on one another, and the need to carry out essential tasks rather than the requirements of an employer or having bills to pay. Time was determined by the rising and setting of the sun, the waxing and waning of the moon and the passing of the seasons.

In all the ways I believe to be most important, it was a society of abundance. It had a strong monastic tradition of scholarship and reflection. The monks were teachers as well as spiritual guides, and in every family in my village at least one person could read. It was a society built around the importance of faith and devotion, the expectation of compassion for every living being and a sense that everything and everyone was valuable.

There was always enough time to talk, to listen and to connect with one another. During the long winter months the animals didn't require much more than daily milking, and the storms were howling outside so we couldn't venture out. We spent hours eating and chatting. We often ate six small meals a day, accompanied by stories and jokes. Life seemed to overflow with laughter, and with love. Even on the most basic level I lacked for nothing. If I was hungry all I had to do was cry and roll over, and my mother would come and feed me! If she was busy or in a bad mood I would simply run off and find another adult, who would welcome me as one of their own.

It was this strong sensation of safety and security that was, I think, the defining characteristic of my childhood, and it has served me well throughout my whole life. Many of the Western people who come to see me nowadays are suffering so much at an emotional level, and for many of them the issue seems to stem from their childhood. They tell me that they do not feel good enough. They do not feel loveable. When they were growing up they were lonely, or emotionally deprived, and they feel insecure and unsafe even as adults. This makes me wonder why so many people grow up in a world of material comfort and individual freedom, with educated and well-informed people around to take care of them, and yet feel a gnawing lack at their heart.

I do not judge anyone and I encourage those who come to me to let go of their often deep-seated tendency to blame others, particularly their parents, for their own distress. Modern society makes it so hard for parents to give their children the emotional support and security they need. There are just so many pressures and conflicting demands on people these days. And, on top of this, most parents did not receive proper parenting themselves. Tibetans greatly value their lineage and the received wisdom going back through the ages, but it strikes me that many parents in the West never inherited a sense of what it is like to be an emotionally integrated human being. To make matters worse, children are under so much pressure to perform academically and become successful. So their only option is to suppress their emotional pain and get onto the relentless treadmill to succeed. When, as adults, they start to meditate, this emotional pain resurfaces – as I later discovered when I began to guide and mentor Western students of Buddhism. My many conversations over the years have made me value even more my own experience of a world where adults and children were together so much, able to listen and pay attention to one another. We children were seen, heard, valued and contained. We knew where we belonged.

Beyond the realm of the extended family, beyond the social dimension, our whole community felt like it was knitted into a vast and interconnected ecosystem of all living beings and of the Earth on which we depend. And, of course, we also felt connected by our belief in the Buddhist teachings and the world of faith that came from them.

Having a strong sense that we are valued by and connected to other human beings is vitally important for all of us, especially children. Even if we have grown up without it, it is never too late to recreate links with others in our own lives, families and communities. Every relationship starts from an impulse to open our self to another being. When we are generous with our attention and our care, empathy flows and compassion becomes possible. Many of the most important Buddhist ideas around joyous and compassionate living begin with the realization that none of us exist in isolation. Interconnectedness is essential to our being; isolation is a delusion. I offer you this thought as a starting point for your own voyage of positive change.

2. Ritual and resistance

As a child I was particularly intrigued by vultures, which are sacred in Tibet because of the crucial part they play in disposing of the bodies of the dead. Since the ground is frozen for much of the year and too hard to dig, our community practised sky burials. When someone died, the lama who lived in the local monastery a little further down the valley would come to perform prayers. He was almost like the village priest, available for ceremonies and consolation as required. We all knew and trusted him.

Once he had finished saying the prayers for the dead, the body was bound in a shroud and carried to the charnel ground, where the covering was removed and the body chopped up. The hovering birds would swoop down out of the sky and eat everything except the bones they couldn't break, such as the skull. Bearded vultures, native to Tibet, are the biggest of their kind in the world and they often have a wingspan of more than 2.5 metres, so they were immensely powerful. The relatives attending to the body would return after a few days and smash the remaining bones together and mix them with the brain so that the vultures would be able to eat everything.

The hope was that not a scrap of flesh would be left behind. In fact it was regarded as inauspicious if a body was not fully consumed, reflecting badly on the karmic status of the deceased. *Karma* is a key doctrine in Buddhism. We believe that all our thoughts, speech and actions, as well as the emotions that drive these actions, shape both the life we are currently living and all our lives to come. When we die the karma we have accumulated in this lifetime, be it good or bad, determines whether we will be reborn once more as a human being, as an animal or as a being of one of the other realms of existence, whether lower or higher. If the vultures were unwilling to consume a particular corpse, it didn't look good for that individual's karmic reckoning. In such cases a further purification ritual by another lama might be required, so every care was taken to allow the vultures to carry out their role.

The Tibetan approach to funerals strikes some Westerners as gruesome. Having visited the lawn-covered cemeteries of England I can see why. We didn't regard the process as horrifying or disrespectful, though. For a start, it was by far the most efficient and hygienic approach. It represented an act of generosity to the birds, and to the interconnected world of mutual support in which we lived. And, of course, all of us believed in reincarnation, so the body was just an empty shell. In Tibetan Buddhism vultures are seen as *dakinis*, or angels, come to help the dead person towards a swift reincarnation. So we believe that being consumed by them is a sacred way to finish your embodied time on earth.

As a young boy I was desperate to catch a vulture. Not to kill it; I just wanted to feel the pull of that enormous, angelic power for myself. This was a foolish notion, unlikely to work out well for me, but it became a fixed idea in my mind. When I was about seven a dog died in the village and I saw my chance and enlisted my friends to help. We decided we would tie a rope to the dog's body and when the vulture came to eat it we could drag the carcass closer to us, luring the vulture until it was near enough for us to lasso it. We thought we were quite clever to hatch such a plan, but when the vulture saw us it simply grabbed the dog and flew off with it. The bird was so powerful that all of us together couldn't keep a hold on the rope.

I didn't give up, however. I was still determined to catch myself a vulture. One day I noticed that a horse had died down by the river and many vultures were coming to eat the corpse. They always start with the soft internal organs, which are the most nutritious part and easily eaten. In a big animal this then creates a natural cage shape from the ribs. I watched the vultures going further and further into the carcass, and noticed that to do this, they had to fold their wings. I came up with the brilliant idea that while one of the vultures was inside the horse, eating its flesh, I would be able to put my arms around it and catch hold of it by its wings. It amazes me that I considered this plan for so much as a second given my earlier experience, which had shown me the vast strength of these creatures. Even at the age of seven I was ever the optimist about my own prowess, and always utterly unafraid.

I lay in wait and when I saw a vulture go into the dead horse's chest cavity, I sprung onto it and managed to grab it by the wings. The vulture wasn't going to stand for that! It was so big that it had no difficulty taking off with me still holding on to it. Terrified, I tried to keep my grip, but it freed itself and I fell to earth. And that was the end of my vulture catching, though it was just the beginning of my taste for recklessness.

When I was ten years old I experienced the first major change to the rhythm of my life. My father announced that my brother Akong Rinpoche had sent a letter summoning us to Dolma Lhakang. My brother the tulku, whom I had heard so much about, wanted to meet me! The visit would be in preparation for my joining him in a couple of years, to become his assistant. I was excited. I had never been further than the grazing lands above my village, so even the act of saddling up a horse and setting off for the four-day journey felt like an adventure.

My father had some business to take care of near the monastery. He was going to trade salt, which could not be obtained in that area, for white barley, which is particularly good for making tsampa. We set off in a westerly direction accompanied by twelve yaks, loaded with sacks of salt. The first night away we stayed with a nomadic family in the area my mother came from. The following day we had to travel through dense forest and cross a river. I couldn't swim and I recall my terror when our horse, which my father had tied me to, began to drift downstream from the narrow crossing point. My father managed to drive the beast on to reach the other side, but I was cold, wet and scared when we struggled out of the water. The second and third nights we spent with other families we vaguely knew, and then, on the fourth day, we began to ascend towards the desert plain where Dolma Lhakang was located, at 4,500 metres above sea level. We left the tree line far behind us and I began to feel overwhelmed by the eeriness of the barren landscape. I just wasn't used to it at all, and I felt small and out of place. We had to cross a deeply frozen lake and I recall our yaks putting their heads down and scraping their horns over the ice, bellowing as if they were calling to some lost companions below the surface.

My first view of the monastery is engraved on my mind. Its central temple building was the largest structure I had ever seen, an adobe construction of pinkish plaster over strong stone walls, its surface rough, the roof made of wood. There was a huge wooden double door set right in the centre of the building. As we approached, across the boulder-strewn terrain of grey rock, the pink walls seemed to glow.

I was still feeling a bit sorry for myself and I had no idea what to expect from the meeting that awaited me. But when my father and I arrived, and once the monks had welcomed us, they told us that Akong Rinpoche was not there. He was away with another young lama called Trungpa Rinpoche, receiving teachings from their *guru* called Shechen Kongtrül Rinpoche, and nobody could say when he might be back. I didn't really mind too much, though I could tell my father was disappointed. These things were inevitable in a society where there was no method of long-distance communication except letters delivered by hand.

My father left me in the care of Akong Rinpoche's tutor for a couple of nights while he went off to do his trading. The man was very kind to me but I did not feel comfortable alone in this new environment. There was nobody to play with since I was the only child there, and I missed my mother's embrace. There was no point in waiting beyond the time required for my father's business, since my brother might not be back for weeks or even months; so after my father's return to pick me up we set off. That return journey was nowhere near as exciting!

When we got back to our village I was ready to forget entirely about the adventure. Going off to see the world hadn't been that much fun, in my opinion, and I was glad to be home with my family and friends. I wanted nothing more than to resume my happy life and forget all about Dolma Lhakang. But my father had different ideas. He set about teaching me to read and write Tibetan, since I would need to be literate when my brother summoned me again to go to him. The training in the routines and procedures of the monastery would be intense, I was told, so it was essential to be ready.

I still couldn't imagine the life that supposedly awaited me. Going away, even for that short time, had made it clear to me that I belonged in Darak. So what need did I have for reading and writing? My father would set out the rice paper, the ink in its copper pot and pens made from bamboo with a sharpened tip. I would study in an unenthusiastic way until the first opportunity for release presented itself – when he left the room to attend to something my mother was saying, for example. Then I would slip out in search of my playmates. I wanted to please my parents, but I wanted much more to indulge myself.

This rebellious streak was a defining feature of the first half of my life. On those tedious afternoons in Darak I discovered I had a knack for escaping from whatever it was that I was supposed to be doing. I spent the next thirty years as an escape artist from any situation or expectation that didn't suit me.

Naturally enough it enraged my father to have to come looking for me out in the fields or in the basement of some neighbour's house. One day, tired of dragging me back to my studies, he hit me on the head with a stick. Tibetan parents generally provide a very nurturing environment for their children, but at this time corporal punishment was still the norm for serious misbehaviour. Unfortunately, on this occasion my father's aim was off and he accidentally hit me in the eye, which swelled up so badly that it provoked my mother's fury when she saw it. She was so upset that she insisted that there would be no more lessons. I was delighted, but it made my life very difficult when I arrived at Dolma Lhakang and embarked on my studies there, for which I was totally unprepared.

Not long after I was released from the burden of study, it was time to begin the preparations for *Losar*, or Tibetan New Year, which was the highlight of our community's year. This holiday typically falls in February or early March in the Western calendar and can last for more than two weeks. I loved it and looked forward to it for months. All normal routines were relaxed, the grown-ups were always in an excellent mood and we got to wear our fanciest clothes, use our nicest things and eat the best food of the entire year. I had a little Mongolian hat decorated with a coral-coloured stone that I was extremely proud of, and a silver food bowl that I was only allowed to use at New Year.

Before the festivities began we would clean our house thoroughly and bring in fragrant woods for burning as smoke offerings. My mother, Auntie and sisters would have been preparing food for days in advance. The custom was to eat fried dumplings made from wheat flour mixed with dried cheese and yak butter and shaped into squares. I loved them more than any food in the whole world. They were served with the meat from a yak's head, which was also a delicacy eaten only at Losar. Those yaks' heads were kept aside throughout the winter until it was time to prepare them. The hair was burned off down at the riverbank, the heads then brought back to the house and the meat chopped up small and cooked for the Losar festivities. We had lots of *krapse*, twisted dough biscuits that were deep fried. And for the grown-ups there was *chang*, barley beer, which was brewed only at New Year. As Buddhists, consumption of alcohol was not done regulary. At New Year it was drank but rarely at other times.

On New Year's Day my whole family would rise early and get dressed in our finest clothes. We then prepared the house by putting out all the softest cushions and the delicate woven rugs we kept for special occasions and for receiving guests. Once everything was ready we sat down to celebrate. For the first two days our immediate family feasted together. Then the other families in the village would arrive, one by one, to celebrate with us. Each day brought a different family, and the celebrations went on long into the night. The adults got a little tipsy and there was music played on flutes, mouth harps and a guitar, with everyone dancing in our big living room. When the party was finished each person was given one square dumpling and a portion of the rich yak meat to take home with them. Meanwhile, every other family in the village was doing the same. It was a whirl of socializing as each family went visiting. When I look back on it now, it must have been quite a feat to schedule all those visits so that there were no empty houses or others where four families had pitched up together. No wonder it took us weeks to get round everyone!

The festivities closed with a religious ceremony in which the whole village took part. We put up a huge baa, or yak-skin tent, and invited our local Lama, all the local Sangha (monks and nuns) from the nearest villages, and any other learned person who was able to read fast. They all came to take part in reading the *Kangyur* (the sacred texts, containing the Buddha's teachings, considered very precious and holy) for the benefit of us villagers. In return, every family chipped in to provide them with the very best food we could offer. When the reading was complete and we had eaten the closing meal, we felt ready to start the new year.

This was the rhythm of existence throughout my childhood. Our community farmed and harvested, rested and feasted. I felt that I was a living part of the fabric of the interconnected world, and I was happy. I credit this with creating an inner core of stability and faith that has never left me, even in my most challenging or confused moments.

It seems to me that human beings thrive when we feel part of a bigger whole. The moment we realize that we are part of the air we breathe and the earth we stand on is a breakthrough that creates a spontaneous wave of compassion and respect for all living beings and the natural world that sustains us. Nothing and nobody stands alone. This wave of loving kindness towards all beings rebounds and envelops us too, and brings about a sense of deep gratitude. Human life is particularly precious to us Buddhists simply because human beings are capable of grasping these truths, which gives us a unique opportunity to learn something about the nature of reality and of the endless cycle of birth, death and rebirth we call *samsara*. This in turn lays the foundation for escaping from suffering's hold over us and taking tentative steps in the direction of liberation. One important part of this process is to learn to appreciate the present moment for all its possibilities. Drink deeply from the cup when times are good and use those moments to foster habits of awareness and positivity, because easy times cannot last for ever.

When I was about seven or eight years old I witnessed something so out of place, so unprecedented, that I stood and stared. A column of Chinese soldiers came marching through our valley and into our village. They wore crisp uniforms with metal buttons that gleamed in the sunlight and their arms and legs swung in time as they moved. I was impressed by their smartness. When I looked at our clothes I saw that they were ragged by comparison and I felt scruffy for the first time in my life. Who were these people and what were they doing here? I had never seen a stranger before but I wasn't scared, just fascinated.

The adults were less taken in. They must have received word that the Chinese People's Liberation Army had launched a military strike on the town of Chamdo in October of 1950, though there had been no talk of it in front of us children. The Communists had come to power in China the year before and the liberation of Tibet was one of the regime's highest priorities. It didn't take them long to launch an invasion. I had no idea, but the poorly equipped Tibetan army had already been overrun and these soldiers were on their way to Lhasa, having received orders from Peking that military force would not be required for the time being. Negotiations with the Dalai Lama's government were about to be opened.

The adults set about performing a ritual to drive the Chinese away. Normally, when dignitaries visited our village the elders performed the *sang*, fragrant smoke offerings from which we expected would come limitless good things for our guests. Instead, the clay pots were filled with burning animal dung. I remember that the stench filled the whole village, so that I felt sure the smart visitors would retreat in disgust. But they stayed put. Seemingly they didn't know they were being insulted and just thought we had stinky rituals.

Then one of my neighbours began a traditional expulsion ritual called *dogpa* that involves clapping the hands vigorously and chanting a *mantra* invoking protective deities. We all joined in, clapping loudly at the soldiers. I wasn't sure why it was necessary to drive these people away but I clapped anyway. To our dismay the men broke into wide smiles and began to clap back at us. As it turned out, clapping is a sign of welcome in Chinese culture. I remember the confusion among my family and neighbours. These strangers seemed impervious to our rituals of resistance. It must have felt like a moment of pure powerlessness to the adults, though the whole incident was just baffling to me.

The soldiers left us after the clapping died down and, as far as I was concerned, life returned to normal. In retrospect, this was the first sign that my world, seemingly eternal and unchanging, was on the brink of being erased.

3. *Return to the monastery*

I had another four years of idyllic life in Darak after that first encounter with the Chinese, but now I can hardly remember them. They have been displaced by my memories of the three years I spent in the monastery, which are still very present to me when I seek them out. Not that I do very often. I have long ago learned to focus my mind in the present moment and leave any discomfort in the past, where it belongs. During the first half of my life I was deeply resentful whenever I thought about being taken to Dolma Lhakang and left there, at the age of twelve. The place was a prison for me. Even after I had left it far behind I hugged my anger and resentment close to me. In that way I recreated its stone walls and its punishing regime within my own mind.

I may have refused to study in preparation for it, or even to think about what awaited me, but the day inevitably arrived when Akong Rinpoche sent for me. All my denial came to an end when my father opened that letter. Once again he and I set off for Dolma Lhakang on horseback. This time he had no goods to trade so we took no yaks. I had virtually no belongings to take with me besides the clothes I wore, a couple of blankets and my little silver food bowl. The Mongolian hat I so treasured was now too small for me, and I left it behind.

I do not remember my mother's final hug for me, though it must have been even longer and warmer than usual since we both assumed it would be the last one for many years. In the normal way of things I would have come home for Losar at some point; perhaps not for three or four years, but before too long. The monastery's inhabitants sometimes returned to visit their families at Tibetan New Year, in the same way that people in the West go home for Christmas.

That didn't come to pass. All of normal life was wiped out when the Chinese invaded Tibet in 1959, three years into my time at the monastery. I did not return to my village during those three years and then I was forced to flee to safety by the invasion, so I never saw my mother again after that day when she waved my father and me off. I used to wish I could remember our last hug but I have accepted that I cannot.

The journey was leaden with my foreboding. I didn't want to go but there was absolutely no way I could not. It was unthinkable that any Tibetan child would defy his or her parents' wishes. In addition there was the will of my brother, Akong Rinpoche, which was even more resolute and even more impossible to ignore. My life's path was set, or so I thought. I would become a monk and spend the rest of my days in the monastery. I could see life stretching out in front of me in a grim and unchanging vista. Ironic, in hindsight, since it would be only three short years before the Chinese invasion would destroy this way of life, along with everything else.

Even if the Chinese hadn't come, at some point I would have learned that, in fact, nothing lasts for ever. This key insight of Buddhism is summed up in the Buddha's famous aphorism, 'This too shall pass.' Darak was over; my childhood had come to a close, but it didn't occur to me that this might support an understanding of impermanence. I was a child, and heavy with the melodrama of children. I felt very unfairly treated, not to say doomed!

The first night I spent in Dolma Lhakang I could barely summon enough grace to be polite to my brother's tutor, or any of the monks, or the servants. I certainly had no positive feeling towards Akong Rinpoche, who was sixteen on the day when we finally met. He received me kindly but with no brotherly warmth. Our relationship was purely one of teacher and pupil. He was a person who felt a deep sense of duty, to the community of which he was a head and the ideal of the Bodhisattva that he literally embodied. He saw his role as being to provide guidance to the Sangha and the laypeople who looked to him.

Akong Rinpoche was not an emotionally effusive person but he had deep compassion. This is a strange mixture for Westerners, who are raised to place a lot of faith in the validity of their emotional life and in displays of emotion. He often came across as immoveable like a mountain, but, as I grew to appreciate, there was an infinite wellspring of loving kindness and compassion within him. My brother was then and continued to be throughout my life a steady and compassionate force, always acting in my best interests. But on the day he received me and for years after there was no sign of special regard and certainly no physical affection. I had not expected it since I knew it was not his role to provide it. Even so, I couldn't help blaming Akong for removing me from Darak. My resentment of him dug its strong roots into my heart on that first day and flourished there for decades.

The great consolation of my time at Dolma Lhakang was another brother, whom I met on the same day I met Akong Rinpoche. Jamyang, my eldest brother, had been ordained as a monk before my birth and lived during my early childhood at Riwoche monastery. Not long after Akong Rinpoche was enthroned as abbot at Dolma Lhakang, aged four, Jamyang's abbot sent him to support his younger brother. It was Jamyang who was kind to me during those first bewildering days at

Dolma Lhakang. It was Jamyang who consoled me when I was upset at my father's departure, two weeks after he brought me. My father was stoical since all of this was simply the way things worked, but when he left I felt that my last link with the safe and secure world of Darak was disappearing out of sight, rising and falling on his trotting horse until he was a vanished speck out on the cold grey plains.

My new living quarters, where Jamyang and I lived with Akong Rinpoche along with some monks in attendance, were in the *labrang*, a second, smaller building attached to the main one. A labrang is the institution set up to protect and preserve the wealth and religious artefacts of a spiritual teacher in the time after his death and before the next incarnation is recognized, which can take years. It is also, on a practical level, the place where a particular teacher lives during his lifetime alongside the treasures and sacred texts that are part of his line of transmission.

The labrang building housed the abbot's quarters and guest rooms, a kitchen and storage rooms, as well as the repository for relics. There was a large courtyard where Akong Rinpoche's horses were stabled. Grand steps led up to the entrance to the labrang's shrine room, which contained a magnificent statue of Padmasambhava, or Guru Rinpoche as he is known in Tibet.

For many Tibetans, Guru Rinpoche is like the second Buddha. 'Guru' simply means 'teacher' in Sanskrit, and though not much is known about the historical person, Padmasambhava was a Buddhist master and teacher in India in the eighth century. He was responsible for bringing the tantric teachings of Buddhism to Tibet at the request of a Tibetan king, who was well disposed to them. Prior to this, the religion of Tibet was Bon, an ancient pantheistic religion that reflected Tibetan people's reverence for the natural world. Ku Lha, the mountain on which Dolma Lhakang was built, for example, had been sacred since the times of Bon religious practice. Padmasambhava himself had visited the mountain and there was a hermitage on the other side of the hill from the monastery, built over the cave where he had sat and meditated.

All these years later, I still remember how cosy and warm the labrang was. Generally the monastery was cold and uncomfortable due to its location so high up in the mountains. Conditions were harsh. Water had to be fetched from the nearest stream. During the long winter it was more a question of breaking ice and filling buckets to drag back and leave to melt in the heat of the labrang's kitchen.

That kitchen was truly a haven of comfort. A fire was kept burning in its central fireplace day and night throughout the winter and there was an ingenious heating system that channelled heat through ducts in the walls. The labrang cooks kept me supplied with butter tea and tsampa whenever I wanted it, and the whole building was warm and welcoming. Since I felt that I had been wrenched from my home and transported to a freezing and alien land, that comfort was particularly welcome.

Mind you, I was largely oblivious to just how fortunate I was to be living a life of such material ease. As always, I benefited from being the brother of the tulku in so many ways, but I was also left isolated by the fact that I didn't quite fit in anywhere. I was not a monk so I could not live in the monastery or join in with its daily rituals and social bonding. The laypeople I encountered in the labrang were servants, so I was not encouraged to interact with them, either. I recall that one of the cooks, who also served us our meals, was fifteen years old; so not that much older than me. We could not be friends, though. I might not have been a monk, much less a tulku, but there was still too much social distance between us in that strictly hierarchical world.

The cook told me that he'd heard Akong Rinpoche had a little dog he kept with him at all times. Was it true? Every detail of Rinpoche's life was of interest, I was discovering. No, I told him. Akong had no dog.

I was thinking to myself as I replied that actually *I* was like Akong's dog. Or perhaps I was like a tiny bird who had fallen silent. I felt like a prisoner, anyway, locked up in the gilded cage of the labrang.

The building was so comfortable because it had once been owned by a noble family, overlords to a few hundred other families in a close equivalent of a medieval European fiefdom. When the first Akong Tulku was recognized, the family offered the parcel of their land and buildings that lay immediately next to Dolma Lhakang to the Akong line, to increase the monastery's prestige.

Western societies are built on the practice of passing property down through a family line, and for laypeople in Tibet the same holds true. In the tulku tradition, land, wealth and religious title are passed to the next incarnation of that spiritual teacher. In most cases the reincarnate individual is from a different family and even a different social caste to his predecessor. Many great teachers have been born into a noble family in one incarnation and into a peasant, nomadic family the next time.

My brother had been recognized as the reincarnation of Karma Miyo Zangpo, a great master and doctor of Tibetan medicine who was the first Akong. The first Akong was born very close to Dolma Lhakang and lived there all his life until his death in 1938, at which point the search began for his successor. When my brother's place of birth was divined by the head of our lineage, His Holiness the Sixteenth Karmapa, a search party of lamas and envoys made their way to our tiny village to identify and retrieve him. He was then put through a series of tests to verify that he was in fact the right child. A number of ritual artefacts that had belonged to his predecessor were mixed with other random objects. My brother, who was just two years old at the time, reached unhesitatingly for the correct cup, book and medicine bowl and was consequently recognized as the authentic reincarnation of the Akong line of tulkus.

I know that reincarnation is a very alien concept for Western people but it is fundamental to traditional Buddhist thought. According to the teachings of the Buddha all beings go through an endless cycle of birth, death and rebirth that has no beginning and no end. This cycle of reincarnation, or *samsara* (as the Buddha called it), is driven by karma. According to this key doctrine, all of our thoughts, speech and actions, and the emotions that drive these actions, shape both this life and lives to come. What breaks this cycle of reincarnation is attaining *nirvana*, or Enlightenment. In the Mahayana tradition of Buddhism, which lies at the heart of Tibetan Buddhism, those who attain Enlightenment and wish to return to help other beings become free of the cycle of rebirth are known as Bodhisattvas. They intentionally seek rebirth in order to carry on their compassionate work of helping to free beings from samsara. In Tibet those who return in this way are described as tulkus.

Reincarnation can be a struggle for Western people (and the specific practice of conscious reincarnation that marks out a Bodhisattva or tulku doubly so), but most people grasp easily the basic idea of karma, which I sometimes paraphrase as

'What goes around comes around.' Every action produces a reaction, in oneself and in others. Our thoughts and emotions flavour our existence. When they are negative they spur us to negative words and actions. Our sum total of unhappiness, anger, resentment, envy, covetousness and self-pity increases. Other people naturally treat us as we treat them, mirroring our negative behaviours back to us. Life becomes a vicious cycle, with damaging consequences for ourselves and for others. This, I trust, is clear to anyone who has reflected on their life even a little. I always say to people who are beginning to explore Buddhism to focus on incorporating a common-sense idea of karma into their thinking, and have faith that this will lead to greater insight as time goes on.

If only I'd been able to open my own mind to any of the teachings, common-sense or otherwise, that my older brothers were trying to impart back in Dolma Lhakang. But right from the start of my time there my mind was closed: sealed by resentment, self-pity and a naive sense that somehow my life was over.

Akong Rinpoche set me to study right after my arrival, and, sure enough, my father's words about the severity of the programme proved to be correct. My brother had just finished a lengthy period of study at the monastery in Sechen with the highly esteemed teacher Jamgön Kongtrül Rinpoche, and he had returned full of inspiration to run Dolma Lhakang in a very tough and vigorous way. He was only sixteen years old and yet he was in charge of a monastery with 300 monks, as well as four affiliate nunneries (one at each corner of the base of Ku Lha mountain) that housed many hundreds of nuns. He never appeared ruffled by all this responsibility, despite his inexperience. He had been born to do this role, and he and everyone else accepted that.

I marvel now at this equanimity, because in addition to the period of study Akong had also witnessed evidence that our whole way of life was in danger. From Sechen he had travelled with his great friend Chögyam Trungpa Rinpoche, another young lama of the Kagyu school, to Palpung monastery. They had been summoned to hear His Holiness the Sixteenth Karmapa give an account of the Dalai Lama's recent trip to China.

His Holiness the Karmapa, flanked by Communist officials, recounted that the Dalai Lama had been warmly received. He explained that His Holiness the Dalai Lama had been informed of all the material progress being achieved in China and Tibet. Reports were passed on of new roads, shops, clinics and schools. But Akong heard no mention of the people's religious and personal freedom. Clearly His Holiness the Karmapa could not express his opinions, or His Holiness the Dalai Lama's, since his every word was being monitored by Chinese officials, but, reading between the lines, it was plain that the regime was growing ever more hostile to our Buddhist way of life.

A month later, Akong had been present at the Dalai Lama's brief personal visit to the monastery of Derge Gonchen, but the general pleasure at hosting His Holiness was curtailed almost immediately when he was hurried away by Communist officials after a mere two hours. When Akong Rinpoche finally arrived back at Dolma Lhakang he came carrying a heavy burden of concern as well as renewed zeal.

It wasn't until much later that I became aware of the crisis. I can only feel admiration for the fact that my brother, like so many other lamas, was able to maintain the communal life of spiritual practice in the face of such severe pressure.

He may have been able to contain his concerns but he certainly didn't hide his determination to give as many of the

Buddha's precious teachings as possible, not only to me but to other members of the community. He was to be my personal tutor except when monastery business, study or visits to the laity of the surrounding area claimed his attention. He drove me relentlessly and beat me when I was particularly obtuse or careless. He was never cruel; it was simply that this was the custom in those days, especially in the monasteries. He wanted to give me the best possible education so that I could eventually serve as his second-in-command. Now I also wonder whether some of his implacability was in response to the escalating threat he had to contend with during these years.

With him there was no possibility of escape as there had been with my father. We began our studies the moment there was daylight enough to see the lines on the palm of my hand. The first objective was to master the Tibetan alphabet. You can be sure that I regretted my former laziness when my brother, amazed that I had not even learned the basics, made me repeat each letter over and over again until I could pronounce it perfectly.

The oral practice of learning was the foundation for recognizing and reading the letters in texts and, eventually, replicating them in my own hand, but I was incapable of clearing even this first hurdle. My throat was permanently sore and my voice grew hoarser and hoarser until I couldn't even croak out a sound. In the end my brother called in a doctor to treat me. These days his methods would be regarded as positively medieval, as much in Tibet as here in the West. The doctor rolled up my tongue and cut the skin beneath it, which attaches the tongue to the floor of the mouth. It was a bloodletting exercise, and of course my mouth did indeed fill with blood. The procedure was repeated three or four times. On one occasion I thought I would choke on my own blood. Naturally, this treatment, instigated by Akong Rinpoche, did nothing to lessen my resentment towards him.

When my brother was away or busy he handed my care over to Jamyang, and my teaching over to the retreat master in charge of the three-year retreat. Then life was much more bearable. My interactions with the retreat master, who was a kind man, were far less charged than they were with Akong Rinpoche. The regime was still tough, mind you. There was no more tongue-cutting, but the hours were long, and the demands endless. Gradually I began to learn to read and write. By the time I left the monastery I could read the prayers aloud very fast, though nothing was ever enough for Akong Rinpoche.

The retreat master's principal duty was the much more rewarding task of teaching the cream of the monastery's crop. The retreatants were those monks who had shown exceptional aptitude for the study of Buddhist texts and who had been selected to undergo the long retreat that would prepare them to become lamas. These retreats, traditionally lasting three years, three months and three days, are unique to Tibetan Buddhism. They were cloistered, so the retreatants had no contact with anyone from the outside world except for teachers and attendants – and unfortunate creatures like me who happened to be the brother of the tulku!

I gained my first real insight into a way of life that would eventually be my own by observing life in the retreat house. The regime was very strict and intense. The monks rose before 4 a.m. and practised in isolation throughout the day apart from some group *pujas* (prayer rituals), until they retired to sleep around 10 p.m. Rather than a bed, the retreatants slept in a meditation box in which they sat cross-legged. The idea was that they continued to sit in meditation posture and maintain some level of awareness even as they slept.

In later life I engaged willingly – joyfully, actually – in long periods of solitary retreat, though by that stage I had turned my mind around and was committed to the path of Enlightenment. But as a young boy of thirteen or so being in the retreat house merely reinforced my sense that I was being tortured and incarcerated.

Throughout my time at Dolma Lhakang all I could think about was escape. But where would I go? It wasn't like being in Darak, where I knew the surroundings intimately, where everyone was either a playmate or a trusted family friend. I couldn't exactly slip out to play in the woods, or down at the stream with my sisters. There were no woods and there were no friends or sisters. There wasn't even a village beyond the monastery walls, only freezing desert. The people who lived close by the monastery were nomads who moved around with their animals. Only a small group of them remained during the winter months, in stone houses built into the shelter of the mountainside. Those who stayed tended to be younger men. There were no families with young children. I missed being out in the sunshine during the warmer months. I missed herding our animals and sleeping out under the stars or on our verandah. Up here, the summer could come and go in scarcely more than a week.

My only real contact with another child occurred periodically when the family of the first Akong came to visit with their twelve-year-old son. For the few days of those visits we played all over the labrang and I felt like a normal boy again. My loneliness when they left was always that much more intense. I missed my mother even more than usual. I bitterly resented my studies. There weren't even any views for me to stare at as I worked, because the windows, sealed in thick opaque paper stretched over a lattice, were set high up in the walls above my head. I felt I had lost everything and everyone I loved.

It was Jamyang who lifted my spirits when I was downcast. Every day I would go to him for comfort and he was always there, with a smile and a hug. He tried to intervene when Akong Rinpoche punished me. He would shield me with his body. But he was in awe of Akong Rinpoche too, of course. I remember him begging me to be more focused when Akong was away and he was left in charge of my welfare. 'Come and study just a little more,' Jamyang would say to me, almost pleading. But at these times I wanted to forget about study. I would leap around him like a puppy, wanting to run and jump and wrestle him to the floor. He indulged me, and we laughed and played together.

When I had been in Dolma Lhakang for about two years, the first report reached us that the Chinese People's Liberation Army had attacked a monastery. I knew that there had already been uprisings against the increasingly authoritarian Communist presence. This armed resistance was met by ever more aggression from the Chinese military. I had been shielded from most of the discussion of what was going on all over our country, but now I couldn't help overhearing fragments of conversation between my brother and his advisers.

Initially I was more puzzled than worried. I could not reconcile the news that Chinese soldiers were ransacking monasteries and insulting monks and nuns with my impression of the smartly dressed strangers I had seen passing through Darak. They had seemed so disciplined, not chaotic or aggressive at all. Then again, they hadn't understood the first thing about us: that was plain from their reaction to our clapping and our stinky smoke offerings. Perhaps they didn't realize what they were doing when they threw texts and relics on the ground? Though to lay hands on another person violently was always wrong. Surely they knew that?

The atmosphere in the monastery grew tense. I was unhappy enough on my own account, but even I noticed that people seemed worried. Jamyang was less inclined to laugh with me. Akong seemed preoccupied. The labrang cooks were morose.

There were more and more visits from lamas with monasteries in other parts of the country, and the news they brought was always bad. Some of them began to talk openly about the need to escape Tibet. Still, it was hard to know how to interpret what was going on. Our Tibetan government had signed an agreement with the Communists back in 1951, recognizing that Tibet was an integral part of China. In return, the Chinese agreed to allow the Dalai Lama to remain in power and the existing social and religious structures to remain in place. In the short term. The ominous subtext was that at some point Tibet would be transformed into a 'people's democratic state', with the complete dismantling of her way of life. Tibetan pleas for international support had fallen on deaf ears, and so the Dalai Lama's government had no choice but to capitulate in the face of vastly superior power.

We Tibetans had grown used to an uneasy sense of muddling along in the intervening years, but was that period of compromise now coming to a close? If so, what would happen next? It was difficult to imagine that the Chinese would actually destroy our society. The cultural and religious links between China and Tibet went back many hundreds of years. Within my own Kagyu lineage there was a long connection between our head lamas, the Karmapas, and the emperors of China. The Karmapas had been tutors of Buddhism to the emperors ever since the time of the Second Karmapa, Karma

Pakshi, in the thirteenth century. All of this shared history made it impossible to grasp that we had now entered a very different era.

The new rulers of China believed in class struggle and the inevitable victory of the proletariat; they believed in material progress. They did not believe in Buddhism. They viewed the monks and lamas as enemies of the people, exploiting the peasants, whom they deliberately kept in ignorance. To us Tibetans, material progress (such as the new schools and roads the Chinese had built over the past few years) was merely changing the outer appearance of things. We were deeply devoted to an entirely different way of seeing existence: as the transformation of the mind on its cyclic journey over many lifetimes. So the Marxist concept of 'liberation' did not ring true to most of us. For us, 'liberation' meant freeing the mind from the prison of self-fixation. This clash of mindsets, combined with China's vast military power, meant that defeat was inevitable. I didn't yet know it but we were already living through the destruction of Tibet.

It was another year or so before Akong received confirmation that the situation was now so desperate that his life, and the life of the Sangha, was actually in danger. Refugees began to flood into Kham from Derge province. They confirmed that monasteries were being looted. Lamas were being rounded up and shot. People were displaced and starving; anyone suspected of having resistance sympathies was being killed. There were informers everywhere and a feeling of panic pervaded every village. And then came the rumour that His Holiness the Dalai Lama had fled Lhasa in fear of his life.

The first I heard with my own ears of all this was from the lips of Chögyam Trungpa Rinpoche. I met Trungpa, who was to have so much influence on my life, in the midsummer of

1958. He arrived at Dolma Lhakang with the now customary bad news, this time of armed troops in Chamdo and increasingly bitter fighting between the resistance and the Communists. I'd heard a great deal about him, of course. The Eleventh Trungpa Rinpoche was a very high lama, abbot of a large and prestigious monastery complex, Surmang, located several days by horse from Dolma Lhakang. Trungpa was also a great friend of Akong's. He had spent six months at Dolma Lhakang two years before my arrival, giving the *wangkur* (rite of empowerment) on the Treasury of the Mine of Precious Teaching, a lengthy and complex teaching that had attracted hundreds of people to the monastery to receive it. He and Akong had also spent many months together in Sechen receiving teachings from their mutual guru, Jamgön Kongtrül Rinpoche, before travelling to Palpung to hear His Holiness the Karmapa's report from Peking and then meet with His Holiness the Dalai Lama in Derge. Trungpa was the same age as Akong and was already a notably learned and charismatic spiritual leader. I was more than a little in awe of him, but he was warm and friendly with me. I immediately formed a bond with him that lasted until his death in the 1980s.

From the day Trungpa and his small party arrived, I knew we had entered a state of crisis. My brother asked him to perform various ceremonies, and I remember that in one address Trungpa said that our way of life would soon change beyond recognition. Everything that we now relied upon would crumble beneath our feet. He had received this insight from a divination, and the impact of his words on all of us was dreadful.

I sat in the temple and struggled to understand what I was hearing. I was appalled at the stories of destruction and death and frightened at the thought of more to come, but I also felt a

43

secret excitement because this wave of destructive change contained within it the possibility of my escape from the monastery.

Trungpa was being asked to give teachings in monasteries all over the district. Before he left Dolma Lhakang he sent a message to His Holiness the Karmapa, asking for advice on what to do. Should he go back to his monastery as one of his senior advisers, Tsethar, the bursar of Surmang, insisted was the best course of action? Or was it preferable to seek safety in Central Tibet, or even escape over the Himalayas to India? To his dismay, the Karmapa said he must make up his own mind. Trungpa then wrote to another high lama, Dilgo Khyentse Rinpoche, but he got a similar answer.

Not long after Trungpa's departure to give teachings at the monastery of Yag, a messenger arrived at Dolma Lhakang with the tragic news that the esteemed master Jamgön Kongtrül Rinpoche had been captured by the Chinese and had died in prison. Akong then got another message, this time from Trungpa, saying that he had gone into hiding as he was being hunted by the Communists. Could Akong join him in the remote valley where he was sheltering, so that they could meditate upon the correct course of action? Not long afterwards we heard that resistance fighters had taken refuge in Trungpa's monastery and the Communists had captured and destroyed it. They had desecrated the tomb of the previous Trungpa incarnation and destroyed the library of sacred texts. Many of the senior lamas had been shot dead and most of the monks taken prisoner and set to forced labour.

Trungpa left the valley where he'd been hiding and, with Akong's help, went into retreat for a few weeks in a secluded cave. He was determined to decide once and for all what to do. He and Akong were both willing to die to defend their monasteries, but they were also concerned that, as tulkus, they were likely to make everyone around them even more of a target. There was also the consideration that they had both received a vast amount of teaching from their gurus, and that if they were killed, all that knowledge and wisdom would be lost. Their commitment to non-violence was of course unshakeable.

As Trungpa meditated on the mountain, Communist troops were moving towards us at Dolma Lhakang from every direction. It seemed now that the only choice was between an attempt at escape or capture and death.

Trungpa's heart and mind were made up. There could be no further delay. He chose the day of the full moon in April 1959 for the start of our escape because this was an auspicious date in our calendar. Akong had discussed matters with his own advisers in the meantime and didn't hesitate to join Trungpa. On the evening of 22 April he informed me that I was coming too, as were my other brother, Jamyang, and a small party of monks and attendants. We would be setting off as early as possible the following day with just a few mules to carry essentials. Akong and Trungpa knew that the bigger the group of people, the more difficult it would be to evade attention. By this point Trungpa had been in hiding for many months and knew from experience that his success in eluding the Communist authorities came down to the fact that he had been travelling with only one or two attendants, at night and in secret. Akong was one of the only people who had been kept fully informed of his whereabouts.

When I was told that we were preparing to leave the monastery and make our way to Lhasa, I felt a surge of excitement. Finally, I was going to escape my personal hell! My naivety makes me wince now. How could I have been so utterly bound up in my own suffering that I took even the overrunning of my country as little more than a personal release? I was fifteen, that's how. I had all the self-obsession of any young person, combined with a great deal of pride and resentment. Change had come for me, at last.

Every life is of course full of fluctuations. My companions and I in Dolma Lhakang had been living in a world ostensibly unchanged in hundreds of years. We had all assumed that it would endure for many hundreds more. In fact it was destroyed in a matter of months. On a moment-to-moment level, though, every one of us – from trainee monks to the servants in the labrang – lived with constant internal change. Our thoughts and moods ran endlessly through our minds. Even I, with my story of how my life had frozen into a predictable shape, had a dynamic inner life. Emotions came and went. I pined for the past and daydreamed about the future. I had glimmers of satisfaction when I accomplished something in my studies. I fumed against Akong Rinpoche. I wondered what my mother was doing. This was direct evidence of impermanence, if I had been paying attention, but I wasn't. And, of course, it is hard to make the connection between change at this level and the kind of change that means losing everything we hold dear.

I spent most of my time feeling resentful at being in the monastery, which made it impossible for me to see it as an opportunity to learn about the wisdom of the Buddha, about myself and my potential. If I had been able to feel grateful for this opportunity, I might have been able to grow. As it was, I hankered after the past and resisted the present. I was truly stuck: a prisoner of my circumstances. So much so that I interpreted the Chinese invasion of my homeland as my personal liberation!

I was, in short, a typical human being.

Most of us live as if we are half asleep. We are distracted and caught up in our thoughts, and as a result we miss so many opportunities. We take as a given that everything will be pretty much the same tomorrow as it is today. We manage to be surprised when change comes, whether it's negative (we get sick; our father gets sick) or positive (we're suddenly all grown up; we've fallen in love!). We overlook the fact that every single moment is always vanishing, and with it our chance to wake up.

Many people I speak to are naturally nostalgic, often prone to melancholy. They experience impermanence – when they start to think about it – as a sad thing. *Good times cannot last*. True. We should treasure them, learn from them and be grateful for them once they've gone. But the bad times don't last, either. Nothing lasts for ever. Impermanence can sometimes be a way out of suffering. It's good to take the time to notice that. And good or bad, in the end, all change is simply part of our path, the material we have to work with. In Buddhism we say the obstacles *are* the path.

'Be careful what you wish for,' I might be tempted to say to my fifteen-year-old self as he steps out into the labrang courtyard on 23 April 1959 and swings himself into the saddle of his horse, part of the small convoy setting off for what we still assumed would be the safety of Lhasa. Then again, I also regard him with amused fondness. He is just an over-excited child, eager to get going. He hasn't yet learned anything about impermanence or the way that our mind shapes our reality, such that freedom is always within our power.

4. Escape

On 23 April we had left Dolma Lhakang without a clear plan. All Trungpa and Akong knew was that it was too dangerous to remain. During their travels over the previous years they had seen enough to understand that the Communists were steadily increasing their grip on our country. I suspect that on the day we set out for Lhasa they must have known that at some point the capital city would fall to the Communists, because the Chinese regime would not stop until it had secured its aim of integrating Tibet into its territory. Why then did we attempt to get there? I didn't ask this question at the time. I asked no questions. Initially I was simply delighted to have escaped Dolma Lhakang. Later, when others did question Trungpa and Akong's judgement, I did not join in. I was too inexperienced. I had no opinions of my own at that stage. And I was too focused on survival. Now I think that we headed for Lhasa for the simple reason that it was impossible to imagine going anywhere else. The city was a symbol of enduring Tibet. It drew our hearts towards it. And it wasn't as if we lived in a world where travel was common. Quite the opposite. Most Tibetans passed their whole lives without straying beyond their neighbouring villages. Bhutan, Nepal, even India were remote places that nobody save high lamas and occasional pilgrims visited.

We were about a dozen people and some thirty horses and fifty mules on the day we rode down the mountainside away from the monastery. It was a relatively small group but, even so, all those animals made us conspicuous. We had brought no slow-moving yaks, but the mules were loaded with sacred texts and treasures as well as provisions for our journey. Our immediate goal was the nunnery at the northern corner of the base of the mountain, where we would spend our first night. From there we were heading for the Shabye Bridge over the river that divided Communist-held territory from an area where the resistance forces were in control. That was about a week's travel away.

I couldn't help feeling excited, as well as nervous. I hadn't left the immediate vicinity of the monastery in three years and now here I was, riding a fine horse with a beautiful golden saddle that Akong had allowed me to use, off on an adventure. It was spring, my favourite time of year. I thought my heart would burst for joy with every step my horse took.

The moment of leave-taking itself had been difficult for everyone else in our party, especially Akong. As we rode out of the monastery grounds I saw monks and laypeople in tears. Akong Rinpoche, their abbot, the heart of their community, was leaving them. Outwardly my brother maintained his usual calm; it was inconceivable that he would let anyone see that he too was upset. But I know it would have been terrible for him. His departure from the community, in such troubled circumstances, was a brutal cutting off from the social and spiritual system that had nurtured him from babyhood, that gave his life meaning and purpose.

The emotion of the people of Dolma Lhakang pierced even my self-interest for a moment and I took care that my face expressed the seriousness of the occasion. I couldn't prevent my spirits from soaring as we descended the valley, though. I had been released from my personal prison, or so I thought at the time.

We had told everyone at Dolma Lhakang that we were going on pilgrimage to Lhasa, though they plainly understood that this was not the case. There were informers and spies everywhere and Akong and Trungpa felt it would offer those who were left behind a shred more protection if they could say with conviction that they knew nothing of any escape plan. The Communists would be looking for us, or, more explicitly, for Akong and Trungpa.

On the third day Trungpa and Akong changed from their monk's robes into layman's clothes. Even my usually stoic brother looked distressed as he slipped his arms into a tunic, belted it round his waist and pulled a hat down on his head. Trungpa told us that he felt naked without his robes. He had been a monk since he was a young boy, as had my brother Akong. This alteration in their appearance made no difference to us, of course. It would take more than a change of clothes for us to see them differently, but the symbolism of those robes was immensely powerful, especially for them.

The following day we were received with all the customary ceremony by the monks and tulku at Kino monastery. Trungpa, who was always more transparent with his feelings than Akong, looked embarrassed at appearing to them without his monk's attire.

We spent three days at the monastery and it was good to rest and prepare ourselves for the next stage of our journey. There was a mood of deep anxiety among our group. We had no idea whether we would walk out and straight into a Communist army patrol. We had heard enough stories to know that if we did, it was probable that Akong and Trungpa would be executed on the spot. I was as terrified as the next person, but my fears were also laced with the adrenaline rush of release.

The next point on our journey was the Shabye Bridge over

the Gyelmo Ngulchu River. If we could cross that we would be in resistance-held territory. Our host, the abbot of Kino monastery, offered to ask some of the local laypeople to go out on reconnaissance and inform us of any Communist presence. This they did, so as we travelled on towards the bridge we felt as if we were protected by a chain of villagers up on trails all around us, who were our collective eyes and ears.

As we approached the river from the highlands everything appeared to be peaceful at the crossing below. We carefully made our way down a sharp descent of 2,000 feet, via a track cut into the sheer side of the mountain. We crossed the bridge without incident but were stopped on the opposite bank of the river by a resistance guard whose duty it was to check us for concealed weapons. He had a rifle swinging over his shoulder and looked very fierce and heroic, though I couldn't help noticing that his uniform was not clean and shiny like the ones I remembered on the Chinese soldiers I'd seen in Darak.

Everyone in our group was wearing laymen's clothing and there was nothing to suggest that our party contained monks or tulkus. One of our number was carrying a rolled-up religious painting and the guard seemed to think it might be a rifle, so he insisted that it be unwrapped. He was mortified when he saw what it was and realized that the person in front of him was a monk. He made a gesture of prayer with his hands and begged forgiveness. I think the mistake was harder for him than it was for any of us, though it certainly made me realize again that we were living in changed times.

What we needed, Trungpa said in reply to the poor guard's offer to help in any way he could, was up-to-date information about the situation on the ground, both in rebel territory and in Lhasa.

The guard was confident that the region was safe from

attack and I couldn't help feeling reassured by this. Trungpa mentioned the rumours that His Holiness the Dalai Lama had been forced into exile in India and that Lhasa was under Communist control. 'We don't believe it,' I remember Trungpa saying, and the guard agreed that it was just Chinese propaganda.

I looked around at our party, who were all now smiling and nodding their heads. I was the youngest person there and accustomed to view my elders, and lamas in particular, as all-powerful and all-knowing. I didn't realize until I saw the wave of relief break over everyone that they had been so worried.

The whereabouts of the Dalai Lama continued to be a great source of preoccupation for all of us throughout the next few months. His Holiness is revered by all Tibetans as a divine embodiment of wisdom and compassion, the glittering jewel of the Land of Snows. He was the very source of our faith and devotion, so the mere possibility that he might have fled was almost too awful to contemplate.

With the guard's assurances we all felt easier. Our anxiety was replaced by cautious optimism. Could it be that the tide had turned in our favour and things were not as bad as we had heard? We relaxed a little and began to enjoy the wonderful spring weather and the pleasure of travelling through unfamiliar terrain. I think now that we had all half convinced ourselves that we really were on pilgrimage. The one thing that puzzled us was that we didn't meet anybody returning from Lhasa; we only passed other travellers who were also making their way towards it.

Two days after we crossed the river we reached the small town of Lhodzong, where we found more resistance troops, all of whom seemed to think that there was no need for us to escape. Trungpa and Akong looked thoughtful.

The first time I saw a road was a week or so into our journey towards Lhasa. I was still overjoyed to be surrounded by trees and vegetation again and I was lost in my contemplation of this beautiful world. Then we came across the road. I thought it looked unreal, as if an immensely long black scarf had been laid down over the mountains by some gigantic being. It was so utterly unlike the rest of the landscape. My horse's hooves looked out of place against this peculiar substance and the horse himself seemed confused.

I glanced at Akong but he seemed unperturbed, as ever. He had made a number of journeys through our province over the previous two years. He must have seen tarred roads before. Probably he had seen cars as well. I could still scarcely imagine such a thing. Trungpa had told me that he'd actually ridden in one. He and his attendant had hitched a lift in a Communist jeep on the road from Chamdo when they were making their way to us in Dolma Lhakang, almost a year before. It had amused him to sit in disguise next to soldiers from the same army that was hunting for him round his own monastery in Surmang. The sickening smell of the petrol was apparently even worse than the sensation of travelling at such a speed. Here there were no vehicles anywhere in sight, thank goodness. The resistance army had only horses and mules, as did we.

From the moment we hit the main road to Lhasa, everything felt more difficult. We passed hordes of desperate people with all their worldly belongings strapped to mules and yaks, leaving the lands they had lived in for countless generations and heading nobody knew where. There were so many resistance soldiers going in both directions that there was no grazing for our animals. Food was expensive. Trungpa and Akong agreed that we should get off the road and continue our journey via a less travelled route.

We made slow but steady progress westwards over mountain passes, until finally the track ran out and we could go no further and had to drop back to the main road. We continued to push on towards Lhasa, up and over the Sharkong-La mountain range. The going was hard and slippery, the weather became stormy, but eventually we struggled over the crest of the pass at 18,000 feet.

At camp the following day, Trungpa, who had a pair of Russian field binoculars, spotted a group of people coming over the pass behind us. Every such moment was uneasy since at a distance it was hard to be sure who anybody was. As the leader of the group drew closer, Trungpa was astonished to see that it was Yag Rinpoche, the abbot of Yag monastery, where Trungpa had given teachings just before our escape. There was great joy when we heard that both Yag and Dolma Lhakang monastery remained untouched by the Communists, though we could not be confident that this would last, as Yag Rinpoche told us that the fighting in Kham continued to be very bad.

The worry increased when Yag Rinpoche said that his small party was just the vanguard of a much larger group of people, as well as hundreds of mules and a large number of yaks. I could see that both Akong and Trungpa were concerned at all this. They had been advised by a number of other lamas to travel alone or with only a few attendants and a couple of animals. Now we would be part of a vast and slow-moving baggage train, impossible to conceal on the mountainside. The rest of the group was some days behind us, so Yag Rinpoche begged us to wait and, of course, Akong and Trungpa agreed. But when they caught us up even I was worried. The group of new arrivals contained another 150 or so people, including whole families with old people and babies. We were going to be slow, and thanks to the babies' cries we would also be noisy! There were hundreds of animals, all of which would need grazing. The survival of everyone depended on our evading attention and now it seemed impossible that we would.

There was nothing to be done except press on, and after a few days we came to a village called Langtso-kha where we camped by a small lake surrounded by rocky hills. I have vivid memories of going on long walks with Trungpa and Akong through valleys bursting with spring flowers. It was early June and the landscape was a mass of colour that reminded me of summer in the hills above Darak. I loved being invited to spend time with Trungpa and Akong and felt a strong sense of peace and wellbeing despite the context of fear and uncertainty. The local landowner was extremely hospitable to us and invited Akong Rinpoche, Trungpa Rinpoche, Yag Rinpoche and a few others of our party, including me, to eat with him. He also allowed us to graze our animals on his land. These were the last days of peace I would know for many months. Our struggle was about to become far more acute.

We had hit a huge obstacle. The track we were following led directly through a gorge on the Tsangpo River where travellers had to cross the torrents of water using a primitive bridge. It was just one plank wide at its midpoint and there were no handrails. Old people and children might be coaxed over, or carried, but it would be extremely dangerous. Could the animals manage the crossing? Would the bridge bear the weight of heavily laden yaks?

These considerations were not even the greatest problem. The bridge had to be crossed in single file and without overcrowding. After we had been camped for a few days, a queue of hundreds of refugees and fighters began to form on the opposite side of the river. As they streamed over, they brought confirmation that Lhasa had fallen to the Communists, though nobody seemed certain whether His Holiness the Dalai Lama had been captured or had escaped. Thousands of people were pouring down the valley and there was no way our enormous party could push against the tide. Why would we want to when our destination, Lhasa, was in enemy hands and the Dalai Lama's whereabouts were unknown?

The mood turned black. This was the moment I grasped that the future was not certain. Up until this point I had been swept along by my persisting sense of relief and excitement at being out of Dolma Lhakang. I trusted that my brother and Trungpa would continue to guide us, as they always had. And whenever I allowed myself to think about the wider situation, I simply couldn't imagine that I was living through the destruction of my world. That seemed impossible. All this complacency crumbled when I heard that Lhasa had been captured. Where should we go now? We could not go on but neither could we stay where we were for long. The narrow valley would not support our large group, despite the landowner's generosity. Besides, he was becoming nervous as the news grew worse. We would have to find an alternative route, but with no destination in mind it was difficult to know which way to go.

That night I thought of Darak. For the first time it dawned on me that I might never go there or see my parents and sisters again. They, along with my other brother, Palden Drakpa, were cut off and there was no way to reach them. What would happen to them all? For once Jamyang could offer me no consolation. He just shook his head when I asked him what he thought would happen to our family.

Trungpa was the undoubted leader of our group and was supported in his decision-making by Akong and Yag Rinpoche. Both he and Akong were still only twenty years old but Trungpa was the highest lama, the most skilled at divinations and a gifted and inspiring leader. It was natural for him to assume command. He now decided that we should retrace our steps and then take a different route, going north-west over many high passes. Lhasa may have fallen but it was still unclear where else we could go.

Looking back I can see that it must have been a situation of terrible pressure for Trungpa. He was naturally brilliant; his resolve and intuition had been strengthened by the intense training he had received in the monastery system, but he was young and he now had responsibility for hundreds of people. No wonder he could not, as yet, think beyond Lhasa as a destination.

The route over the mountains was harder going than the valley pass we had been forced to abandon and it took a week to slog through the highlands until we reached another valley that allowed us to change course and head westward once again.

Then we received two pieces of devastating news in quick succession. Travellers coming east confirmed that the Communists were in control of the main route to Lhasa and that if we continued we would certainly be captured as we were walking straight into the enemy's ranks. We had run out of any plausible reason for continuing our course in that direction. Every hour more and more refugees were arriving and halting to absorb the impact of this news. There was total confusion. Trungpa and Akong spoke with several other lamas but there was no consensus on what to do or where to go.

This was one of those moments in life that happen to many of us, in different contexts, when we realize that those we trust to lead us or care for us do not know what to do about a difficult situation. For many of us the first such moment is when we realize that our parents are not infallible. During times of political crisis we might feel that we are lurching from one such moment to another. As I observed the debate between the lamas, all of whom had different opinions, I felt as if the boundaries of my world were crumbling.

Trungpa and Akong did not give in to panic. On the contrary, they drew on their reserves of insight and fortitude and remained calm, even as we heard something truly unexpected. Apparently His Holiness the Karmapa, the head of our spiritual lineage to whom Trungpa had written asking for advice some months before, had fled Tibet. He had escaped through Bhutan to India, accompanied by several lamas, including Dzogchen Ponlop Rinpoche and Sangye Nyenpa Rinpoche. He had left his monastery in Tsurphu several weeks before the fall of Lhasa. This news provoked some consternation as well as more confusion. His Holiness was renowned for his exceptional clairvoyant powers, so why had he not given some indication of his opinions and plans to Trungpa when he was asked?

Trungpa seemed unconcerned about that question. He simply reminded everyone that he himself was being asked for advice constantly and felt unable to give any as he still had no clear sense of what was best even for our group. The situation was simply too chaotic and fast-moving. Akong agreed. It was impossible to think otherwise but I was still left feeling almost winded by the shock.

One positive thing to emerge was clarity about where we were now heading. If the Karmapa had fled to India we must follow him. Lhasa had vanished as an option. Tibet was finished. India was now the goal.

We turned south and began to walk. The weather was bad, even though it was still summer, and we headed up and then down the other side of endless mountain passes, finally struggling over a pass called Nupkong-la. From there onwards none of us knew where we were going. It was uncharted territory and we would never have chosen to travel through it in normal times.

That was a tough week. Any lingering sense of adventure had been vanquished by the enormity of realizing that I, along with everyone else in the party, was heading into exile. I wondered what my family were doing in Darak and whether they were safe, but I couldn't think about that for long. I had to focus my energy on the present moment and the immediate need to deal with its next challenge.

Eventually we dropped down onto the same valley track that we had been forced to abandon when we realized we could not cross the bridge over the perpendicular gorge. We were many miles further down now but could just make out the gorge in the distance. What a lot of effort to come virtually full circle.

The going was at least easier again and we had left the cold weather behind in the highlands. We fell in with a train of refugees. When Trungpa asked one man where everyone was heading, he simply said that they were following the group in front. The crowd was huge and there wasn't enough grazing for all the livestock. We began to pass the carcasses of animals that had died of starvation. As the days went on, the warm summer air grew thick with the stench of rotting flesh. My own horse began to grow skinny. It had been weeks since the local landowner above the gorge had fed us and our animals so generously.

I was amazed at how well people seemed to be coping, despite all this. My spirits were flat but others seemed relatively buoyant. Prayers continued to be said. There was chanting and music and the sound of beating drums echoed off the valley walls.

Jamyang was as kind as ever. I slept next to him in our tent every night and his familiar presence was a simple comfort when my mind strayed to the subject of our parents or what awaited us on the way to India. He told me he was positive that all would work out for the best. Like so many others in our party who continued to pray and to meditate, he was living out the maxim that the obstacles are the path, even when those obstacles are impassable mountains and hostile Communists! I can't say I saw it that way, but I trusted him and our leaders and I knew there was no alternative but to continue.

Finally we encountered people who had been witness to events in Lhasa. A group of bedraggled resistance fighters fell in with our group. They had escaped from Norbu Lingka, the Dalai Lama's summer residence outside Lhasa, when it was shelled by the Communists. Most of their companions had been massacred. They had previously seen the Potala Palace under fire and told us that the Communists had completely crushed the resistance army with their modern artillery. Any survivors had fled. To the crucial question of whether His Holiness the Dalai Lama had escaped, they could tell us nothing useful, and the uncertainty made our anguish worse.

Not long after we spoke with the resistance soldiers, we ran into some monks who were escaping from the monastery of a well-known high lama, Khamtrul Rinpoche. The People's Liberation Army had entered their monastery and all the lamas had been lined up and shot one by one. The monks had escaped imprisonment, because they had been in the retreat house, so when they heard the shooting they simply grabbed what they could and ran. Our peaceful way of life was being destroyed. There was now a terrible sense of urgency. I remember the nausea and exhaustion that come from living with your nerves permanently strained tight. I lived with that sensation for months.

Everyone agreed that in the light of what we'd heard it was simply too dangerous to travel along the road. Once again we turned off and began to pick our way over the mountains along perilous tracks. Up and up we climbed, heading for a plateau that lay at 17,000 feet and where we could camp and plan our next move. The ascent was steep and before long it was under a deep blanket of snow through which we had to wade. We must have climbed a dozen steep, narrow mountain paths. One horse plunged to its death when it lost its footing and slipped over a precipice. I couldn't even see where it had landed when I peered over the edge.

That climb felt like an eternity but eventually we arrived at the plateau. Any sense of relief was tempered by the fact that it was full of people, all of whom were as confused and desperate as we were. Resistance fighters were mixed in with refugees and escaping monks and lamas. One of the soldiers was trying to persuade every able-bodied man to join the army. A particularly revered lama tried to convince Trungpa and Akong that exile was unnecessary and that rather than escaping to India we would do better to treat the journey as a pilgrimage and take a detour to visit some sacred sites in the next valley over. When Trungpa pointed out that we had whole families and many animals, the lama reiterated that escape was unwarranted.

Trungpa and Akong were sceptical, but others in our party were more inclined to put their faith in his suggestion. Some people began to voice their criticism of Trungpa's leadership. We had received news that a large group had set out from Dolma Lhakang and Yag under the leadership of Tsethar, Trungpa's former bursar, but walked for just five days before stopping. They weren't convinced it was necessary to leave. This made some in our party wonder whether Trungpa might be mistaken, since other senior lamas who were older and more experienced than him were not persuaded that desperate measures were necessary. A few of our group seemed half minded to try to make their way back towards home.

Trungpa decided to go into retreat to find some clarity. He spent several days camped at a distance from us. As well as meditation he performed *tra*, a mirror divination, invoking the help of protective deities to reveal to him the best course of action. He was renowned for his skill with this practice. On one occasion when there was no mirror available I saw him perform the divination simply by licking his thumbnail to make it shiny and then gazing into it!

After a few days of contemplation Trungpa returned to us. He was resolute. He sent a monk off to Tsethar's party with a message saying that we were definitely heading for India.

Meanwhile, we waited. Conditions on the plateau were bad. With so many people and animals the camp was dirty and overcrowded. It proved impossible to protect our horses from the bears that roamed that area and we lost so many animals. I grew used to waking up in the morning and opening the tent flap to see another horrifically mauled carcass. One day I came upon the body of a horse that had been savaged and then hoisted up into a tree. We began to wonder whether this wasn't evidence of the infamous yeti. How could a bear, or even two bears, have managed this grisly feat?

It was a desolate time and the collective spirit was fraying. Everywhere we sensed danger, from wild animals and the Communists who might overrun us at any moment. Autumn was almost upon us and we were still hundreds of miles and many mountain ranges away from safe territory. Now that I have spent years purifying my mind's tendency to give in to fear, I can see that this was the point at which we began to feel that we were surrounded by a malign force. Long-strained nerves were succumbing to terror.

Some weeks later Tsethar finally arrived, with another large group of people. Trungpa and Akong welcomed them all and we rejoiced that so many more companions had managed to make it this far, but Tsethar had hardly been there five minutes before he began to openly criticize Trungpa's leadership. He said that Trungpa had changed his mind too many times over which way to go. A long discussion followed and tempers flared. This shocked me greatly. It alarmed me to think that there was no unity of purpose among our leaders.

While we were waiting on the plateau we had heard news from the wider world. Somebody in another group had a battery-operated radio that could pick up broadcasts from both Peking and Delhi. The Communist broadcast stated that Lhasa had fallen and Tibet was under the control of the People's Liberation Army. The Indian broadcast informed us that His Holiness the Dalai Lama had already reached Mussoorie in northern India. While we could not be absolutely certain whether this was simply more propaganda, these accounts chimed with what we had been told by the resistance fighters, and they supported one another. There was some relief in hearing that His Holiness was safe, but it was a cold kind of comfort.

As rumour trickled in that the Communists were advancing on the plateau, our party readied to split into two groups. Trungpa had used his skill at divination to pinpoint a route towards the border with India that would take us via unknown territory towards a completely untried route over the Himalayas. Tsethar declared immediately that this was a bad idea. A small group that included a noblewoman, the Queen of Nangchen, and several lamas were similarly unconvinced. Many of the families with young children decided that it was going to be too hard to cross such remote passes. But Akong's faith in his friend's abilities was unshakeable. We were going with him. Yag Rinpoche likewise elected to stay with Trungpa. In the end, and despite his grumbling, Tsethar also came with us. On the day we set off we said goodbye to the smaller group in a hurry, wondering whether we would see them again. Tragically, we found out much later that they were all captured. Some of the lamas and the Queen of Nangchen were imprisoned and tortured.

Our group began the descent from the plateau. We dropped down 7,000 feet into a valley and the first few days were relatively easy-going, but before long Trungpa gave the order to abandon all our animals. We were going to have to pass along another steep gorge and the path was simply impassable for horses and mules. We would have to head for the village of Rigon-kha on foot. I was sad to say goodbye to my horse and didn't relish walking, but there was nothing to be done about it. This leg of the journey was slow-going and exhausting. We crossed countless small rivers and had to build makeshift bridges every time. I felt my spirits sinking. Trungpa and Akong still seemed confident, however, and Jamyang didn't allow me to be morose for long.

We made it to Rigon-kha in early September and rested for a few days. Then we traded whatever we could spare for more food supplies, repacked our bags and set off again for the Tso-phu valley. Trungpa managed to secure the services of a local guide to lead us in the direction of Lower Kongpo. That was reassuring and I remember a night, around this time, when we camped near some herdsmen's huts and stayed up late telling each other stories. I can visualize everyone's faces, smiling in the firelight. That was the last night of relative ease I felt for a long time.

We were still a large party of almost 300 people, including some old folk and children. We had no animals with us any more but we were still travelling slowly, hampered as much by the deep snow as anything. The only way to struggle through the snow-bound passes was for two or three strong men to lie down in the snow and flatten it, then tread down the track so that others could pass. This was exhausting but there was no alternative.

Days turned into weeks. Even our guide didn't know where we were. We kept thinking that at the next peak we would see the Brahmaputra River. This was our goal. Once we had crossed the Brahmaputra we would at least be beyond the reach of the Chinese, though we would still face the formidable obstacle of having to cross the Himalayas to reach Tibet's border with India. I didn't think about that; I just fixed my attention on getting to the river. But at every peak we saw only another mountain range.

Trungpa and Akong were worried about the food running out and urged everyone to be sparing, but, of course, it was difficult. It was November by now, two months since we had last stocked up on supplies. There was no longer any vegetation with which to supplement our tsampa and cheese. People grew weaker and the cold grew more intense. One day we were climbing a particularly steep pass and an old man dropped dead in his tracks just in front of me. We had to leave him where he fell. He wasn't the last. More than once I looked around as we set up camp in the evening and realized that somebody was missing, had been left behind on the mountainside. It was heartbreaking but what could we do?

We trekked on blindly. People continued to join in the daily chants and prayers led by Akong and Trungpa. The weakest passed their packs to others who were stronger. There was, somehow, a sense that we would survive. I recall feeling exhilaration at the extremity of what we were attempting and the vastness of the landscape. I felt tiny and insignificant but I was not despairing. There was no alternative but to keep going. Somewhere over there must be the river. We had to reach it.

In the seven months that had passed since I trotted out of the monastery I had been forced to dig deeply into the lessons it had taught me. I hadn't noticed at the time but Dolma Lhakang had given me a basic training in forbearance, faith and trust. Unwittingly, I had absorbed enough of these qualities to survive the suffering that awaited me.

In Buddhism we say that *dukkha*, or suffering, is inevitable. It comes as an integral part of being alive. The situation I found myself in was an extreme one in terms of external afflictions, but, then, every life is full of suffering. The people we love don't love us back. Or they die. We are disappointed at work. We want to have a child and are unable to. Or we are in conflict with the children we do have. We get ill. We lose our job. The list of ways in which we suffer is endless. It is how we respond to these painful events that will determine the extent and duration of our suffering.

The Buddha told us something very powerful about this in one of his teachings. He remarked that all of us will be struck by the arrow of suffering and most of us will be struck by a second arrow. The first is the inevitable pain of life: all those hurtful experiences we've just listed. Even the most highly realized person will be afflicted in this way. It's the second arrow that does the real damage, though. It lands in the same painful spot as the first and aggravates the wound. This is the arrow of resistance to or avoidance of the pain. The Buddha called it 'resistance obsession'. It typically takes one of three forms. The first is characterized by a desire to escape the pain through reliance on a numbing substance such as alcohol, or rumination on the past or daydreaming about the future. The second is to fight it by being judgemental and controlling, with oneself or others. The third is simply to tune it out by distracting oneself in some fashion, such as with excessive busy-ness. None of these reactions is very effective in the long term. In fact they simply encourage the original wound to fester.

To these two arrows you might want to add a third: the belief that because we have been struck by these arrows there must be something wrong with us. We conclude that if we have failed to evade the second arrow we must be terribly flawed and uniquely unworthy. I have observed that this third arrow is very common among Westerners. It has almost fatally wounded many of the people who come to see me.

When I think back to this period of my own life, I can see that during my time in Dolma Lhakang I was grievously wounded by the second arrow. I tried to escape the pain of being wrenched from the world I knew by daydreaming about it constantly. I also fought it with resentment and aggression directed at Akong. Once our escape was underway, though, something changed in the way I responded to painful events. The arrows of pain kept coming at me but I reacted to them far less.

I can't say that this was because I had learned to be wise and apply the balm of compassion to those arrow wounds. I was still only fifteen and a long way off any such insight. Now it is plain to me, though, that I had learned enough to grasp that my suffering, as we slogged over the mountain passes and my belly began to cramp with hunger, would only be made worse by railing against it. The situation was so extreme that it demanded neither fury, nor avoidance, nor passivity, but forbearance. And, somehow, I managed that. There was the example of my brother Akong and Trungpa, who were my teachers, and there was the collective effort among our whole group to evade that second arrow. We only succeeded partially, of course, but it was enough to ensure that we survived.

5. Crisis

It was a bitterly cold morning in November 1959, eight months since we had left Dolma Lhakang. We had stopped for a rest. Our guide had no idea where we were or how much further we had to go before we reached the Brahmaputra. He and Trungpa had climbed ahead to the crest of the pass we were slogging up and they were handing Trungpa's Russian field binoculars from one to another, scanning the horizon.

I heard a shout and looked up to see Trungpa waving at Akong and me, gesturing for us to come up. 'Look!' he said, pointing to a spot in the distance as we scrambled up beside him. 'There it is!'

We all took turns to peer through the glasses and, sure enough, I saw the gleam of water far away but unmistakable. The river was like a coiled serpent, looping its way to India. I could just about make out the smoke from fires in the villages on the banks of the river.

This discovery electrified us. We had a purpose again, though we were now walking directly towards the critically dangerous part of our journey. To make matters worse our guide realized that we had not been bearing east as much as we should have, and were still in an area where the river was too wide to cross. We knew that the Chinese had control of the main crossing point, so we would have to trek eastwards until we had passed it and found a safer, more discreet point to attempt the crossing. The low-lying region we were heading for was far more densely populated than the highlands we'd been wandering through and the villages were full of Communist spies. Trungpa insisted that we should travel at night to avoid detection. We were just too visible: a train of black ants against the white of the snowy landscape.

I felt a massive surge of adrenaline as we set out on our first night trek but it was soon washed away in cold rain. Visibility was terrible in the darkness and fog so we were travelling more slowly than ever. We stumbled on blindly, walking at night and camping by day. Our food supplies were getting low. Every day more stragglers simply dropped away.

At one point Trungpa performed another divination to determine which was the best way to reach the river. We followed the indications and crossed a high peak and three more ranges. I remember thinking that surely we must be about to see the river in the valley at our feet. I felt crushed when, cresting the third range, we saw yet another line of mountains across our path.

Trungpa called a halt and sent our guide on ahead to reconnoitre the ground. When he returned some hours later he had astounding news: he'd seen a brand new road, less than a quarter of a mile from where we were camped. It had to be the Szechuan to Lhasa road, but nobody had had any idea that there was now a highway running through Lower Kongpo. Our guide told us that it was busy with People's Liberation Army lorries and jeeps, travelling in both directions. I was about to have my first encounter with motorized vehicles.

We now had two perilous crossings to make: firstly the road and then, at a distance that we still couldn't make out, the river. We were hungry and exhausted, but somehow we had to muster the strength to overcome this challenge. The road was busy night and day, but in the darkness the vehicles were at least easy to spot thanks to their headlamps.

Trungpa's plan was simple in theory but terribly risky to carry out: we would wait for nightfall, then walk in single file down the mountainside. We must all conceal ourselves among the boulders at the side of the road and maintain total silence. On Trungpa's orders we would all stand and cross as one.

As we neared our objective my heart felt as if it might pound out of my body. Suddenly, when I was about twenty yards away, I saw the beam of a vehicle's headlamps flash round the bend below us. Everyone flung themselves to the floor. One nun close to me was so distressed that she was saying mantras to herself in a loud voice and Trungpa had to tell her quite sharply to say them under her breath.

I lay on the rocky ground and tried to slow my breathing and control my legs, which were feeling weak and shaky. I could scarcely comprehend the sight of the lorry bearing down on us. Its grinding noise of moving metal parts and the stench of its fuel made me nauseous.

I watched the lorry's rear lights recede in the darkness. We were now very close to the enemy that we had been running from for months. Then, just as I thought we must be about to receive the order to move, another set of headlamps flashed round the bend in the road and were almost upon us. One man had actually stood up and he flung himself to the ground as the noise of many voices talking fast and loud in Chinese flashed past us. For a second I thought they were shouting because they had seen us, but the lorry did not screech to a halt and it too disappeared into the darkness.

I concentrated on my breath, trying to slow my heart rate as I listened for the whispered order.

When it came, all 300 of us stood and then ran as fast as we could, in complete silence, over the road. I dived for cover on the other side. Had we made it without being spotted? I looked around to see whether we had lost anyone. We were all here. I stared wide-eyed at Jamyang and then he pulled me up.

Trungpa had ordered two men to sweep away our footprints and the rest of us reformed into single file and walked as fast as possible away from the roadside and along the valley.

That night we found a sheltered spot to camp that was sufficiently protected to risk lighting fires. I drank a little tea from our almost exhausted stocks and felt much better. We spent the following day there, resting after the ordeal of the road crossing, but then we had to press on. There were still mountains between us and the river. Our guide was almost certain that a particular snow-covered mountain in the far distance was on the other side of the Brahmaputra. All we could do was trudge on towards it.

I heard noises coming from a group of monastics who were walking directly behind the lamas' party. The nun whom Trungpa had calmed down at the road crossing was in a terrible way. She had suffered a complete mental and physical collapse, and Trungpa, after doing what he could to support her to keep walking, took the awful decision that we must press on without her. We gave her what food we could spare and continued.

By now people were beginning to feel the bite of hunger and this, combined with the effects of exhaustion, made them careless. That night several fires were lit, even though the order had been given that it was too risky since we were out in the open and the smoke might give us away. Trungpa had to speak severely to people, which he hated. I could see that he was under an awful strain. Akong did his best to bolster his mood.

That night we camped in a wooded area up on the hills above the river valley. We were drawing close now. It was time to find a crossing point. The difficulty was that this area was full of villages that spread along the river valley and up into the hills behind. We could see smoke and hear dogs barking. It was a cruel reminder that those villages contained the food supplies that we needed. We couldn't risk trying to source provisions, though. We had seen no evidence of Communist troops, but it was safe to assume that there would be informers everywhere.

Luckily we found a valley that was full of dense scrubby vegetation. It was almost impossible to pass through, but that meant that there were no people around, and we slowly forced our way through the scrub until, finally, we found a spur that led down to the riverbank. This was the spot for us to attempt the crossing, Trungpa decided.

It was the evening of 12 December. We pitched our tents and tried to get some rest. Despite my exhaustion, I felt excitement growing. It had been nearly eight months since we left Dolma Lhakang, more than two months since we had had to leave our animals behind and journey on foot, carrying everything we owned. The next few days would determine whether or not all our efforts had been for nothing. On the other side of the river, where the Communist hold on the land was much weaker, we might find some villagers who were prepared to sell us food. But we had to get there first.

The following morning, at sunrise, we set about making as many coracles as we could. There was a particular monk who was skilled at this task and he directed all our efforts. I went to cut long slender branches that could be bent into bow shapes and then lashed together with stronger straighter branches to make a boat. Other people were tasked with soaking the yak skins we had been carrying on our backs for three months so that they would soften, ready to be stretched over the light wooden frames. Pine resin was gathered and rubbed into the leather in order to make it more water-resistant.

It took two days to make eight coracles. Each one could take six passengers with another two men rowing, so it was going to take many trips to get everyone across to safety. Late in the afternoon of 15 December, Trungpa decided that we would all travel that night. He had spotted a narrowing of the river a little upstream. We would have to pass dangerously close to several villages to reach it but it seemed like the safest place to cross. The opposite bank was covered in holly, which would offer protection. There was a spur with what looked like a backwater between us and the other bank, but it seemed that there was a strip of land we could use to reach safety.

Everything was ready. There was nothing to do but wait for nightfall.

I felt nearly sick with adrenaline and nerves. We had heard from our guide, whose Kongpo clothing meant he was able to move around without attracting attention, that he'd spoken with a local scout, who had informed him that the passes on the other side of the river were already impassable with snow. He'd also discovered that two of our party, who had gone missing the night before, had stolen a bullock in one of the neighbouring villages and the authorities were now looking for them.

The mood became hysterical. A row broke out about someone having stolen a small bag of tsampa that had been saved for Trungpa. He insisted that it was unimportant and that everyone must calm down. Our success depended on discipline and it seemed to be falling apart.

In the early hours of the morning we moved off towards the spot on the shore that Trungpa had designated. I heard a dog barking and then saw a man in local dress who turned and walked away when one of our number approached him. Then another man with a rifle appeared. He didn't shoot but he too disappeared as soon as he saw us.

There was not a moment to lose. As the full moon rose, the first coracles were launched. I was in the lead boat with Jamyang, Akong, Tsethar, Yag and Trungpa among others. We were all squeezed in tightly, like sardines in a tin. As the boat rocked in the strong current and the two men who were rowing struggled against its pull, I felt time slow down. My life had brought me to this point and it seemed to stretch out for ever. Then suddenly we were landing. Jamyang turned straight round and returned with the rowers to fetch the next boatload of people. More boats were landing around us. I followed Akong along the spur of land that we had calculated would lead us over the backwater to the other bank. But to our horror we saw that the water had risen. There was no spur and we were now stuck on an island.

Then the shooting started. It was coming from the bank that we had just left, where all our people were. We heard screaming in Chinese and bullets were whizzing all around us. I had never heard gunfire before and I was bewildered by the noise but strangely calm until I saw the terror in the eyes of Yag, who was lying on the wet sand next to me. Then I too became engulfed in total panic.

I could see that others from our group were trying to launch more coracles and were being shot at. Bullets continued to scream overhead. Yag opened my hand and pressed some relics into it. He said that we would all be killed and that the relics would help us on our journey into the next life. I too was convinced that I was going to die.

I felt hands pulling at me, forcing me to crawl on my belly to the water's edge. We had to get off that island.

I plunged into the narrow but fast-moving strip of water. The shock of the cold seized my body and for a second I couldn't move or think. Then a surge of adrenaline coursed through me and I shouted out to anyone who could hear, 'This water is absolutely terrifyingly cold!' None of us could swim. I waded but I was soon up to my neck.

I saw that someone had retrieved a waterlogged coracle and that Trungpa and Akong were heaving themselves into it, but somehow I became separated from them and then they were moving away, taken further downstream by the current.

My foot struck shallower ground and I was able to wade until finally I managed to drag myself out of the water.

I was now on the south bank of the river, soaked from head to foot, freezing, shivering but alive. I was also alone.

Some luggage had washed ashore. I searched through it and to my delight I found some tea and a kettle. Then I heard a woman's voice calling me. It was one of the nuns from our party. We scrambled through the dense holly bushes to get away from the river. I could still hear the panicked cries of all those stuck on the island, the opposite bank or afloat midstream. There was no let-up in the gunfire.

We had no choice but to turn our backs and walk away from the awful sounds of the attack on our group. We began to climb the hillside. Trungpa's plan had been to make for a settlement we'd heard about and hope that the villagers would be prepared to sell us some food and keep our arrival secret. I had no idea which direction to head in but I felt that we must keep moving.

Just then I saw someone up ahead. It was Akong. I ran to him and saw that he was with Trungpa, Tsethar, Yag and everyone else from our boat and that they were all unharmed. I had been numb with panic and cold but that moment warmed me. There was still hope.

There were just thirteen of us in our little group, of the 300 who had gathered to attempt the crossing. Some others had made it to the south bank but had fled immediately and were now gone. We had no idea how many people had drowned in the river or been shot by the Chinese. Jamyang was missing. I couldn't bear to think about that.

We began to walk, straight into the Himalayan winter. We had all thrown away our big bags when the shooting started, on Trungpa's orders. Many of them had contained precious scrolls, paintings and relics, all the treasures of the monasteries, which we had been carrying with us for months. Now Tsethar, in a state of shock and mourning this awful loss, began to grumble and criticize again.

I realized that the relic Yag had given me had washed away. We had virtually nothing between us, just a couple of small packs with some remnants of food. No drinking water. The morning sun did not hit this part of the mountain and the cold as we passed through the dark forest was intense. Our soaking wet clothes began to freeze on our bodies. We could hear shooting that seemed to be on this side of the river. Apparently there were Chinese troops in the area and they were hunting for us.

We pushed on until we found a holly grove that offered good protection and we hid there until darkness fell. Then we walked through the night until dawn, when we camped again. The cold was terrible. Trungpa's attendant found a small quantity of tsampa at the bottom of his pack, which cheered us up but did nothing to alleviate our hunger, which was now becoming intense. At nightfall we set off again. Our guide had no idea which way to go. He'd never travelled in this region. We could see no signs of habitation. For now we simply pressed on away from the river.

After a couple of days like this we reasoned that we were far enough away from the Communist-held areas to walk by day.

By the third day we had climbed to a very high altitude and could see behind us the many mountain ranges we had crossed since we became separated from our companions at the river. I remember sitting with Akong on a ridge and both of us staring in silence at the distance we had come. I was so sad when I thought of all those we had lost. My brother and I were in a place that neither of us could ever have imagined. We were lost, suffering from desperate hunger and exhaustion, but we were calm. In that moment I felt closer to him than I ever had before.

By now we were reaching the limits of human endurance. We hadn't eaten for more than a week and the only thing we had left that was in any way edible was our yak-skin bags, which we now resorted to boiling so we could chew the leather. The skins were roughly cured and still contained a lot of fat, so there was some nutrition there, but not much.

On 19 December we reached snow level. Our frozen clothes made a clinking sound as we walked; we felt like walking ghouls. Once again Trungpa resorted to divination to determine which way we should go. He received a very clear vision that we should climb a mountain to our right and then we would see another range in the distance. Three gaps would be visible between its peaks. We must hike through the centre one. The divination stipulated that this would be the last high range we would have to cross.

This was the encouragement we needed to keep going. As we were walking through the central gap a snowstorm engulfed us and I wondered whether we would be buried alive by snow, but we pushed on and eventually began our descent. The way was terribly slippery and one lama lost his footing and nearly fell over the precipice. He was only saved when his clothing caught on a rocky outcrop and we all rushed to haul him back to safety. That night we made a fire, drank a little tea and chewed on the last of our leather bags.

As we picked our way down the southern slopes of the Himalayas the air grew warmer but I couldn't shake off the cold. I felt frozen to my core. The terrain was tough and the vegetation thick and alien to us. We saw trees with yellow fruits that we'd never encountered before. I know now that they were bananas but, of course, at the time we had no idea that they were edible. We were getting to the point where if we did not eat soon we would die. Every day the walking was harder. My mind was starting to feel foggy.

On 22 December we weighed up our few options. Everyone's face was gaunt, eyes were sunk into their sockets and our tattered clothes hung off our skinny bodies. Somebody suggested surrendering to the Chinese, but everyone else insisted we should continue to India even if we died in the attempt. Besides, we had seen nobody since we crossed the river, so surrendering was not a realistic option. What could we do but keep going in the hopes that we would find a village?

The following day we walked as far as we were able, but then we could go no further. We found a cave in which to shelter and lay down to rest. Our guide told us that if we did not find food within the next day or two, we would all certainly die. He left us and set off to see if he could see any signs of life.

While we waited for his return we kept our spirits up by chanting as we boiled the leather from our shoes. Our weakened jaws could hardly chew the tiny pieces we cut. I was totally depressed at this point. I believed I was going to die.

I woke from a fitful sleep feeling scarcely alive. It was the morning of 25 December. Our guide had not yet returned and Trungpa decided that we could wait no longer. Our last chance was to stagger as far as we could in the hope that we would stumble across someone or something that would lead us to food.

I was almost crippled by starvation and fatigue. I followed Akong blindly up a shallow hill. When I heard a shout I couldn't immediately understand the words, or what I was seeing. It was our guide, on the path ahead of us. He was carrying a large bag and grinning and waving at us. Was this our salvation? I sank down to the floor and had to be helped up. When we reached him I saw that the bag contained tsampa, lots of it. Akong and Trungpa plunged their hands into the bag and passed out food to all of us and I ate and ate until finally I could comprehend what our guide was telling us. By some miraculous piece of luck he had stumbled across my brother Jamyang as he was returning to the cave where we were all sheltering. Jamyang was with three nuns. They had all escaped from a Communist prison camp down at the river, foraged some food and headed for the border via the mountain road, so their journey had been much faster and easier than ours.

I couldn't believe what I was hearing. I had given my beloved brother up for dead and now, not only was he safe, but he had saved us all from certain death with this miraculous bag of tsampa!

'Where is he?' I asked our guide, who took us to a nearby cave, where to my astonishment I saw Jamyang safe and smiling at me. That embrace was the sweetest of my life.

We all sat down and Jamyang told us his story. After we were separated at the riverbank he grabbed what money and relics he could from the shallows where we had thrown them and then he started walking, with no idea where he was going but in the hope that he would find us. It was dark when he arrived at the outskirts of a village. He was immediately arrested by the Communists. The soldiers interrogated him closely. They knew that Akong, Trungpa and other lamas had escaped and were searching for them. Jamyang gave nothing away and pretended to be sick to bring his questioning to an end. This turned out to be a fortunate strategy, because he was left behind when the soldiers marched all the other male prisoners away to a forced labour camp.

Jamyang came up with a plan. There were several nuns also being held captive. They were sent out every day by the authorities to beg for food for the upkeep of the inmates. He asked one nun to get him a supply of tsampa and directions to the Doshong-la pass, the main crossing over the Himalayas. This she did. During the change of guard that night he managed to untie his hands and feet and roll away through the undergrowth, taking three nuns and a young boy with him. This group had travelled along the main road while we were taking our circuitous route through the mountains and had ended up overtaking us. Some four days after the escape Jamyang had bumped into our guide as he was searching desperately for food and now here we all were, reunited in the most extraordinary way.

By dusk, news of our ordeal had spread. A group of people from a nearby village arrived at the cave with pork and wheat flour to make dumplings for us. There was no Chinese presence in this area, they told us. We were safe.

That night, as we feasted, I struggled to grasp that the crisis was past. We were out of danger from starvation and Chinese soldiers alike. It was too much to take in. I fell asleep in my customary position next to Jamyang with a terrible stomach ache but so happy that I would wake in safety and with more food to eat!

Our journey was not over, but from this point onwards we were at ease. Our anguish at the fate of our companions was still raw, but we knew that we would achieve our objective and arrive in India. We had come very close to dying, though. It's possible that we would have stumbled into the nearest village by chance, but the more probable scenario is that we would have died of the effects of starvation if it had not been for that chance encounter between our guide and Jamyang. It still feels almost miraculous to me now, more than sixty years later.

I have been asked how I overcame this ordeal. First of all, it's important to note that many of us did not survive. Even a mentally disciplined and physically fit person is no match for prolonged starvation and exposure.

Part of the explanation is a practical one: I was travelling with the lamas' group and we were always protected and provided for as much as possible. We did not eat our fill even as others were going without, by any means, but the lamas' attendants ensured that there were as many provisions as possible for their masters, and they hung on to those supplies. I had also, as I've said, learned more about forbearance and withstanding the second arrow of suffering than I had realized, during my time in Dolma Lhakang.

The wider explanation, I believe, is that I was surrounded by people who knew something essential about how to trust in their innate wisdom and goodness. Akong and Trungpa were able to stay positive and committed to the idea that they were doing their best. Their courage did not falter, because their faith in their inner Buddha potential did not falter. Trungpa trusted in his divinations and we trusted him. There was a collective discipline in the way that we were able to stay optimistic and support each other, even when it would have been easy to give in to despair.

This inner Buddha potential, or 'Buddha Nature' as it is

generally called, is that quality of basic goodness, unconditional compassion and clarity of mind that is the essence of
every single person. When we can trust in this, and unclench
our anxious minds, everything becomes easier and we discover that we are capable of more than we ever thought
possible.

The Buddha told a story that illustrates how easy it is for
human beings to miss this vast richness we carry within ourselves. A beggar spent his whole life bemoaning his misery.
He had no possessions, and only rags for clothes, and he slept
on a dung heap at night. Every day he raged at his lack and
bemoaned his fate. Eventually he died, without ever discovering that beneath his dung heap was a big nugget of gold. He
was always rich beyond his dreams but he didn't know it. We
must not be like the beggar and die without discovering that
everything we need is within reach. Each and every one of us
is more capable than we know, more courageous, compassionate and calm.

I was too young to embody all this myself during our eight-
month journey over the mountains but I was sustained by it,
even so. I was surrounded by capable elders and a circle of
mutual support. That is something that we can all try to build
in our own lives. When we offer support to others out of compassion, we are open to their compassionate support. This will
sustain us in the tough times and enrich our lives in the good
times. There is no need to be a Tibetan lama to create this way
of being. Every one of us, thanks to our Buddha Nature, can
do so.

On 31 December we reached the village of Pedong. We had
spent three days trekking down the southern slopes of the
Himalaya, crossing the Brahmaputra once again, then moving towards the Assam region of India. When we reached

Pedong, after an arduous climb, we decided to call a halt and rest properly before the final leg of our journey to the newly constructed border post, which was a day's walk away. We were welcomed warmly by the locals and spent two weeks there. It was such a relief to enjoy the luxuries of a full belly and a restful night of sleep, and then to awaken to safety.

One feature of village life that was new to all of us was the custom of drinking beer. Fresh water was in very short supply. The women had to walk down one of the valleys and dig a hole into which water slowly trickled. So beer was the preferred drink. At first all the monastics in our party refused it since intoxication was forbidden, but after a while and out of necessity they relented. The beer wasn't very strong but we drank quite a lot of it. I have wondered whether Trungpa's subsequent problems with alcohol might have their origin in that time.

On 17 January 1960, feeling refreshed and renewed, we arrived at the brand-new border post between Tibet and India. Next to the Indian soldiers' hut was a gleaming white *stupa*, a domed monument containing sacred relics, which delighted all of us. It was wonderful to see this familiar symbol of our Buddhist faith in this alien setting. Next to the stupa stood a sentry from the Indian Army, who greeted us politely. The freshly painted sign behind him read 'Bharat' in Hindi and 'India' in English, against a background of the Indian flag. We had made it.

6. Refugee

I left the Himalayas on 23 January 1960. I've never lived again in the harsh and beautiful world of the mountains, where I grew up. On that final day I clambered into a cargo plane alongside my companions. We were strapped down on the floor for the duration of the flight because there were no seats. We were each handed a bag and told that we could expect to be sick from the turbulence. Then the plane took off and we were flown down towards the plains of India and away from our old lives.

I was astounded by the impossible fact of being inside this contraption, high up in the sky. The noise and the stench of chemicals from the fuel were terrible. The only way I could tell how fast we were travelling was by peering out of a window and tracking the shadow of the plane on the ground far below. I didn't look down for long. It was all too overwhelming.

Then I felt my stomach heave and I vomited over and over again into the bag. Looking round I saw that everyone else was in the same predicament.

Fortunately the flight was short. We were being taken from the mountain town of Tuting to Dimapur in the state of Naga-land. Our final destination was the transit camp at Missamari in neighbouring Assam, which the Indian government had commandeered to process the exodus of Tibetan refugees.

When we touched down at Dimapur I felt a massive wave of relief. I couldn't yet comprehend having survived the nine-month-long trek to get there or even that short but bewildering flight. I was simply desperate to get off the plane and for the sickness to stop.

I stepped onto the hot tarmac of the airstrip and my foot sank a little into its sticky softness. The heat was difficult to believe. We were all used to the pure cold air of the Tibetan plateau. I immediately began to sweat in my thick sheepskin coat that was stinking and encrusted with the grime of many months. I thought I might pass out.

Jamyang steered me away from the plane and towards a jeep that was waiting to take us to the camp at Missamari, several hundred miles away. My mind was now so numbed by the new sights, sounds and smells that I barely registered the landscape I was passing through. I don't remember anything until we were approaching the bridge over the Brahmaputra. I looked down at the brown sluggish water. I couldn't connect this wide slow river with the freezing fast-moving waters where we had been shot at by the Chinese soldiers. The attack already seemed as if it had happened in a different world, a lifetime ago.

I was so tired that when we eventually arrived at the camp I could hardly follow the instructions about where we should sleep and eat. One thing I did notice, though, was that the person in charge was a white woman in Indian dress. I had never seen a white person before. European travellers were virtually unknown in Tibet and in fact had passed into folklore as bogeymen to scare children with. Back in Darak my parents used to tell us that if we were naughty a white-skinned man with a long nose would come and eat us!

A refugee camp in Assam was scarcely a more likely place to find a Western woman than the Tibetan highlands, but there she was. She introduced herself to us as Mrs Freda Bedi and she took pity on us immediately.

Freda Bedi would become one of the most significant people

in my life, in all our lives. She was instrumental in ensuring that the Tibetan Buddhist culture embodied in the lamas and tulkus was not lost, and went on to be a key figure in disseminating Tibetan Buddhism throughout the West. Freda later wrote in her account of working in Missamari that we were the most pitiful group of refugees she had yet seen, our bodies emaciated and eyes sunk deep in their sockets.

On that first day she invited us back to her tent for sweet tea and to tell her our story of escape. When she discovered that several of our group were tulkus, she promised to do what she could to assist us.

But as she led us to our spots in a huge tent and I stumbled after my brother Akong, I could not imagine what she might do to help. All I could take in was squalor and what seemed like thousands of miserable people. I was choking on the filthy dusty air and I still couldn't believe how hot it was. I knew I should be glad to be alive but in that moment it seemed to me that we had swapped a freezing hell for a hot one.

The modern state of India was still only thirteen years old on the day I arrived at the camp. The authorities were doing their best to cope with the influx of refugees but they were seriously over-stretched. It was a delicate political situation for India, given the size and might of neighbouring China, but Nehru's government had received His Holiness the Dalai Lama with all due respect and given him assurances that the Tibetan people would also be welcome. This generous offer of humanitarian support was extended partly because of the long cultural and spiritual ties between Tibet and India, but also as recompense for having failed to object to the Chinese annexation of Tibet back in 1950. We were grateful, but the situation was desperate on the ground.

Freda Bedi was an extraordinary woman, British by birth

but Indian by marriage and inclination. She had been jailed for campaigning for Indian independence and was famous throughout India for her political and social work. She had overseen the relief efforts for refugees in Kashmir after the horrific fighting unleashed by Partition and was also deeply sympathetic to Buddhism and a close contact of the Prime Minister, Nehru. So when she heard that the Tibetan exiles were suffering in terrible conditions, she badgered Nehru into sending her to do something about it.

By the time we arrived, Freda's efforts had already improved things, but they were still bad. There were about 1,000 people in the camp, which was a run-down army base that hadn't been used since the end of the Second World War. There were temporary bamboo structures that had been put up for the first wave of arrivals, but they were all full by the time we got there, so we simply headed for a tent made of sacking, on the edge of the camp.

There wasn't enough water even for drinking let alone for washing, so conditions were squalid, and there was a desperate shortage of medical attention. New arrivals were suffering from injuries, malnutrition and frostbite. Many of us had lost toes, fingers or noses during the winter climb over the Himalayas. There was plentiful food, but it was not what we were used to and we didn't know how to cook it. Worse, our bodies struggled to digest the rice, vegetables and spices. I thought I would be sick the first time I tried to eat dhal and rice and it took me a long time to learn to like it. Conditions grew worse and worse. The camp was actually shrinking despite the constant stream of new arrivals, because there were more people dying of malnutrition and disease than there were arriving. We were completely vulnerable to diseases such as measles and tuberculosis that were unknown in our country, and they began to spread like wildfire. Then there was the problem of unsanitary conditions, which led to outbreaks of dysentery and cholera.

But perhaps the greatest challenge of all was that created by the ordeal we had undergone. We had lost our families, our homeland, our entire way of life. I saw parents whose children had died on the journey and children who had been separated from their families and were alone. There was a mood of desperation, of terrible grief. Now that the crisis was past and we had obtained our objective, what would become of us? We were alive but how could we heal? We had nothing. Where would we go and what would we do?

Trungpa and Akong had no more answers than I did to the practical questions, but, as ever, their faith was unshakeable. On the day after our arrival they set about leading us in prayers and encouraging people to continue their practice. I tried to join in but had little appetite for it.

Those of us who had escaped together stayed in a tight little huddle. Jamyang tried to reassure me that once we moved beyond the transit camp things would improve, but I simply could not understand this world I found myself in. It was all too alien. At Tuting, the border town up in the mountains, I had seen shops and restaurants for the first time. I'd heard three or four different languages being spoken. I'd ridden in a trailer being pulled by a tractor to the airport and then flown in the cargo plane to this hot, dusty place. After the single-pointed focus of our escape, all was now confusion. Even the traditional social structure based on deference towards tulkus, monastics and elders was difficult to maintain here. In Dolma Lhakang I had got used to a life of privilege as the younger brother of the abbot of the monastery. But here our special status meant nothing. We were all simply refugees, fighting for survival in this foreign country.

The Indian authorities insisted that nobody could leave the camp unless they had funds to support themselves, or an external sponsor. All the men, young and old, monks and lamas, had to work on the road-building programme to earn an income. In the intense heat this amounted to a death sentence for many, since we were so weak from hunger and disease. Though we were nominally safe, the situation was distressingly similar to what the Chinese had imposed.

Freda Bedi was appalled by all this but she was unable to prevent it, though she did write to Nehru asking him to put a stop to using refugees on the road-building, and after his personal intervention things eased up for the elderly and the lamas. Freda really admired the wisdom and dignity of the tulkus and was especially impressed by Trungpa, whose brilliance and exceptional capacity for learning English she identified straight away. The two of them very quickly formed a close bond. In fact within a couple of weeks he was acting as her interpreter as she went on her rounds, visiting the sick and overseeing the food aid.

A week or so after our arrival there was an outbreak of dysentery and I was struck down. It was a terrible time. I felt that all the life was draining out of my body. There was little to be done except wait and hope. Akong, who was a skilled physician, did what he could for me and for the many others who were afflicted. I recovered, but some of the younger children and the elderly did not.

We remained in Missamari for about a month and then we were transferred by lorry to the main refugee camp at Buxa Duar in West Bengal, where I was to spend the next few months of my life. Days after setting out I struggled down from the lorry to take a look at our new home. I had recovered from dysentery but had developed the first signs of what turned out to be tuberculosis, as had Yag, Tsethar and both my brothers. We were a sorry and bedraggled bunch as we stood and stared at Buxa.

The camp was close to the border with Bhutan and was at a higher altitude than Missamari, so it was cooler. There was a stream running through it, so water was plentiful, but, none the less, the stench of excrement hung in the air as so many people were simply too sick to walk to the primitive latrines. There was still a terrible shortage of medical supplies.

Thanks partly to Freda's interventions and even more to a personal request by His Holiness the Karmapa, none of our group was sent to work on the road-building programme. As always, I was the beneficiary of special privilege because of being Akong's brother. Trungpa and Akong tried to make themselves useful to Freda when she visited Buxa and she continued to single them both out, particularly Trungpa.

For the first few weeks after we arrived at Buxa I was utterly demoralized. I thought back to the village of my birth and how safe and happy I had felt there. I grieved for the loss of that time and place and for my parents and sisters, my family and friends. Even Dolma Lhakang seemed in retrospect like paradise compared to the escape over the Himalayas and my current reality, displaced and disoriented in this foreign land.

Though I felt completely lost there were in fact a great many efforts being made to give us Tibetans a new start. Even the road-building programme was an attempt, albeit misguided, to provide the employment that people needed. The problem was that we lacked the skills that might make us more employable in a modernizing economy. We were the product of a highly sophisticated culture but one that was completely out of step with twentieth-century life. When I arrived in India I believed, as did all my companions, that the Earth was flat. There was a huge gulf between us and a worldview shaped by industry, technology, commerce and Western secular thinking. His Holiness the Dalai Lama had quickly grasped the urgent need for us all to be helped to adjust to our new world, and when he met with Nehru he asked the Prime Minister to focus on education as the single most beneficial measure beyond essential humanitarian relief.

So a school was founded in the camp at Buxa. The first places were given to monastics and lamas, since they were the most educated class and were therefore expected to make the quickest progress. As many as 1,500 monks from all four of the main Tibetan Buddhist lineages were sent there, and Akong, Trungpa and Jamyang were, of course, prime candidates. They had both Freda Bedi and lately His Holiness the Karmapa himself advocating for them.

His Highness the Karmapa was already at Rumtek, his monastery in Sikkim, by the time we arrived at Buxa. When news reached him that we had made it to the camp he wrote to Trungpa and Akong welcoming them to India and instructing them to attend the college. Somewhat to my surprise he also stipulated that I should attend, even though I was not a monk. So off I went, though I was, if anything, even less motivated to study than I had been at Dolma Lhakang. I struggled to see it as an opportunity. What was the point in studying when the future looked so hopeless? I was ill, a refugee who didn't speak the language of my new country or understand anything about it. But if His Holiness had seen fit to single me out then I wasn't going to argue. There were no alternatives in any case. So I began to learn Hindi and geography and some basics about contemporary affairs.

The food was just as dreadful at the college as elsewhere in the camp and before long we all had parasitic tapeworms. One of the boys with whom I was friendly told me that if you drank the liquid paraffin we used for our lamps it would kill the worms and wash them away. One of my jobs was to collect our weekly ration of paraffin and one evening I decided to drink a whole mug of it. My stomach felt as if it contained a fire ball and I was sick continuously for hours, but luckily I suffered no long-term ill effects. And to my delight it did the trick and killed the horrible long tapeworms!

Not long after we began at Buxa College we got word that Freda Bedi had collapsed, her health destroyed by strain and overwork. She had left the camps and returned to her family home in Delhi to recover, though she continued to work part time for the Social Welfare Board in the Ministry of External Affairs.

Trungpa didn't stay long at Buxa after Mrs Bedi's departure for Delhi. He was as restless, driven and curious about the world as ever. When he received another letter from His Holiness the Karmapa, this time inviting him to come to see him at Rumtek, Trungpa didn't hesitate. He began to plan another escape. The Indian authorities had not relaxed their ban on anyone leaving the camp without a means of support. Political tensions with China were worsening all the time so it was even less likely that they would give permission for a high-profile lama to travel. But Trungpa was determined to visit his spiritual leader. Yag Rinpoche and Tsethar said they would go with him. They were grievously ill but they wanted to see His Holiness the Karmapa one more time before they died. Along with Trungpa's faithful attendant, Yonten, the group escaped in the middle of the night by scrambling under the camp's high wire fence where it crossed the stream.

Akong decided not to go with Trungpa on this occasion. He himself was not well and neither were Jamyang and I. He preferred to stay behind and do what he could to treat the diseases that were afflicting us all. Akong was a physician of great renown in Tibet, here he had no access to the Tibetan herbs and, besides, he had never seen these illnesses before. He and I seemed to be struggling along in a state of semi-recovery, but to my great distress it became clear that my beloved older brother was gravely ill with tuberculosis. The conventional medical services lacked the resources to treat the hundreds of people who were suffering from this and numerous other diseases. There was little to be done.

Some months after Trungpa's departure, Akong received a letter from him explaining that he had been in Rumtek but had decided not to accept an invitation to begin a new life as a teacher within His Holiness the Karmapa's establishment. He had then been with other exiled Tibetans as well as various Westerners in Kalimpong and had made a commitment to move further into the modern world rather than stay in the familiar Tibetan monastic system. He was heading for Delhi with the vague aim of trying to learn more about the contemporary world that so excited him, and how best to bring the teachings to life in this new context. He planned to ask Freda Bedi for assistance and invited Akong to join him. This time, Akong agreed. He had recovered. I was out of danger and Jamyang . . . well, there was nothing he could do for Jamyang.

Not long after Akong's departure, Jamyang began to deteriorate fast. I tried to relieve his discomfort but quickly realized that all I could do was keep him company in this stage of his journey. I was there when he died.

Afterwards I was grief-stricken. Jamyang had been my

consolation, my comfort and my link to the loving secure home of my childhood. Now he was gone. Akong and Trungpa were in Delhi. I was the last one left in Buxa of the little group that had struggled from the banks of the Brahmaputra River to the border with India. I felt utterly alone in the world.

In the face of this personal catastrophe my mind turned of its own accord to the profound Buddhist teachings on impermanence. The lifetime we are currently experiencing is like a gathering of friends and family at a marketplace. There is much activity and laughter and convivial conversation, but then all too soon the market comes to an end and people disperse to go home. Life had never seemed so fragile and fleeting as it did to me on the day Jamyang died.

I was not left alone with my misery for long. Some weeks after Jamyang died, Akong arrived at the college to take me back to Delhi with him. I left the refugee camp gladly but with little excitement about what lay ahead of me.

On that long dusty bus journey, Akong told me of his life in Delhi. He and Trungpa were staying with the Bedi household. The family lived in a small three-room government flat. Akong and Trungpa had been welcomed with open arms on the day they knocked on the door and asked for assistance. It seemed that Trungpa had been in contact with Freda while he was in Rumtek and had informed her of his decision not to stay there but to embrace the modern world. She was delighted to hear from her lama in shining armour and replied with her address and another assurance that she would try to help. So when Trungpa and Akong got to Delhi they were able to track her down. I don't know whether Freda had actually envisaged taking the two of them in, but that's what happened. They had been sleeping on mats on the small verandah for the last few months. When word reached Akong that Jamyang had died and I was now alone, Freda had agreed immediately that he should go and fetch me. Which is how I came to live with Freda Bedi, her husband and their three children.

The flat was tiny and very basic, though of course it was wonderful compared to the camp. I slept on a rug on the floor of the verandah. I felt a bit like a little dog in the corner. For washing we had a cold tap and a mug for splashing water onto our face and bodies. There were no cupboards or drawers in which to put anything. There were no chairs, only cushions and mats and a hard bed-seat covered by a Tibetan rug. In one corner of the sitting room there was a Tibetan shrine with lighted butter lamps. There was hardly any floor space that was dry or clean. Rats regularly scurried back and forth below our feet. This was how people lived in Delhi in those days. I thought back to my time in the monastery at Dolma Lhakang and how I had lived a life of such luxury there but had been unable to appreciate it.

Despite the squash we were treated as part of the family. I was now nearly seventeen and Akong and Trungpa were twenty-two. Two of the Bedi children were of similar ages and they considered us brothers. We all ate together and talked and joked. It should have felt like a new beginning but I still carried a terrible burden of loss and resentment. When I saw Akong and Trungpa laughing and teasing each other I felt excluded and it made my misery sharper. I still wasn't warming to Freda so that made everything tense, especially since Akong and Trungpa clearly adored her and she them. Soon they started calling her 'Mummy', and then 'Mummy-*la*', which pleased her greatly. (The suffix denotes high esteem.)

Mothers are revered in Tibetan culture for their compassionate care of their children, but beyond that, in the Mahayana school of Buddhism – which is the heart of Tibetan Buddhism – compassion is the cornerstone. One way to begin to cultivate compassion is by meditating on the great kindness of our own mother in rearing us and enduring many hardships for our sake. We then extend this feeling of compassion to all living beings, since over the countless lifetimes we have all lived they too have been our mother at some point. This practice of universal compassion becomes the basis for *Bodhicitta* – the deep aspiration to attain Enlightenment so that we may bring all other sentient beings to Enlightenment too.

There is no doubt that Freda Bedi embodied this ideal of compassion, but at the time I simply didn't want to call her 'Mummy'. I missed my own mother terribly. Once again I felt I was on the edge of a group that didn't include me fully. Since I was not a tulku I was of less interest to Freda. I could not hide my misery or my resentment, and my refusal to address her as 'Mummy' increased the bad feeling between us.

When she got home from her government job, Freda would tutor Akong and Trungpa in English and sometimes take them along to parties at foreign embassies so that they could meet important and influential people. She had already come up with a plan for the lamas and tulkus that she so admired. She had a vision of them teaching the Dharma in the West and was laying the groundwork for this to happen. Trungpa, of course, was her favourite because he loved to study and was exceptionally good at it. Akong applied himself diligently too. True to form, I was utterly uninterested and rebellious. After a while she gave up trying with me and insisted that I go with her to her job so that I would not distract the others. I would loiter around the ministry car park while she got on with her work. For her I was the worst kind of Tibetan. I became her example of how you might turn out if you did not do things the right way – which meant her way!

Freda's plan required more than her tutoring Akong and Trungpa in her evenings. She realized that a properly resourced college was necessary for the tulkus if her vision of them as spiritual ambassadors to the West was to be fulfilled.

It all seemed very unlikely to me. Most of us Tibetans were still stuck in the squalor of the camps or on the road-building programme in the far north and south of the country. Besides, for many Tibetans the West was impossibly remote and full of spiritual barbarians. I wasn't sure anybody would even want to go!

But Freda persisted with her vision. She was determined to establish a school for lamas in Delhi so that they could learn English, Hindi and the basics of a modern secular education: science, history, geography and contemporary affairs. Each pupil would also receive religious instruction in the tradition of his own Buddhist lineage.

Freda drew on her close relationship with Nehru and her network of influential and wealthy people. Nehru promised government funding, and with that in place everything else followed. In the autumn of 1961 the Young Lamas Home School was opened in Green Park, a modern suburb on the outskirts of Delhi. His Holiness the Karmapa came from Rumtek at Freda's invitation to conduct the opening ceremony. Trungpa was installed as the principal of the school and Akong was the manager. Each boy was given a new set of robes as a welcome gift and then settled down to a strict regime of study. Freda started off with twelve tulkus and the number soon grew to twenty.

I was not one of them. I wasn't eligible, not being a tulku, and, of course, I had already proved to Freda that I wasn't a worthy candidate for making an exception! In fact our relationship went from bad to worse after the school opened. I did odd jobs and studied a bit of English, but most of my energies went into leading Freda's pupils astray and dreaming up little tricks to drive her mad. I was still an expert with a catapult and I once shot stones at the young lamas' balloons and destroyed them all. Akong was very upset with me and gave me a sound beating. Since I was Akong's brother and had nowhere else to go, Freda had to put up with me, but I always seemed to be on the outskirts of things, causing trouble.

Then I contracted measles, as did Zopa Tulku, another pupil (who later became the co-founder of the Foundation for the Preservation of the Mahayana Tradition in the West). Freda locked us up in quarantine and finally, when our health did not improve, she sent us to the local hospital, where we were both diagnosed with tuberculosis as well as measles. Zopa's condition was not as bad as mine and he responded well to treatment and was soon discharged. But I got sicker and sicker. The infection was severe, and very close to my heart. Eventually the doctors sent me to a specialist tuberculosis hospital in Rajasthan, hundreds of miles to the west of Delhi. The medical staff there were similarly unable to treat my disease and I spent some weeks languishing, feeling as if I were hanging between life and death. I had watched Jamyang die of this illness and now it seemed that it would claim me too. I was almost numb with fear and loneliness.

The next thing I knew was that a fancy American doctor was going to come to the hospital to perform an operation to remove my infected lung. He was the most eminent man in his field and this procedure had never been carried out in India before.

Once again, Freda Bedi had taken compassionate action to save my life. When she heard that I was likely to die she mobilized her network of favours and arranged for me to have the operation. It was a success, though the recovery was agonizing and felt interminable. Two and a half of my ribs had been removed, as well as almost the entirety of one lung. I could hardly sit up in bed, my body had been so weakened. (I still have difficulty sitting up straight for long periods of time, which makes it challenging to maintain good posture for meditation.) I was the only adolescent on a ward full of Indian adults and could barely communicate with anyone. But I was alive, and slowly I began to get better. I started to believe that it was not my time to die.

I had been in India for just over two years when my life was saved by Freda's intervention and the actions of the American surgeon. I was seventeen years old. Many people seem to be appalled on my behalf when they comprehend the things I lost in the course of those three years, between leaving Dolma Lhakang and nursing my scars in the tuberculosis hospital in Rajasthan. If I list them, it does make for a daunting read. I lost my homeland; the only way of life I had ever known; hundreds of companions. My family. My beloved older brother. My health. Very nearly my life. This affected me deeply, of course. I was bewildered, grieving, and I continued to seethe with resentment towards Akong as the ultimate author of my troubles, and latterly Freda as well.

I was also receiving a profound lesson in two of the key tenets of Buddhist teaching: impermanence and compassion. I was learning, once again, that nothing lasts for ever. We can choose whether to regard this as a tragedy or a liberation from self-centred concerns and an opportunity to practise compassion, towards ourselves and others. I always say that in Buddhism, mind is king and how we view things is key. When we witness suffering, and even more so when we experience it for ourselves, our heart and mind can awaken to compassionate action. The tough times become an opportunity to learn, to empathize, to turn towards the positive and to change.

In Buddhism one of the symbols of compassion is the lotus flower, which grows out of mud to bloom upon a beautiful lake. The seed for the flower of compassion germinates in the stinking mud far below the water's surface. The mud is understood to be all those difficult or unpleasant emotions and tendencies that we like to keep hidden from the world and ourselves. Anger, resentment, jealousy and pride, our selfishness, greed and the neurotic patterns of thinking that limit us: they're all part of the mud. Typically we want to get rid of this festering mulch in our hearts and minds but, actually, it's more constructive to see it as the manure for the seed of compassion. If there were no mud then the seed would not germinate and grow up through the waters of the lake and finally burst into flower in our conscious experience and manifest in our daily life.

So rather than try to clear our minds of all negativity, which seems impossible, we can welcome the feelings that make us uncomfortable as a source of transformation. When we face them and engage with our pain and the pain of others, the seedling of compassion begins to grow. We nurture it by being mindful and by practising patience and kindness, until eventually it bursts into flower. Without the darkness, compassion cannot awaken and without compassion, we remain trapped in darkness.

As I lay in that hospital bed it was not lost on me that the two people I most resented had been my saviours. Freda did not like me, I'm still quite sure, but that did not stop her from responding with compassion to my plight. She did not merely feel pity: she took action to alleviate my suffering. This is the essence of compassion, which must be both active and ever-expanding if it is to be meaningful. The Buddha teaches us to show compassion to every sentient being: our friends, but also those we dislike or fear and those who are as yet unknown to us. In the round of infinite lives that we all pass through, even our enemy has been our mother at some point. We will be their mother in a future life. If you struggle with the idea of reincarnation, come back to the law of karma, or cause and effect, which teaches that we will reap what we sow. This insight and the call to action it inspires is of course the cornerstone of all major religions and ethical systems. But I was a slow learner in many ways and even this lesson faded as my pains lessened.

One day Akong arrived at my bedside. He had come to tell me that he was leaving India and travelling to England with Trungpa, who had been awarded a scholarship to study at a famous university in a place called Oxford. Freda had been busy again. I remember that Akong gave me a present, a beautiful wristwatch. I turned it over in my hands as he talked. He seemed excited.

I nodded when he said that Ato Rinpoche, who was taking over at the Young Lamas Home School, would look after me. In truth I was indifferent to the fact that my brother was leaving. I had been feeling so alone for such a long time that I was beginning to get used to it. Besides, my relationship with Akong was still based on fear and a grudging respect laced with resentment, rather than affection. I did not consider his departure a particularly significant loss.

When he stood up to leave he gave me a blessing. I would not see him for another six years. The next time we met was in an airport in Scotland, and my life would once again have been transformed.

7.   *Outsider*

I spent my late adolescence and the early part of my twenties in various different parts of India, which I eventually left in 1969 when I was twenty-five. I was a young man without family, part of a community of exiles. Some of the time I was reasonably content. Some of the time I was lonely. I was always without any sense of purpose. I spent years half-heartedly studying and then working in admin jobs until finally I encountered His Holiness the Sixteenth Karmapa in person for the first time, and a seed of motivation was planted within me. It would take years for it to flourish.

When I was eventually released from the tuberculosis hospital in Rajasthan, Ato Rinpoche came to take me to the new location of the Young Lamas Home School, which was now the only home I had in the world, though I was no lama and had no interest in schooling. Freda Bedi had moved the institution out of the stifling heat of Delhi and up to Dalhousie, a beautiful hill town built across five peaks with views of the Himalayas in the distance. It had been a summer retreat for the British during the time of the Raj and there were churches and large houses built in the English style.

I returned to Mrs Bedi's school knowing that I owed her my life but still unable to fall in line with her imperious way of organizing everyone. I was supposed to be studying but I was very much an outsider, not a lama or even a monk, though not a typical layperson, either. And, of course, we Tibetans were all outsiders in India, though I felt that less strongly in

Dalhousie than I had in Delhi because there was already a Tibetan community in exile when we arrived. That was one of the reasons why Freda had picked the place. That and the cheaper rents and blessedly cooler temperatures and cleaner air. It was also not too far from Dharamshala, another former hill station, where His Holiness the Dalai Lama had established his government in exile.

When I followed Ato Rinpoche through the iron gates I saw a large brick and half-timbered house with a verandah and a gabled roof. The colonial villa was the grandest building I'd been in since I left the monastery, and though it was now a little shabby it was still comfortable and had beautiful gardens full of roses.

I was given the job of attending to the young English teachers that Freda employed to teach her beloved lamas. I used to keep them supplied with bread and butter and cups of tea, which they seemed to prefer to Indian food. They were young idealists, most of them with an interest in Buddhism, whom Freda knew from her political and social work. Some of them had been in India for a while, others were recently arrived from England or the States. We used to have lessons out on the lawns as the monkeys that lived in the pine forests screeched above our heads.

There were some peaceful times but not many. I felt dejected and alone. I was resentful of Akong, who had brought me to Delhi and the Young Lamas Home School and then left me there. I missed Jamyang and Trungpa terribly. And I could not tolerate the blind adoration that both Tibetans and the teachers seemed to feel for Freda Bedi, and that she seemed to require. She was an extraordinarily able, energetic and compassionate person, but she was also bossy and demanding. You had to do things her way, and she seemed to me to be too comfortable with flattery. In other words she was a complex human being, like all of us, but I was not willing to see her in those terms. I was too blinkered by my own pride. Our bad feeling escalated into conflict. One day she shamed me by saying that a friend of mine was destined to become a prime minister of Tibet, while I would always remain a nobody because I was not attending to my studies and was disrespectful to my elders. Ironically, that lama emigrated to America, suffered terrible mental health problems and tragically died of his addiction to drugs.

One day I was having a picnic on the lawn with a group of young lamas. We were in good spirits and playing at wrestling one another. I beat one after another and was beginning to enjoy my new status as unofficial wrestling champion when I fell awkwardly with my left hand behind my back. When I stood up I couldn't feel my left arm at all. Ato Rinpoche took one look and decided it must be dislocated. So he wrenched it back into its 'normal' position. That was even worse. So he had another try . . . I was in so much pain that Freda sent me off with an American teacher to the hospital in Pathankot, where they confirmed that my arm had been broken in two places. Whether that was from the fall or Ato Rinpoche's attempts to help, I'm not quite sure.

The doctors put my left arm in a full cast and I had to stay overnight in hospital. Despite the discomfort, I was excited to be away from the stifling regime of the school and within striking distance of fun. I had spotted a cinema showing Hindi films as we were walking up to the hospital. The movie billboards with their bright colours and promise of music, romance and drama were calling to me. I decided that I should not miss this opportunity. I was an old hand at hospitals by this point and it wasn't difficult to time my escape for while the nurses were elsewhere. The ward was on the ground floor so I simply climbed out of a window and sauntered down to the cinema. When I got back to the school the following day, all the tulkus signed their name on my plaster cast and I felt like something of a celebrity.

That was the start of my obsession with Hindi films. From then on I regularly used to slip away from the school and run down into the valley to spend my evenings in the many little movie houses and cafes. I made friends with local boys and flirted with the rich Punjabi girls. I was a bit of a dandy, very proud of a beautiful denim jacket and pair of jeans I'd managed to acquire via one of the young American teachers. I had a full head of curly black hair then, like an Afro. I thought I was quite the thing. I loved teasing the girls and had a habit of sneaking a needle into the cinema with me and stealthily sticking it into unsuspecting girls' bottoms!

As you can imagine, none of this endeared me to Freda, who was becoming ever more devout in her own practice of Buddhism. So when a letter arrived from Akong suggesting I transfer to a different school for Tibetan refugees, in Mussoorie, Freda leaped at the idea. I was a little sad to leave my circle of friends, both tulkus and local people, but I welcomed the opportunity to start again somewhere new. I was twenty by this point and as restless and unfocused as ever.

Mussoorie is a beautiful hill station in the Dehradun district of the northern state of Uttarakhand. The school was a brand-new venture, founded by a Bönpo lama called Sangye Tenzin whom Akong had met in England. Sangye Tenzin had been invited to teach at Cambridge University and had met an eminent professor there who was fascinated by the pre-Buddhist Bon shamanic religion. The professor became Sangye Tenzin's pupil and helped him to fundraise for the school.

I spent two directionless years in Mussoorie. I wasn't sure why I was there, really. I'd only been accepted because I was Akong's brother. I drifted in and out of lessons and spent most of my time in the town cinema, watching films in Hindi and English. My language skills benefited but I wasn't achieving anything else. I missed Jamyang. Any time I wondered about what had happened back in Darak, I distracted myself from those thoughts by seeking out company, conversation and flirtation. It worked well enough in the moment but, of course, I was storing up trouble for myself.

When the decision was taken to move the school thousands of miles south to the state of Kerala, where there was a large community of Bon Tibetans, I was very unhappy. Kerala had a swelteringly hot and humid climate and life was hard there as the local population were extremely poor. Then Sangye Tenzin began to teach Bon philosophy and practice as part of our core curriculum, which didn't sit well for us Buddhist students. When I said that I didn't want to take part in Bon lessons the teachers said they would expel me. That fired up my rebellious nature and I led a protest by all the Buddhist pupils. We simply refused to come to school. There were only a handful of Bönpo kids and a few teachers left, and the place was forced to close not even a year after it had opened. I had ruined their project.

I'm full of remorse when I look back on my destructive behaviour, but at that time I was essentially selfish and full of pride. I had no interest in learning and no curiosity about Kerala or the people who lived there. The fundamental problem was that I was struggling to process the loss of my family, culture and homeland. It had been six years since I arrived in India and I had no idea what to do with my life. If I were still in Tibet I would have been a monk by now, helping Akong to run Dolma Lhakang. I was glad to have escaped that fate, but this life was hardly more rewarding. I was single at an age when a layperson in Tibet would have been long married. I enjoyed dating when the opportunity arose but had no interest in settling down or starting a family. How could I even contemplate it when I had no sense of my future and knew nothing about myself, or about my own mind?

Naturally I didn't tell Akong anything about what had happened in Kerala. I just made my way back to Delhi with a small group of other disaffected students. I was twenty-two years old and was surly and miserable.

The Tibetan government in exile paid for our return and then offered to send many of us, including me, to university. By that time the plight of the Tibetan diaspora was attracting a lot of sympathy from all over the world and they had received numerous scholarships from overseas governments. I was more or less given my pick of opportunities. I was crazily fortunate, in some ways, though that future was not necessarily a healthy one for everybody. Many other young Tibetans did go to Europe and the USA but lots of them struggled to adjust to the Western lifestyle and some ended up dropping out and slipping into addiction. I think the Tibetan people were struggling with the legacy of traumatic loss and for some of them it was all too much. It might have been especially hard for the tulkus and other high lamas, because they were treated in the West almost as exotic creatures rather than human beings. The contrast between the feudal society they had come from and the consumerist individualistic culture they encountered was just so enormous. In the West at that time Buddhism was very much associated with the counterculture rather than the mainstream, so many Tibetans, especially the teachers and tulkus, found themselves in a setting where drink, drugs and free love were the norm. They were completely unprepared for this. Often they travelled alone or with just one other companion, so they were isolated and revered at the same time. I certainly found the adjustment very hard myself, when I arrived in Scotland in 1969, and I had a lot of support compared to some others.

When I was offered the opportunity to study abroad at the end of 1966 I turned it down. I wasn't interested in the West or in further study for its own sake. Instead I opted to stay in Delhi and enrol on a course to train Tibetans in the administration skills required to build and manage the network of camps, schools, hospitals and other facilities for the Tibetan community in India. In Tibet no such training had existed and there was a desperate need for people with these skills. I already spoke good English and Hindi, and I thought this was work that might give me something useful to do.

For the first time in my life, I was right. When I finished the course I was asked which refugee camp I wished to be assigned to. I chose Tashi Jong in north India, where the Tibetan government in exile was buying land for a new settlement. My job was to oversee a programme to teach Tibetans the agricultural skills they needed to farm in India, since the conditions were so different from what we were used to. I helped to set up tea plantations and other farming settlements and I loved the work. Most of the people were from the Kagyu and Nyingma groups, and I felt a particular affinity with them. I was often still very lonely but I was starting to feel settled for the first time in years.

Then I was told that I was going to be transferred to a much larger Tibetan settlement in the south of the country where they badly needed administrative officers. It was a big opportunity, the sort of thing that might have made my career. But

I didn't want to go. I'd had a terrible time in the south of India at the Bon school and, in any case, I was tired of moving around. I'd been transplanted so many times in my life and I wanted to put down some roots. The government official I spoke with wasn't very sympathetic. I had no idea what to do.

While I was trying to decide, His Holiness the Karmapa visited Delhi. I happened to be there at the time, because I had been dating one of his nieces and I was visiting her. I was very keen to meet him. I'd heard so much about him but I'd never so much as laid eyes on him.

My girlfriend arranged a personal audience. I arrived, full of curiosity and some trepidation. His Holiness was a larger-than-life figure renowned for his extraordinary clairvoyance, charisma and ability to relate to people in just the way they needed. Some found him playful, almost childlike, while others experienced him as terrifyingly wrathful. He was, as I would discover, one of the wisest, most compassionate and powerful people I've ever met. He was magnetic.

As I bowed to him I had the disconcerting sensation that he could see into my mind. He spoke as if he'd known me for a long time and knew all my faults. He was extremely severe with me and he was very blunt about what I should do. 'You bad man,' he said. 'What are you doing messing around here? Come to Rumtek with me!' When I protested that I had a job, that I was supposed to be going to the south to oversee a big project, he ignored me. I felt absolutely frozen to the spot and unable to say anything to resist his argument. But I also felt a deep and instinctive trust that His Holiness knew what was best for me. That, in fact, he knew *me*, that he had known me over the course of many lifetimes. So I found myself agreeing to go with him, to his monastery. This filled me with nervousness but also deep relief.

I left that encounter and went straight off to ask my employers for a month's leave. In the end, I never did go to the big camp in the south of India. My career with the government in exile ended there. Instead I spent fifteen months in Rumtek with His Holiness the Karmapa, acting as secretary and translator but being treated more as his son and receiving many teachings. It was an absolutely precious time in my life, though, true to form, I was resistant to much of its transformative effect. At least in the short term.

Within a few weeks of arriving at Rumtek at the end of 1967, I was on my way to Bhutan, accompanying His Holiness the Karmapa on a formal visit to the royal family. The Karmapas had been spiritual advisers to the kings of Bhutan for many hundreds of years and over the course of many successive reincarnations, as they had with the emperors of China. The current king of Bhutan was absolutely devoted to the current Karmapa and invited him for an extended visit. The others in our group were elite monks who were assisting the Karmapa with religious duties. We all had a wonderful time. We were given quarters in the royal palace and stayed there for two months. I couldn't quite believe my luck. This was a level of comfort and luxury I'd never seen before. After so many years of hardship, it was very welcome.

The king took our group on a pilgrimage of Bhutan's holy sites. One that particularly moved me was the famous cave called Tail of the Tiger, perched high up on a cliff face, where the great eighth-century master Padmasambhava, or Guru Rinpoche as he is known to Tibetans, sat in meditation.

Guru Rinpoche is particularly dear to us because he brought Buddhism to Tibet from India. His was the large statue in the abbot's temple in the labrang, back at Dolma Lhakang. He is famous for having tamed the powerful negative forces at work in our country at that time through his skill in turning adversaries into allies of the Buddhist teachings. His speciality was teaching the path of *tantra*, which flowered in the sixth and seventh centuries CE and became one of the hallmarks of the Tibetan tradition.

The Sanskrit term 'tantra' refers to the warp of a loom or the strands of a braid. It also means 'unbroken continuity', and refers to our Buddha Nature, that innate goodness and wisdom which can never be tarnished or diminished despite the many troubles that befall us in life. It is like a seamless thread running through all our thoughts, words and deeds, and when we recognize it, our life can change. We then act from a place of inner confidence and clarity instead of lack and confusion. This teaching was to affect me powerfully in later years but at this time I could not really hear it. I was not yet mature enough. It lodged in my heart, though.

When we returned to Rumtek I settled into my new life. The monastery had just been completely rebuilt with the generous help of the royal family of Sikkim, and it was a spectacular and beautiful place. The Karmapas had had a monastery on the site since the seventeenth century but it had fallen into ruin. When His Holiness the Sixteenth Karmapa fled Tibet he was determined to rebuild this ancient seat of his lineage and had sketched its original design from memory without any recourse to plans or books. It took four years to build and was inaugurated on Tibetan New Year 1966, a year and a half before my arrival.

There were a couple of very comfortable guesthouses and I fancied staying there rather than in the main complex. It would make it easier for me to pursue my leisure activities of gambling, movie-going and chatting up young women. But His Holiness had other ideas. When I told him that I wanted a little freedom because I was a layperson not a monk, he was blunt with me. 'I will make the decisions, not you! You will stay in the temple!'

That was the tone of our whole relationship. I was constantly pushing for freedom, special dispensations and preferential treatment, and he was adamant that I would do as he said. Though, actually, the Karmapa did single me out and treat me very kindly. The main temple complex only had accommodation for His Holiness and his four Heart Sons, the high lamas who are the Karmapa's closest disciples and lineage holders. Even the relatives of the Sharmapa, one of the Heart Sons, slept on the floor. But I insisted that I needed my own room and I was allotted a small bedroom next to the Tai Situpa, another of the Heart Sons. I am amazed at my own arrogance when I look back on it now. I always demanded that everything go my way.

My day job was to act as personal secretary to the Karmapa. My administrative skills made me very useful to him. I dealt with correspondence and answered the telephone, which had just been installed and took me a while to get used to. I also acted as his translator with the Hindi- and English-speaking visitors we received. The Karmapa's fame attracted many students to Rumtek.

As well as working I was receiving instruction from the esteemed Khenpo Thrangu Rinpoche, who was teaching the key treatises of our Karma Kagyu lineage to the four Heart Sons. (A *khenpo* is akin to someone with a PhD in the West.) The Karmapa asked Thrangu Rinpoche to teach me the Four Foundation practices, which are the core preliminary practices of Tibetan Buddhism. The Tibetan term for them is Ngöndro. They are very vigorous and time-consuming and lay the foundation for the higher tantric practices. The first of them involved doing 100,000 full-body prostrations to an image of the lineage masters of the past. The idea was to develop humility – which I certainly needed then – and confidence in one's own Buddha Nature as embodied by these great masters of the past.

The second is Dorje Sempa, which is a purification practice that involves reciting a 100-syllable mantra 100,000 times. The main focus here is sincere regret for one's negative thoughts, speech and actions along with a commitment not to do them again. The third is Mandala Offering, which is concerned with accumulating merit and wisdom. Merit means generating a momentum of positive energy in the mind that provides the context for realizing that all things are interconnected, so not separate and set apart. This realization is wisdom. Merit is generated by offering a symbolic representation of the universe to all the Buddhas and Bodhisattvas, 100,000 times. The fourth foundational practice is Guru Yoga, which consists of praying with devotion to one's guru or teacher to receive the grace and blessing that comes from their lineage (in this case the Kagyu lineage). We can use the analogy of a cup to understand how the Four Foundations prepare our mind to receive the higher tantric teachings. The practice of prostrations is like turning an upturned cup over, so that liquid can be poured into it. Dorje Sempa purifies the impurities, as if we are cleaning the cup. Mandala Offering is like repairing any cracks in the cup and then Guru Yoga is receiving the liquid in the cup, or receiving the blessing. Blessing really refers to our mind becoming more positive, through a process I call 'alchemy'. The aim of the Four Foundations is to provide the appropriate conditions for the alchemy to take place: turning the mud of a negative mind into the gold of a positive one.

You probably won't be surprised to learn that I was not a

good student. I couldn't see the point of doing countless prostrations, so I didn't complete even this first of the four practices. I was nominally a Buddhist but in reality had no interest in deepening my practice, despite the exceptionally privileged position I found myself in at Rumtek, with access to some of the most revered masters. The prostration practice felt more like punishment than anything else. So I would slip away and head off to meet my friends outside the monastery to gamble, or flirt, or drink beer. We used to play cards for hours on end. The only problem was that I was not very good at it, so I lost whatever little money I had.

The Karmapa always seemed to know what I was up to. He would bellow out at the top of his voice, 'Where is Jamdrak? Where is that scoundrel?' and then, without waiting for a response, he would send a young monk off to drag me from whichever gambling den or local cinema I was hiding out in. When he'd done this one time too many, he insisted that I carry out the prostrations in the most sacred of all the shrine rooms, where he performed the Black Crown ceremony, a ritual for directly transmitting the energy of enlightened wisdom. The Black Crown had been presented to the Fifth Karmapa by the Chinese emperor Yongle in about 1410 and was said to have been woven from the hair of 100,000 dakinis. (In the Christian pantheon these might be described as angels.) The Black Crown shrine room was right next to His Holiness's quarters, so there were no more escapes for me. I had to knuckle down.

I spent three months doing prostrations. I would use a *mala*, which is similar to a rosary, and a small pile of pebbles on the floor to keep track of how many I'd done. Each time I did a prostration I turned over one of the beads on the mala. When I reached the last bead (there are usually twenty-seven of them), I would place one of the pebbles forward on the floor. When I finished my session I would count up the pebbles on the floor and enter the figure into a little book. I managed about 80,000 but my heart wasn't in it and I learned very little. This was the pattern for my time at Rumtek. I was given so many opportunities that are not normally extended to a lay-person, let alone one with so little practice to his name, but I didn't make full use of them.

Freda Bedi arrived at Rumtek during my time there and was given full ordination by His Holiness the Karmapa. She was the first Western woman to become a Tibetan Buddhist nun. Afterwards she asked to receive the Vajrayogini and Karma Pakshi empowerments, so that she could undertake their respective practices. Vajrayogini is one of the main tantric deities of the Kagyu lineage. She is red-coloured and slightly wrathful. Karma Pakshi is a specific Guru Yoga practice. Before doing these practices you need three things: empowerment, scriptural transmission and teaching on the practice. They can only be imparted by a highly accomplished master such as His Holiness the Karmapa, initially via an empowerment ritual. I too received them, as well as the scriptural transmissions for the various Guru Yoga practices, including Karma Pakshi. I think Freda was a little astounded to find me there, alongside her. I can't blame her, because the truth is that I was blind to the power of the sacred tantric tradition of Buddhism at that time, though these teachings certainly came to my aid many years later when I was in solitary retreat in New York.

Despite my lack of application, I continued to feel enormous admiration and respect for His Holiness the Karmapa. He was not a man who ever felt the need to explain himself in words, but I felt that he was refusing to give up on me. He saw something in me that I could not. I never lost my sense that he could read my mind, which meant I was always a bit frightened of him. There was something so obviously powerful about him. It was as if he emanated a luminous energy. I also loved and trusted him completely. And he continued to accept me as I was: selfish, closed-minded, rebellious and arrogant. He would allow me to sit cross-legged opposite him as he was making the sacred black pills for which the Karmapas are famous. The secret recipe dates back to the time of the very first Karmapa in the twelfth century. The pills are given to people at the time of death and are believed to help the person's consciousness navigate the *bardo* – the forty-nine-day interval between death and rebirth. One day when I was sitting at his feet I cheekily asked him for some pills. Nobody else would have been so irreverent, but I didn't know (or care) anything about protocol. He just laughed and amazingly, considering how precious they are considered to be and how inappropriate a person I was to receive them, he actually gave me one large pill and five small ones. I have given the small ones away over the years, but I still have that large precious pill on my shrine.

To add to my increasing ambivalence about being at Rumtek, I kept meeting young Westerners, who were arriving in ever-greater numbers. As well as those who were very committed to deepening their Buddhist practice there were Peace Corps volunteers and hippies fascinated by Eastern religions and the search for Enlightenment. I had met mostly English people at the Young Lamas Home School. Now I met people from the United States and all over Europe as well. My curiosity about the outside world was growing, alongside my restless sense that I could not stay in Rumtek.

So after I'd been there for almost a year I wrote to Akong, asking him to help me. I had decided that I wanted to go and join him and Trungpa. They had recently founded Samye Ling in Scotland. Named after Samye, the first Buddhist monastery in Tibet, it was the first Tibetan Buddhist centre outside Asia. Could Akong send me the money for the airfare and help me to get the necessary travel documents to leave India? My brother was keen for me to join him and wrote to the Karmapa asking him to release me. His Holiness was absolutely furious, with both of us. He replied to Akong that it was his choice to keep me at Rumtek and that Akong should do nothing to help me to leave. He said it was his business how he treated me, not Akong's. At the time I felt a bit like his property, though I now appreciate that His Holiness wanted me to stay because he already had plans for me. In any case, my brother stopped communicating with me from then on.

I think it was this that cemented my determination to leave. I could not abide the feeling that I was not free. Ironic, since I had closed my mind to the most profound teachings that would have brought me to true freedom. But it simply wasn't my moment to receive them.

It might seem that I missed endless opportunities to learn, to choose the path towards ordination as a Buddhist monk that I eventually took. But looking back, I do not see it that way. I was learning about other matters, such as the addictive pull of material things and the trap of self-indulgence, which have been necessary in order for me to become an effective teacher here in the West. I prefer to see seeds of positive change that were sown and that have flourished eventually, often in surprising ways.

Many of us struggle not to look back on our pasts and castigate ourselves for having failed to grasp an opportunity, learn a lesson or appreciate how lucky we were. Why did we miss our chance? Why did we choose to remain stuck? I meet many people who have struggled with lifelong mental health issues, deep sadness or addiction. They are often filled with regret and self-hatred. When we first meet they seem to assume that I have always been content in myself and sure of my vocation. I laugh and tell them that until I was thirty-seven years old I was a mess. My mind was all over the place. Change is a complex process and we must give it time. So long as we persist in sowing those good seeds, nurturing them as lovingly as we can, and treat our past and present selves with deep compassion, we will find that we have been moving in the right direction.

Just over a year after his first visit His Holiness the Karmapa was once again invited to stay with the Bhutanese royal family. This time I remained behind to help with the running of the monastery. Then I got word that Trungpa had returned to India for the first time since his departure. He had been studying with many different masters and would be coming to Rumtek. I was overjoyed to see my old friend. It had been six years since I'd spent much time with anyone I'd been close to in Tibet. Trungpa was his old self: jolly and warm, funny and brilliant. I implored him to take me with him, back to the UK. He knew all about Akong's exchange with His Holiness the Karmapa but he was never one to follow orders, and he agreed immediately.

After he'd set off for Delhi I took a fifteen-day leave of absence from Rumtek and went to stay with him. Through his connections to the Canadian High Commission, I managed to get a visa to England. My only form of identification at the time was an Indian identity card. Sorting out the papers would probably have taken years without Trungpa's help but it was all managed very quickly. My brother sent me the money to buy the airfare, reluctantly since he did not want to go against His Holiness the Karmapa's wishes. But I didn't care. I sent word to His Holiness the Karmapa that I was leaving India and that was that. I was twenty-five years old and I felt free.

My departure from India was luxurious compared to my arrival, nine years previously. Early in 1969 Trungpa and I boarded a plane for Paris. Trungpa wanted to stop off there on the way to Scotland, to see a girlfriend. I was rather taken aback by this because I had always known him to be a celibate monk. But as I had discovered during our chats in Delhi, young people in the West were rejecting the old ways and exploring alternative lifestyles, values, politics and spirituality. Trungpa, with his natural authority, charisma and boundless curiosity, was very much part of this movement. He was nearly thirty by this point and had been in England since 1963, watching the social upheavals of the sixties up close. He was increasingly rejecting traditional Tibetan ways, though his faith in Buddhism and love for the Dharma had not and would never falter. He told me that his recent time in India and Bhutan had merely consolidated his belief that he must shed some aspects of his religious identity should he become an effective teacher of Buddhism in the West. He had decided to return his monk's vows to His Holiness the Karmapa. He was now a layperson. All of this, not to mention his stories of indulging with alcohol and many girlfriends, was slightly shocking to me but exciting. I loved Trungpa deeply and trusted that he would be my guide to this new phase of my life. As would Akong, of course. My heart sank a little at that prospect.

8. Rebel

On the day we were reunited after six years apart, my brother was distant and simmering with irritation. Understandable in one sense, since he had been waiting for Trungpa and me for more than a week. When we didn't show up at Glasgow Prestwick airport at the expected time he assumed we'd be on the flight the following day. When we weren't on that either he reported us missing to the police. By the time we eventually arrived at Samye Ling he was really worried. He'd been back to Glasgow to speak to the authorities and seen our faces on posters, but found no trace of us. So we were not exactly received with open arms when Trungpa strode into the entrance hallway to Johnstone House. I could say that Akong and I got off to a bad start in Britain, but, really, it was a continuation of our always difficult relationship.

It was typical that neither of us had let Akong know that our plans had changed. We ended up spending three days in Paris. Dazed from my first encounter with the West I barely left our cheap hotel, but Trungpa seemed to have a lot of fun. From Paris we flew to Birmingham, and from there we drove up to Samye Ling via Manchester. Trungpa wanted to stop in there to visit another lady friend. I can't remember anything about the drive or the blur of English cities flashing past outside the car window except that it was raining and everything was grey. I had been used to blue skies, fierce cold and bright sunshine in Tibet. It had cost me, but over my ten years in India I'd adapted to the heat of the Indian plains. England was neither hot nor cold, just damp.

With all these detours, it wasn't until a week after we left Delhi that I arrived at my destination and had a chance to look at this new world I'd chosen. I wasn't at all impressed. Samye Ling was just a single building in early 1969 when I arrived. It was housed in a Victorian former hunting lodge just outside the village of Eskdalemuir in the Scottish Borders. The River Esk wound through the grounds and the countryside reminded me a little of the area around Darak, but the house itself was damp, dilapidated, cold and gloomy. Previously there had been hooks in the roof's gables where the gamekeepers had left the game to hang after a successful day of sport. Akong and a team of volunteers had carried out some basic renovations after they took over the building in 1967 and the hooks had been removed, but I found it ironic that this temple to blood sports was now dedicated to the Buddhist philosophy of non-violence. Ironic and rather unpleasant.

From the moment I arrived at Samye Ling and for years afterwards I felt I had made a mistake in coming. When I followed Trungpa into Johnstone House and saw Akong's impassive face it felt as if I were returning to my own past. Samye Ling was not Dolma Lhakang, I was not a child any more and yet here I was, under his influence again. I felt the old resentment close around me, like a trap. In Rumtek I had at least had useful work to do, assisting His Holiness the Karmapa with admin and translating. Here I had no job, no role, no purpose. I was back to being the little brother, the one who wasn't a tulku. Outside it was raining and cold. The local people I'd passed on our way here seemed baffled at best by the presence of two Asian men, one in monk's robes. I had been an outsider in India, but here I was an alien.

Samye Ling is my home now but it has taken a long time and a personal transformation for me to see it that way. Back in 1969 it turned me into a rebel, but, unlike Trungpa, I couldn't make common cause with the young Westerners who came seeking new answers to old questions. The only cause I ever had was resentment of authority. I felt as alienated from the new ways as I did the old.

On my first day I walked into the dining room where all the residents and guests ate together and felt overwhelmed by the noise of English and Tibetan being spoken and the smell of vegetarian food and damp, musty clothes. The place was full of people of roughly my age, with long hair and colourful clothing. They seemed smelly and untidy to me, not like the teachers at the Young Lamas Home School or even the Peace Corps volunteers and visitors at Rumtek. In those days Samye Ling was full of characters, many of them hippies and spiritual seekers. Some of them were very sincere but many were dabbling, and they came and went leaving a trail of marijuana smoke behind them. I didn't know it but there were already tensions building between Trungpa and Akong over the drug use and many other things besides. They had completely opposing approaches to spreading the Dharma in the West. Those tensions were about to bubble over.

Samye Ling had been a joint labour of love for Akong and Trungpa. They were offered the building in 1967, by the trustees of the organization that owned it. The place was already being run as a Buddhist centre, but the Canadian-born monk in charge was going home and the centre needed new directors. After his studies at Oxford University were completed, Trungpa had established a name for himself as a teacher and was beginning to attract quite a following. Trungpa and Akong were well connected within the small British community of Buddhists and Buddhist sympathizers, and were well liked. They had leaped at the opportunity. It was particularly welcome for

Akong since he had spent the years since his arrival in Britain working as a hospital orderly at Oxford's Churchill Hospital, earning a wage to support himself, Trungpa and other lamas. He had sought out this job since it took him as close to medical work as he would be allowed, given that his Tibetan traditional medicine qualifications were of course not recognized. But it was hard for a man who had grown up in a position of privilege to clean toilets and wheel hospital trolleys for a living. Years later he told me that at the beginning he might have despaired if he hadn't had his faith to fall back on, though in the end he was grateful for the experience. It allowed him to practise humility and compassion.

On the day I arrived there were just twelve residents, including Trungpa and me. The only other monk was an Englishman called Lodro Thaye who'd been ordained in the Tibetan tradition. There was also a famous Tibetan artist and former monk called Sherab Palden, who had painted a series of traditional *thangkas*, religious artworks depicting divinities and lineage masters, around the top of the walls in the shrine room. Sherab had given up his robes when the Chinese invaded and then joined the resistance fighters in Kham. He'd escaped not long before us and made his way to India. I had met him in Mussoorie during my time at school there and we'd become quite friendly, so I was pleased to see another familiar face. Everyone else was British or American. The cook, who was from America, made terrible macrobiotic food that neither Trungpa nor I could stomach. A macrobiotic diet was practically compulsory for anyone interested in the counterculture of the sixties. It derived from Zen Buddhist principles of the need to balance yin and yang in the body in order to be healthy, but in practice it seemed to mean eating raw vegetables, a lot of brown rice and not much else. For a while we used to bring him lamb from the local butcher's but he didn't want to cook it and it always ended up burned. Cake was my salvation in those early days. I developed a terrible sweet tooth from eating so much cake!

As well as the full-time residents there were always lots of visitors, many of whom stayed in the rather dilapidated huts at the side of Johnstone House. Whenever a course was being run, some of us residents would have to move out there or up into attic spaces to make way for the paying guests. Trungpa gave the instruction and Akong took care of the practical side of running the centre. There was only one shrine room at the time. It had a huge bay window and it was the brightest, most comfortable room in the house, though it was cold, like everywhere else, since we couldn't afford to keep the creaky old central heating running. It was painted in rich yellows and crimsons and there were butter lamps and incense as well as a little Tibetan dog called Sengdruk who was like the discipline master. He would sit quietly while people meditated, and if anyone shuffled in their seat or made a noise he would bark and stop them in their tracks!

Though I loved Trungpa I didn't attend his teachings. Akong did not insist that I attend prayers, get a job or do anything at all. I spent most of my time loitering in my tiny bedroom, listening to Hindi pop music on a portable radio. I missed India. After a while I stopped coming down for meals, because I couldn't face the people downstairs. Sherab would bring food up to me. On the one hand I was very spoiled, but I was also completely adrift and unhappy. I hadn't known what to expect from a new life in the West but it wasn't this chilly and purposeless existence. I cut myself off from the life of the community and felt even less engaged with Buddhism than I had in Rumtek. I missed out on all the powerful teachers who began to arrive as more and more

Tibetans left India. Samye Ling was the only Tibetan Buddhist centre in the West at this point, so every lama and tulku came to give teachings. I missed out on other experiences too. Both Leonard Cohen and David Bowie came to Samye Ling in 1969. Bowie had been seriously interested in Buddhism a couple of years before, when he was studying with Akong and Trungpa's friend Chime Rinpoche, at his centre in north London. He didn't stay for long at Samye Ling as his interest was softening by then. I had no idea who he was. The same went for Leonard Cohen. I was too busy sulking in my room to have any interactions with them. I was sorry about that later when I discovered Western pop music and their songs.

I did make one friend among the hippies who came to stay. He was a young aristocrat and I found it easier to be around him as he didn't take drugs and was less smelly than the others. He had a flat down in London and he gave me the keys and told me I could stay whenever I wanted. So when I was feeling particularly fed up I would get the train and go there for a few days. He seemed to have a very busy life so I hardly ever saw him. Most of the time I was on my own, drinking whisky, which I'd started to develop a taste for. My friend was out on the town in Swinging London but I didn't join him. I felt as if I didn't fit in anywhere.

My one pleasure at Samye Ling was to go for long walks in the countryside. Often I would walk for hours in the afternoons with Akong and Sherab. We watched the seasons come and go and I loved to see the changes in the landscape, which were more gradual than in Tibet. The colours of autumn and the birth of the lambs in spring gave me particular delight. The animals reminded me of my childhood in Darak.

Trungpa was as kind to me as ever but he was busy with his own concerns. He and Akong were falling out badly, and though there was no overt hostility between them, the tensions were felt by all of us. Gradually two camps emerged: Trungpa and his mostly Western and younger devotees on one hand, and Akong and a small group of Tibetan and older people on the other. The fundamental dispute was between Akong's traditional approach and Trungpa's modernizing one. Akong wanted to preserve the time-honoured traditions of Tibet as the best way to spread the Dharma. Trungpa didn't think that would work. He wanted to adapt to Western norms, especially since there was a social revolution going on that meant more and more people were open to Buddhism. This difference was always going to be a problem but it was made more personal, and more antagonistic, by the fact that Trungpa was drinking heavily and sleeping with his female students. He was clearly breaking the precept to refrain from intoxication and Akong was concerned that he was also breaking the precept to refrain from sexual misconduct. He didn't voice his concerns, because of their old friendship and the enormous respect he had for Trungpa both as a person and as the embodiment of a long lineage of tulkus. Trungpa was also conscious of their friendship and all the experiences they had shared, in their current lifetime and over many previous ones. Nevertheless he had no intention of changing his behaviour or approach.

I colluded with him in his drinking and helped him to get alcohol. Trungpa was still hiding the extent of his drinking and drug-taking from Akong and Sherab at this point, but I knew what was going on. I felt a lot of sympathy for Trungpa. He had always been a great friend to me and, of course, I was in rebellion against Akong's authority. Also Trungpa was felt to be exceptional, not just by me but by everybody who encountered him. It was almost as if the normal rules did not apply, because of his obvious gifts and also because he was such an important and senior figure in our very hierarchical culture. I could not refuse him when he asked me for help.

Things got worse when Akong went back to India in 1970 and left Trungpa and me in charge. Trungpa was drunk and out of control much of the time. He went out and bought himself a red Triumph motorcar and took to racing around in it. He hadn't even passed a driving test. He'd taken several but he kept failing, and in the end he asked an English follower of his to dress up in robes and take the test for him. That's how he got his licence!

One day Trungpa was driving to Newcastle to see one of his many girlfriends. He was completely drunk and as he was passing through Carlisle city centre he took a bend much too fast and crashed his car straight into the window of a joke shop. Luckily nobody else was hurt, but he was badly injured and was taken to hospital, where he spent several weeks recovering. Initially he was paralysed on the left side of his body and was unable to speak. I visited him often, and to my relief he made a good recovery, though he walked with a limp for the rest of his life. After the accident his energy seemed to change. He was less gentle and even more full of zeal to teach in his own way. His mind was as brilliant as ever and he made the decision to set aside his robes. He no longer wanted that division between him and the people he was teaching.

I felt terribly guilty about his accident. I had been complicit in his drinking habit and I knew he was driving while intoxicated and without a licence. He might have been killed. He might have killed others. Remonstrating with Trungpa was impossible, though. I held him in such high regard. We simply didn't have that kind of relationship. He needed a lot of help after he was discharged from the hospital, and I continued to support him in any way I could.

By the time Trungpa was released, Akong had returned from India. He was very upset by the accident. Trungpa for his part was drinking even more than before. He was an exceptional person but he could be destructive, and this trait grew stronger after his accident. His behaviour began to enrage Sherab, who previously had been totally devoted to him. He had thought that it was Akong who was causing all the bad feeling, but after a while he could no longer ignore the evidence of his own eyes. When Trungpa admitted the extent of his drinking and drug-taking Sherab was so angry that I had to stop him from punching Trungpa.

The other great worry for Akong and Sherab was Trungpa's habit of sleeping with his female students. One of them, Diana Pybus, was only fifteen when she began to visit Samye Ling. She was from a wealthy family living in London and she returned many times without the knowledge of her parents. She had developed a passion for Trungpa and they quickly became sexual partners.

Not long after he returned from hospital, Trungpa decided to go to convalesce at Garwald House. Garwald was a mile or so away and was owned by a couple of wealthy local people, Christopher and Pamela Woodman, who had become devoted followers of Trungpa. Most of Trungpa's group consequently decamped with him.

I continued to be Trungpa's accomplice. Despite my feelings of guilt, I carried on supplying him with cigarettes and alcohol. I didn't go with him, though. The atmosphere at Garwald was not to my liking, and for this reason and out of loyalty to my brother I stayed at Samye Ling with Akong and Sherab. The Woodmans were experimenting with the alternative lifestyle of the times. There were a lot of hippies in their house, and drugs of all kinds, and everyone seemed to be engaged in free love. Pamela was beautiful and used to walk around naked. She slept with Trungpa as well as others. Trungpa required a woman in his bed every night: he said he could not get to sleep otherwise, so I used to find partners for him. Luckily there was a German woman who was very large and very obliging. If I could not find anyone else she was always prepared to be a consort for Trungpa.

My whole life – in fact the life of the whole community – was now dominated by the tension between Akong and Trungpa. It became impossible to ignore. The final rupture occurred when Akong received a phone call from Trungpa announcing that he had eloped to the Highlands with Diana but that he didn't have the money to pay for the marriage licence. Could Akong meet them and bring cash? Diana had just turned sixteen and the law in Scotland allowed sixteen-year-olds to marry without the consent of their parents, which she did not have.

Akong and Sherab went to find them. They stayed for the first part of the proceedings but could not bring themselves to witness the whole ceremony. Akong was devastated that Trungpa had chosen someone English, a novice in Buddhism and so very young, to be his consort in life.

Everybody put a brave face on it when Trungpa and Diana returned after their wedding. They stayed in Samye Ling again as the Woodmans had made it plain that they were no longer welcome at Garwald House. There seemed to be some general jealousy among Trungpa's group, now that he had chosen Diana for his wife. The dynamic was altered and everybody in his previously tight band of followers started to fall out. Not that his marriage stopped him from sleeping with other women. Diana once caught him kissing a student in the private interview room next to the shrine room in Johnstone House. Trungpa explained very gently that their relationship was special to him but that he would continue to be intimate with other women. In the end Diana came to accept this and they were married until his death, seventeen years and four children later.

There was a sort of truce between Akong and Trungpa but their differences were by this point too great to resolve. The tension was making everybody extremely miserable. It was Diana who eventually suggested that she and Trungpa should go to the States and begin a new life there. There was a small group of American Buddhists and another in Canada who had received teachings from Trungpa and were great supporters. One of them offered to buy a property for him to establish a Buddhist centre in Vermont. So in 1971 they left Scotland for the United States, travelling via Canada.

I was absolutely devastated when Trungpa left. I had been in Samye Ling for almost two years by then and still did not feel at home. I had spent most of my time and energy serving Trungpa in any way he required, and trying to avoid getting too caught up in the bad feeling that swirled around me. When he left I felt I had once again lost my main friend and support. As usual I blamed Akong. What would I do now?

There were big changes in Akong's life happening at the same time. He too decided to set aside his robes and form a family, though the partner he chose was a Tibetan nurse named Yangchen he'd met in London. When she fell pregnant they got married. Akong would continue to administer and, increasingly, to teach at Samye Ling, but he moved his young family out of Johnstone House to a large house in Dumfries and I went with them. There was a long tradition of married

131

lamas in Tibet so this was not particularly unusual. With Trungpa gone, the atmosphere at Samye Ling stabilized. Akong began his life's work of establishing a thriving Buddhist community.

It felt to me that everybody else was moving on but my life remained the same. I continued to go down to London, simply for something to do, though all I ever did was drink alone. I had girlfriends but I was selfish and egotistical, unwilling to form an attachment to anybody. I behaved in bossy and thoughtless ways and none of my relationships lasted for very long. Most of this behaviour was pure self-centredness, but I do wonder whether some part of me knew that I was not going to make a life partner for anybody because buried within me there was a slowly ripening seed of a vocation to be a monk.

I knew I needed to earn my keep, but for several months after Trungpa left I had no idea what to do. My mind was still closed to the possibility of finding any purpose through the activities at Samye Ling. I had no desire to lend a hand in the administration, though it was what I had trained to do. I felt adrift. I couldn't bring any awareness to the habitual thoughts that took up space in my mind, so I was stuck in old ways of seeing events and people. My mind was like a jar of muddy water in which resentment, a sense of disconnection and confusion were constantly stirred up. I was unable to let them settle so that the water of my mind might become clearer.

In the end I decided to ask Akong to set me up with a clothes shop in Dumfries. He was completely obliging, as always, so I opened a shop selling Afghan sheepskin coats as well as incense and candles, Indian textiles and ornaments. I'm not sure where this idea came from, though I was certainly a complete dandy at the time. I'd loved Western fashion ever since my first denim jacket back in Dalhousie, and since I'd been in Britain my taste in pop music had expanded too. I think I just thought it would be fun to have a shop where I could hang out and play Stones and Hendrix records. A girlfriend had once told me I looked a little like Jimi Hendrix, with my curls and skinny denim jacket. I was delighted with her comment!

I turned out to be a terrible shopkeeper. For the first few weeks there were quite lot of customers. There were no other shops selling youth fashions in Dumfries at the time, and there certainly wasn't one blasting out Hendrix and staffed by a Tibetan refugee! So initially I had a flurry of sales and I enjoyed chatting with the people who came in, who were all curious and friendly. But after a while things quietened down. Then I got bored and impatient, as usual. I would turn up late or not at all, so eventually people stopped coming. I must have lost an awful lot of Akong's money but still he didn't complain.

Yangchen, his wife, was much less restrained. My other great love, apart from clothes, pop music and whisky, was fast cars. Or motorbikes, I wasn't fussy. It drove her absolutely crazy that Akong indulged me in this and bought me vehicle after vehicle, even though I kept crashing them. My adventures in driving had begun when I took some lessons with a former taxi driver from New York City who was staying at Samye Ling at the time. He taught me in the centre's official car, and one day I was recklessly speeding over a narrow bridge and crashed into a car that was travelling in the opposite direction. Both cars were a write-off but, miraculously, nobody was hurt. The other driver had his two young sons in the back and I could easily have killed them, so he was understandably furious. I apologized over and over again and tried to shake his hand but he refused. I didn't have even a learner's licence and the man had called the police, so I asked my friend to pretend to run off into the hills so I could claim to the police that he had been driving. He was heading back to the States the following week, so he obliged and the other driver was too shaken up to have noticed who had been driving. I got away with this deception, my friend was not pursued and I just carried on in the same reckless way.

You'd think that after Trungpa's experience and my own close shave I would have learned something, but no. Akong bought another car and I crashed that too. The car rolled several times but I just got up and walked away, escaping without even a scratch and nothing more than a fine. I felt as if death couldn't touch me. So then I asked Akong to buy me a motorbike. I got myself some German biker's leathers and used to whizz around like a total speed freak. One Samye Ling resident once described me as 'a shadowy figure who came and went on his motorbike'. I was on the edges, as always.

One day I had a disagreement with Yangchen. She worked incredibly hard, running part of their family home as a B&B. By this time they also had a son, Jigme, as well as a daughter, Kami. Yangchen wasn't happy about having a good-for-nothing brother-in-law living with them. I loved to play with the children, but I didn't do any work round the house and I was running through Akong's money. So we had a row. I stormed off, got on the bike and set out for Samye Ling. I was coming too fast round a sharp bend when I came up behind a lorry and couldn't get past. I swerved, skidded, the bike hit a stone and careered off the road, throwing me into the bushes. Once again I was completely unhurt, though the bike was a mangled mess.

This time I felt really ashamed. I trudged to a bus stop with my helmet in my hands and got the bus back to Dumfries. When Yangchen opened the door to me I felt like a dog with its tail between its legs. She told everybody what had happened and after that nobody would ride in a car if I was driving. I was just too reckless, too careless, with myself and other people. I couldn't look after possessions or other people's feelings. I was no good to anybody. Akong never told me off, because he knew I would explode in anger. He just kept patiently and generously giving me whatever I asked for and remaining calm when I threw a tantrum. I was like a naughty brat who would do anything to upset his family, even if it meant risking his own safety and happiness and other people's.

I was drinking and smoking heavily throughout this time. One of our family friends was a man called David Robison whose wife, Etta, attended yoga classes put on by Yangchen. He was a successful and wealthy businessman who owned the second largest construction company in the south of Scotland, and he and I became close. The Robisons hadn't been able to have children of their own and they were both absolutely devoted to Akong and his whole family. Etta was fascinated by Buddhism and spent her days looking after Jigme and Kami, taking them on excursions, and even helping with cleaning and other chores.

David and I were drinking buddies. He was a member of the masonic lodge in Dumfries and spent a lot of time there, playing cards, drinking, chatting with his friends. No women were allowed in the club and anyone who wasn't white wasn't welcome, either, but David was an important figure locally, so he pulled some strings and got me in. It was smoky and dingy but I had fun there. I don't remember ever experiencing any hostility. Being David's friend meant I was granted exceptional status. It wasn't always so easy being one of the few Asians in a small town, though. There had been abusive phone calls in the early days of Samye Ling, calling us devil-worshippers and telling us to go home. But nobody was ever racist to my face. I was certainly an object of curiosity, still exotic, but in the club I was also just another player round the card table. And I always got my round in, which counted for a lot!

We used to play cards and snooker every Friday and Saturday night, for hours on end. Whoever lost had to buy a round of whisky for everyone else. My card skills hadn't improved since Mussoorie so I lost a lot. I always ended up broke and drunk after a night with David, but, since Akong gave me more money and I didn't suffer hangovers, I felt free to carry on. There were no constraints. Was this what I had been looking for when I left India? I couldn't remember.

I arrived in the West at a moment when it seemed that everyone under thirty was obsessed with developing their own personal freedom. Looking back, I think I must have swallowed the Kool-Aid. The Western people who came to stay with us wanted to explore new ways of thinking, and a new spirituality. They were chasing freedom from their problems, from their worldview and from social convention. For many of them and for some of us Tibetans, the supposed personal liberty of the West seemed to mean the freedom to live without care or responsibility. It often led to self-destructive behaviour.

That was what happened to me. I thought I was following my curiosity and getting to know my new world, but actually I was trapped in my confused mind, as were many others who came to Samye Ling at that time. I felt lost and without purpose, torn between so many different options and values. I was still resentful, arrogant and alienated from everyone. In fact I was drifting further and further away from any possibility of true freedom, which does not lie in breaking rules, taking drugs or drink, or even choosing a new spiritual path, but in training our minds to see things as they really are. A confused mind will be its own prison, whatever we're doing and whatever we tell ourselves. We become free when we are able to tame our minds and cultivate compassion, insight, an attitude of openness to everything that happens to us and oneness with everyone around us. This sounds like a lot to expect of ourselves, but all we really need to do is learn how to stop struggling and let be.

I was still a long way away from this. The barrier I had constructed between Akong and me was high and thick as a prison wall. The first time I felt it really shift was when I again broke the fundamental Buddhist precept against killing. I went on a fishing trip with David up in the Orkneys. I wasn't comfortable about participating in a blood sport, but I was too busy enjoying our boozy road trip, driving around in David's Jaguar car and staying with his many friends to give it much thought. When we got to the Orkneys we hired a small boat and rowed out into the middle of a lake. David had brought a bucket full of worms for bait. They made me feel squeamish, so he baited the hook and then passed the rod to me. Each time I cast a line, I caught a fish. David was amazed. I seemed to have providence on my side. I pulled out fish after fish and he took them from me and killed them by battering their heads on the side of the boat. This made me uncomfortable and a little nauseous, but I was enjoying the sensation of being a master fisherman. At the end of one successful day, David lined up all the fish in front of me on the shore and took a photo.

When we got back to Dumfries, David showed the photo to Akong, who was devastated. He didn't say anything to David, because he knew that fishing was a traditional pastime in Scotland, but once David had left he turned to me with tears in his eyes. 'I promised our parents that I would take care of you and raise you with Buddhist values,' he said. 'I have given you everything you ever asked for. I have protected you from adversity and suffering. But now I feel like a failure. I have let our parents down.'

This tore me apart. I had never seen him so upset, not when we were fleeing Tibet, nor when Jamyang and others died, nor when he was in conflict with Trungpa. My brother, who was always impassive like a rock, was in tears. And it was my fault. My heart broke. The walls I'd built around it and between us began to crumble. All my life I had done everything I could to hurt him. I took a vow, silently, deep in my heart, that I would change. I wanted him to be proud of me.

My life did not alter in obvious ways just yet but something in me had shifted. I had been able to bring some awareness to my own behaviour. I had made a vow to move from negative thinking and action to a more positive way of being. These were crucial steps in my journey towards the transformation that was awaiting me.

9. *Wild days in the USA*

I have never been a quick learner, either in school lessons or in life. Then again, very few of us are able to change our habits overnight, especially our habits of mind. It takes patience and repeated work to purify the mind's preference for aversion from that which it finds unpleasant, attachment to that which it desires and ignorance of the true nature of reality. My vow to make my brother proud did not wipe away all my lifelong resentment. Neither did it turn me into a devoted practitioner of Buddhism, though it did create the necessary openness to the next turning point in my life.

In 1974, when I was thirty years old, we heard the news that His Holiness the Sixteenth Karmapa was coming to the West for the first time. Trungpa had invited him to the States. Akong asked the Karmapa to come to Samye Ling on his way back to India. He would be travelling with Sister Palmo, who had been my nemesis and my saviour when she was still Freda Bedi, as well as a group of monks and lamas. As soon as I found out about the visit I was determined that I would go with His Holiness the Karmapa to the States. My motivation was, on the one hand, quite straightforward and self-serving. Once again I needed to escape my life. I was bored, restless and fed up with chilly damp Scotland and living in Akong's shadow. But, on the other hand, and more positively, I remember very clearly my sense that I could not miss this opportunity simply to be with His Holiness the Karmapa again. To serve him. He had been an exceptionally positive influence on me and I longed to be back in his presence. I was also very keen to see Trungpa. Opportunities (and valid excuses!) to travel were few; this was too good to miss.

So I put it to Akong that I would be useful to the Karmapa's party. Aside from Sister Palmo none of them spoke good English. I had previously acted as translator to the Karmapa back in Rumtek and volunteered to do so again. This was agreed to be a good idea and I was added to the trip. I was jubilant.

The group was flying from Delhi to London and then on to New York, so they took a few days in London to rest. I travelled down and made an appointment to see His Holiness the Karmapa. When he saw me he simply smiled and nodded his head, as if he knew exactly what I had been up to and knew too that I was now, once again, within his sphere of influence.

There were fifteen monks in the group and most of them were quite elderly. They were used to the wild open spaces of Tibet and the chaos of Indian towns, but not to airports or Western hotels. They had already caused the Karmapa some worries by wandering in and out of airport security zones and getting lost in London, so he asked me to be the group's discipline master. This is a role that's not usually assigned to a young layperson, but, with my English and my familiarity with Western ways, I was equipped to do it. I followed them around like a little dog, shepherding them this way and that!

My first flight to New York was almost as thrilling as riding away from Dolma Lhakang had been, fifteen years before. I was so pleased to be getting away from Akong, Samye Ling and my failing shop in Dumfries. I had stepped into a different world, one where everything was easy. I was given special treatment, not because I'd done anything to deserve it but because of my link to His Holiness the Karmapa. From the moment we took our seats on the plane we were all treated like royalty. Trungpa had arranged everything, with funding from a multi-millionaire Chinese-American businessman called Dr Shen, who was devoted to the Karmapa. Money was no object. Even His Holiness's sacred Black Crown had its own seat on the plane! Dr Shen had been a minister in the Chinese Republican government before the Communists came to power. He escaped via Taiwan before coming to the States and founding a shipping company. As well as being extremely wealthy he was very devout. He donated more than a million dollars a year to Buddhist causes and had promised to do whatever he could to help establish the Dharma in the States.

When we arrived we were met by a fleet of limousines and driven to Dr Shen's mansion on Long Island. He was not present since his main home was in Chicago and he was travelling for business, but we spent a couple of days resting and being waited on by his staff and Trungpa's Western students. Then it was time to launch into the programme that Trungpa had scheduled. It was to be a two-nation tour taking in cities across the States as far as Los Angeles, then up to Canada and eventually back to the Eastern coast.

I was overjoyed to be reunited with Trungpa. Not that we had much time to talk during my first few weeks in the States as we were all too busy, but it was just so good to see him and feel that he was the same as ever and that our bond was intact. He was still relatively unknown at that point, though his reputation as an outstanding teacher of the Dharma was already growing. Just the previous year he had founded a big new centre in Boulder, Colorado, called Vajradhatu, which means the 'Diamond Realm', a metaphysical space inhabited by the Five Wisdom Buddhas. But it was the Karmapa's visit that allowed Trungpa to really establish himself. Trungpa had a gift for taking the essentials of Vajrayana Buddhism and making them accessible to the Western mindset. Vajrayana is the third of the three historical phases in the development of Buddhist teaching and practice, which occurred from the sixth century onwards in India and was brought to Tibet by Guru Rinpoche in the eighth century. It includes the tantric teachings, which are very complex and rich, but Trungpa had a knack for talking and writing about them in terms that ordinary people could grasp. He was thriving and appeared far more at ease than I had seen him since we left Tibet. American ways seemed to agree with him.

Sister Palmo was also delighted to be with her 'lama in shining armour' again. I could see that she was proud of what Trungpa was building in the States. He was as affectionate to her as ever. He always acknowledged how much he owed to her, his first English teacher and champion.

Over the course of the trip she and I also grew closer. I observed that His Holiness the Karmapa trusted Sister Palmo completely and this helped to soften my former resistance to her. She was kind enough to be appreciative of my efforts and I was better able to see her many good qualities and her achievements, which were undeniable. When she was still Freda Bedi she had spent years working for justice and social welfare in India and her diplomacy was vital to Nehru during Partition. Above all, her role in the spread of Tibetan Buddhism to the West was absolutely vital. The Young Lamas Home School, where the tulkus learned English, was key to the spread of the Dharma beyond India. Without her, it is doubtful that we would all have been in the United States on that influential trip. His Holiness the Karmapa later said that Sister Palmo was an emanation of Tara, the female deity of compassion and action who is regarded as a protector in Tibetan Buddhism. She truly was an exceptional person.

I was immediately caught up in the excitement of the trip and of the glitzy world I had entered. New York was like a jolt to the senses, especially considering I'd spent most of the previous four years in small towns. Even my little trips to London had not prepared me for the Plaza Hotel and Central Park, Broadway and Greenwich Village. And we weren't just tourists, we were being treated as VIPs. After our rest at Dr Shen's mansion we moved into the Plaza, where Trungpa had hired the top two floors of rooms for our group, as well as the conference suite so that His Holiness the Karmapa could perform the Black Crown ceremony. I was completely astounded by the luxury, and yet, as usual, I also took it as no more than my due.

I was on my best behaviour throughout this time as I was very much back within the Karmapa's influence. I also needed to be clear-headed in order to translate. Some of the American accents were a little difficult for me to tune into to begin with, so I had to really listen and concentrate. I could see that Trungpa was still drinking and smoking but I didn't indulge, aside from eating as many huge steaks as I could order! I loved the American food, which was so abundant and so varied. I had meat at every meal.

The response to His Holiness the Karmapa's presence was extraordinary. He didn't give teachings, he simply performed the traditional Black Crown ceremony for which the Karmapas are famous. People were so moved by it and by his exceptional powers that they began to come in their hundreds. By the time we got to Los Angeles there were thousands of people who wanted to see him and attend the ceremony. I remember that David Bowie, who by this time was a huge star, came to see His Holiness the Karmapa. I was a big fan and I didn't waste a second opportunity to tell him so!

From New York we flew to Washington DC, where we were met by more limousines and stayed with a senator at his home. He invited us to attend an event at the White House and we visited the Smithsonian Museum, where we were introduced to Neil Armstrong. This was the pattern of my first trip to America. I only met the elites. Everywhere I went, the effect of the Karmapa's grace was such that I too was treated like royalty.

In some part of my mind I had the uneasy sensation that all this worldly excitement was not the whole story, maybe nothing more than a distraction. I certainly knew that I hadn't earned any of it on my own account. But for a while I was content to enjoy the reflected glory. I was charmed by the bright and cheerful manners of the Americans I met. They made most of the Scots and English people I'd known seem rather cold and dour by comparison. It was all so seductive, after years of feeling lonely and at a loose end in Scotland.

Los Angeles was like nowhere I had ever imagined. The sun, the light, the ocean all made me happy. I loved the atmosphere of laidback ease that the city projected. By the time we got to California we were all feeling very relaxed. I was being close to His Holiness. News of the Karmapa's almost mystical power had spread and the crowds were huge. I felt as if I were living in a dream, one where high lamas were treated like rock stars! From LA we flew to Vancouver and spent two more weeks on the road until, finally, we made it back to Toronto. It was almost the end of our trip. I can't say I was looking forward to going back to Scotland and my ordinary life.

One of the last things that had been arranged for us was an excursion to Niagara Falls. After we had spent some time admiring the power of the water, His Holiness asked me and Tenzin Chonyi, a young monk from our party, to go with him to the US side of the Falls, where we would meet Dr Shen. I hadn't known he would be there, and I was curious about our benefactor, but I had no particular expectations of the conversation beyond being able to thank him for his generosity. I was not in the least prepared for the discussion we were about to have.

After the introductions Dr Shen began to outline an offer to the Karmapa. If His Holiness wished to establish his own Dharma centre in the States, his headquarters in the West if you like, then Dr Shen would be honoured to offer him 250 acres of property in upstate New York, about fifty kilometres from the city. He would fund both the building of the centre and the cost of bringing lamas from India to teach and live there.

I was impressed by the size of this gift, even after all the evidence of Dr Shen's generosity and commitment, but the Karmapa betrayed no surprise at all. He thanked Dr Shen very politely and then, gesturing at us, he said, 'Jamdrak and Tenzin will start the centre and get it going.'

I couldn't believe what I was hearing. I was standing right next to him but he didn't ask whether I wanted to do this, or for my opinion. He had come up with a plan and he simply announced it.

Neither Tenzin nor I said anything. We were dumbfounded. I knew from experience that it was impossible to say no to the Karmapa. Unless I was going to run away from him again, just slip off with no warning as I had from Rumtek, then I was going to have to do what he commanded. This time, I knew I would not run away. I'd love to tell you that my heart was full of gratitude for this opportunity and fervour to acquit myself well. There was some of that. There was also the fact that although it sounded like hard work, it also sounded better than going back to Scotland.

So that is how I found myself with the task of polishing my rusty administrative skills and putting them to work in a completely different culture and in a foreign language. I really had no wish to run a Buddhist centre. I'd spent years avoiding exactly that in Samye Ling. I was lazy, inexperienced, selfish and feckless. Hardly even a Buddhist! Tenzin Chonyi was almost as much of a spoiled brat as me. He was the son of an aristocratic family from Lhasa who had entrusted his care to His Holiness the Karmapa. He didn't even speak English. But here we were, standing on the boardwalk as the water poured endlessly over the Falls, suddenly in charge of a million-dollar project. I got back in the limousine to drive on to Toronto feeling absolutely bemused. My life had just been turned upside down. As we drove I remembered that I had wanted to do something to make my brother proud. Perhaps this would be my chance.

Three days later our party arrived at Glasgow airport for the European leg of the Karmapa's tour. His Holiness had already made it plain to Tenzin and me that we would not be travelling on to mainland Europe with him. Once I had settled things in Samye Ling the two of us would be heading back to the States to begin our work. The reality of this had started to sink in and I was happy about it. I've never been somebody who worries about how things will turn out. The ability to inhabit the present moment rather than projecting into an uncertain future or ruminating on the past is an essential skill in meditation, and this at least has always come naturally to me. I don't get stressed or worried.

That said, even I was a little apprehensive as we approached airport security in Glasgow. How were we going to pass through with all these caged birds that the Karmapa had brought with him from the States? His Holiness felt a special affinity with birds. He had visited numerous pet shops during the course of our trip and bought many of them, with the intention of releasing them in his enormous aviary in Rumtek. But he didn't have permission to ship them. It was extraordinary that we had managed to get them this far, given that it was against airline regulations to travel with animals of any kind in the cabin. I couldn't understand how it was possible that nobody had remarked on the many cages. True, the birds had behaved extraordinarily well during the flight, but the cages were still visible to me, perched on the laps of various monks. It was as if the check-in staff and hostesses could not see them. Surely now we would be required to leave the birds behind? There were quarantine laws to stop animals from crossing international borders.

Nobody said a word to us about it. The Karmapa simply strolled through with his habitual smile for everyone, while his attendants carried the birds in their specially made wooden cases. The creatures were silent. And then, as we emerged into the arrivals hall, I saw that Akong and a small group from Samye Ling had come to greet us. Others who were there that day told me that as the Karmapa walked towards them they could see nothing but light emanating from him. They were entirely unaware of the cages full of exotic birds. His Holiness later told us that many of the creatures had been his students in previous lifetimes and he simply had to rescue them. He truly was a miraculous man.

When Akong heard from His Holiness the Karmapa about his plans for me, he went along with everything but I could tell he wasn't convinced. Sure enough, when we were alone he said to me, 'How can you promise to His Holiness that you will run this centre when you can't even look after yourself?' I simply told him that I couldn't say no to the Karmapa, an answer he didn't seem to find reassuring. I think he was concerned that I would let His Holiness down and bring shame on the Kagyu tradition. I wasn't worried about that, or anything else. I was excited and already looking forward to leaving. I trusted that things would work out and I felt I had no ties to cut in Scotland. My brother's lack of faith in me didn't surprise me. I had never given him any reason to think any differently. I felt a brief flash of disappointment, whether in myself or him I didn't know, and then I got on with arrangements for my return. In truth there wasn't much to do. I left the packing up of the shop to Akong and more or less ran back to the airport.

Tenzin and I arrived back in New York, installed ourselves in a bungalow on Dr Shen's Long Island estate and immediately set to work. I had shaken off Akong's discouraging words but I wanted to make sure I didn't disappoint His Holiness the Karmapa. His presence was very clear to me, having just spent months with him, and though I still had no zeal for the project itself I was truly devoted to him. Quite quickly I remembered that I was good at this kind of organizing work. There was a lot to do. Tenzin spoke very little English, so all the phone calls and meetings fell to me. Eventually Dr Shen insisted on paying for intensive private lessons for Tenzin and he gradually became much more involved as his English improved, but for the first few months I did everything.

Before long I realized that the rural location was not an ideal place to build. It would make it hard to attract attention for the project of spreading the Dharma. What we really needed, I insisted to Dr Shen, was a central New York location. It didn't need to be a big place, just somewhere that we could seed the project, but it should be easy for potential students to get to. Fortunately the ever-obliging Dr Shen could see the sense of this and he rented us a posh place on the Upper West Side, at West 84th Street and West End Avenue. We were four blocks from Central Park and just one block from Broadway. It was perfect, and I began to feel that my confidence in my skills had not been misplaced. The day Tenzin and I moved out of the bungalow in Long Island and into the house in Manhattan, I almost had to pinch myself.

The next step was to start bringing lamas over. I wrote to the Karmapa and reported that we were almost ready to open. Could he send us some good teachers? He and Dr Shen arranged for Khenpo Karthar, Bardor Tulku, Lama Ganga and another Tibetan monk, named Zigma, who became our cook, to travel to New York. (In those days Tenzin and I were so hopeless that we could not even cook for ourselves!)

I knew Lama Ganga and Khenpo Karthar, a particularly renowned scholar and teacher, from my days in Buxa College. We had all been refugees in India and now here we were, about to open a Dharma centre in Manhattan. When I went to the airport to meet them I saw that Khenpo Karthar, who was in his early forties by then, was still as skinny as he had been fifteen years previously. He had never fully recovered from tuberculosis, which he, like so many other refugees, including my beloved Jamyang, contracted in Buxa. He may have looked frail but he was a steady and gentle presence from the beginning of our new relationship, and would go on to be one of the most significant teachers in my life.

With our city base up and running, Tenzin and I turned our attention back to the land Dr Shen had bought upstate. It would be wonderful to have a bigger centre in a stunning location where we could build a temple as well. But when we began to seriously investigate the costs it was clear that the location was so remote that the cost and difficulty of constructing a temple would be huge. Dr Shen did not begrudge the money, but it didn't seem like the most efficient way to accomplish our goal. So we started to look for a more practical and auspicious alternative. In 1976, a year and a half after my arrival in the States, we found it in Woodstock, close to the original site but more accessible, smaller and with a beautiful old house already on site. Dr Shen very obligingly agreed to sell the other land and purchase this property, and in 1977, when His Holiness the Karmapa returned to the States, he confirmed that it would be his seat in the West and blessed the site. Building work immediately began on what would become Karma Triyana Dharmachakra (KTD). My friend Lama Tenzin Chonyi was appointed president of our newly formed centre and I was its general secretary.

I was full of satisfaction. Tenzin and I, both young, under-equipped and spoiled, had nevertheless achieved what we'd set out to do, which was to realize His Holiness the Karmapa's vision in the United States. There was a huge amount of work still to do to establish the centre but I felt that I had played my part. I had proved to Akong that I was up to the job, and that pleased me.

In fact, I was rather too pleased with myself. There was an egotistical element to my satisfaction, a sense that I had triumphed and proved my point. This was the sign that although I had done useful work it had not been with a completely pure motivation. I had wanted to prove my brother wrong rather than be a vehicle for the spread of the Dharma. And now that I'd fulfilled my part of the bargain I felt entitled to turn my attention to self-indulgence, materialism and worldly pleasure.

I hadn't seen that much of Trungpa while I'd been busy with the job of setting up the centres. He was based in Boulder, Colorado, and though he came regularly to New York to lead courses, when he was in town he was even busier than me. He always made time for us to get together, though, and I found him as kind, warm and inspiring as ever. He was so generous with me. He knew I loved fancy clothes and would take me shopping to boutiques, where I picked up the latest fashions.

Now that I had a lot more free time I wanted to spend it with him. I would go to Boulder for weeks on end and hang out with Trungpa and his students at the centre. By 1977 he had established centres all over the States, and once a year all his students gathered in Boulder. I attended that gathering in 1978 and saw how he was able to communicate with American people and how they responded to him. He was determined to transform the hierarchy between guru and pupil and to shed the formality of Tibetan teachers. There was always a lot of drinking, drug-taking, smoking and partying mixed in with the teaching. He slept with his students' wives and encouraged Diana to sleep with the students. It was free love in action. Trungpa wanted to immerse himself in the prevailing culture of the time and absorb its confusion and chaos so that he could help others to purify it within themselves. His approach was to allow everybody to indulge themselves, then once they had drunk fully from the cup of desire and seen that it contained no lasting fulfilment, he would shift his focus and insist that they begin to introduce more discipline to their practice. He asked them to do a lot of *shinay* (calm-abiding) meditation, to settle their minds. Then when their minds were stable he would insist on more and more rigour and discipline. Trungpa always reminded people that it was not acceptable to walk the Dharma path in a mindless ego-driven way. If we become proud of our spiritual discipline, our virtuousness or our accomplishments in meditation, then we are falling into the trap of spiritual materialism, which is just as destructive as any other kind. Trungpa could not tolerate any spiritual pretentiousness at all!

I was fascinated by all this, though with hindsight, and especially now that we live in very different times, I can see how some of it was open to misunderstanding. There's no doubt that Trungpa was a paradox. How was it possible for someone who did not observe the precept of refraining from intoxication, and someone whose sexual behaviour might look questionable, also to be an exceptionally gifted teacher?

At the time I definitely believed that Trungpa's so-called 'crazy wisdom' was a valid way to connect with people in the United States, which was being transformed by the counter-cultural movements of the sixties and seventies. Crazy wisdom is a complex idea that has its roots in early Buddhist texts and could be described as a state of innocent awareness that rejects social conventions. Some highly realized masters who have attained crazy wisdom can make use of behaviours that might appear wrong, in order to open people's eyes to their own behaviour. Many of his followers have said that Trungpa embodied this notion of crazy wisdom, though it's not a term I use about him as I recognize that it might, in other circumstances, be used as an excuse for bad behaviour.

I maintain that Trungpa's legacy of making the Dharma accessible throughout the West speaks for itself. The traditional Tibetan approach would not have worked in the United States at that time. It's also vital to say that I do not believe that Trungpa ever behaved in a way that broke the Buddhist precept to refrain from sexual misconduct. Yes, he had many partners, but that was in keeping with the promiscuity of the times. Diana was of course at liberty to do the same. Coercive sex is of course always a different matter, but there has never been any suggestion that any coercion was involved. Trungpa lived his life from a position of wanting to help people. He was a sincere person. But he could certainly be confusing.

At the time I was just happy to fall in with his approach of indulging desires, though I was still too immature in my thinking to grasp that it was a step on the way to their purification. When I was partying with him there wasn't any thought of anything else in my mind. On one occasion Tenzin and I visited him at his centre in Vermont. By this time Tenzin was no longer a monk and he and I were both delighted to find that Trungpa had a cellar full of *saké*, Japanese rice wine. He asked Tenzin and me to make *momo*, steamed dumplings, which are a Tibetan delicacy. I'd learned a few skills from our cook by then, so I tried to oblige, but I drank so much *saké* that I dropped and broke one of his very expensive sets of porcelain plates. He just said, 'Don't worry, let's have another glass!'

He was such a complex man but I still believe that he was one of the most highly realized people I've ever met. Despite all his crazy behaviour he was able to communicate the essence of the Dharma in a way that people could really understand, and his books, such as *Cutting Through Spiritual Materialism*, were unique and powerful contributions to the spread of the Dharma in the West. Trungpa managed to find a way of teaching that directly related to people's minds and life situations, and so he became very popular.

Not everybody was convinced, of course. I remember one occasion in Boulder when Trungpa and I had been drinking for hours, even though he was supposed to be giving a talk. Eventually, four hours after the scheduled start time, he decided to head off, by which point he was not only late but very drunk. An angry American student confronted him, saying, 'Mr Trungpa, it seems to me that you are full of shit!' To which Trungpa replied, 'Yes, that is true, but most of the shit is yours!'

One day he came to speak in New York. The room was full to overflowing and as usual he was drunk and arrived very late. I was sitting next to him on the podium. When his talk was finished we walked outside and someone ran up to him in the street and said, 'I went to see Dudjom Rinpoche and he needed gold, so I offered him gold. What do you want, Rinpoche?' Trungpa turned to him and said, 'Oh really, is that true?', and then took out his penis and peed on this man's shoes! Trungpa was crazy, completely unpredictable and outrageous, but he was also brilliant, kind and a great teacher.

I spent the two and a half years after KTD was founded indulging in (almost) all the pleasures and vices New York could offer a young man in the seventies. I still didn't touch drugs. I'd been put off by seeing how people abused them at Samye Ling. But I went to nightclubs in Manhattan, slept with and discarded women with no thought for their feelings, drank whisky until I passed out. I was the driver for visiting lamas and would tear around in the official car, a red Cadillac, not caring if I got into road battles or bumped other vehicles. I became very nasty on the road. I had two big fat lamas sitting next to me when I drove to collect teachers and Tibetan dignitaries. If I bumped into someone else's car then I would say to the driver that my two companions were Kung Fu experts, so they had better watch out! I had slipped back into total wildness and closed my heart to the great masters around me who were suggesting I was on the wrong path and urgently needed to tame my mind.

Was I happy? No. Sometimes I was having fun, but I was increasingly tormented by my memories, my resentment and anger. I had been having nightmares for years and they got worse and worse. They were always about crossing the Brahmaputra River. In the dream I was swimming to escape the bullets as they rained into the water around me, which was full of bodies. I would awake with my heart pounding, in a state of panic.

I was increasingly out of control. Most mornings I would wake up feeling deeply ashamed of myself. I'd open my eyes and try to work out what had happened the night before. Was I alone or was there a woman with me? If so, who was she? Had I fought with anyone last night? Who had I upset?

By this point I had ruined my reputation among the Tibetan community. Tibetans are very conservative and ethical in how they go about their lives, because of their belief in karma. People would say, 'Whatever you do, do not end up like Jamdrak!' I knew that Akong would have been kept informed of all my misdemeanours and this only increased my fury and shame. It meant everything to me that His Holiness the Karmapa never wavered in his support. I felt he saw me not just as a scoundrel but as someone with deep potential, albeit deeply buried! Long ago he had recognized something in me, some kernel of goodness, that I could not see. And because he kept faith with that part of me, eventually I was able to find it for myself.

One night I was so drunk that I was sick all over myself and had to be cared for by Trungpa's students. I woke up in my room in Trungpa's centre in Boulder with a terrible hangover. The place was littered with empty wine and beer bottles and my discarded clothes. My head was pounding. I felt totally empty. Deep down in my heart I felt that something big was missing and as a consequence my life was going nowhere. That was the moment I realized that I had to change.

I have talked to so many people about their 'rock bottom' moments and every single one is different. Some of them are very dramatic. Some of them are more like a series of gradual realizations. Some people come to me feeling powerless and without any direction, others need little more than a nudge of encouragement. Whoever they are, whatever they have done or not done, I tell everyone the same thing. All change begins with the resolve to turn away from negative thoughts and actions and towards the positive. It begins with the commitment to sit in stillness and face ourselves, to face the negative habits we have become enslaved to and feel remorse for the suffering this has caused, both to ourselves and to others. If we keep looking, the deep wellspring of positive potential that each of us has in abundance gradually begins to surface. We may have to repeat this process over and over again; in fact we certainly *will* have to do it many times, but we can do it. *You* can do it.

On that morning in Colorado I was ready. It was a crucial moment in a long series of many such moments. Seeds that had been planted in Rumtek, in Scotland and in the States were finally bursting into life, nurtured by the mud that clogged my mind. My anger, fear, shame and self-disgust were the material from which the seeds of Dharma were about to burst forth. I just had to find the humility to do nothing except allow the process to run its course without fighting it or running away. My pride had always prevented me in the past. I had spent years dancing in its grip. I thought I had proved myself invaluable to His Holiness the Karmapa when, in fact, he had been invaluable to me. It was only when I had drained the cup of materialism and self-obsession to its dregs that I could see clearly what remained for me. My pride finally quietened down enough to make way for the grace within me to flower.

10.   *Transformation*

The turning points of our lives are sometimes vivid and some-times muted. On occasion we don't even know, at the time, that a particular day *is* significant. If we have been living for years in a rut of negative thinking, then it is hard to believe that any day is different from the others. I know from experience that change is a process, not an event, and I always insist on this to people who are hoping for a miracle in their own life. Out-side of Hollywood films, change usually happens in fits and starts over years, not with dramatic gestures that alter every-thing in ten seconds flat. I have also observed that change rarely takes place on a smooth upward curve. It's messier, more circular; we must slide back before we go forward, or we stall and drift, sometimes for years, as was the case in my own life. So it's fair to say that I don't have much faith in epiphanies, but, even so, I vividly recall the impact of that hungover morning in Colorado in the spring of 1980. I felt disgust. I saw that I had lost control and lost my dignity. I had a strong sensation that I absolutely did not want that life any more. I returned to New York feeling chastened and concerned. What should I do with this feeling that I could not go on as I was? What could I do differently?

I was too busy to focus on the matter for long. His Holiness the Karmapa was coming in a few months' time to inaugurate KTD and I had work to do. But my mind was restless. I spent every possible spare moment in Central Park, which was my favourite place in the city. It felt like an oasis of nature. I would sit on a park bench and just try to let my mind calm so that I might understand what to do next with my life. Akong had sent word that after the inauguration he wanted me to return to Samye Ling to help him with the running of the centre. Now that I had acquitted myself well, he wanted me back. Perhaps he was also concerned about me going off the rails in the big city and with Trungpa relatively close by. I think he wanted to have me back under his wing.

The problem was, I had absolutely no desire to do more administrative work. It would have felt as if my life were moving backwards, returning to Scotland and that world where Akong ruled. But what could I do instead? Time seemed to be running out for me. Where were the freedom and purpose I sought? I had thought I would find them in the States, but here I was, thirty-seven years old, five years after I arrived, and still so confused.

I would try to get my thoughts in order as I watched people come and go. Central Park might have been beautiful on a sunny afternoon, but in those days it was regarded as dangerous and there were always a lot of policemen (mostly white), stopping and searching mostly young African American and Puerto Rican men. If they didn't have the right papers, the unspoken rule was that they would have to slip the cops some money. The police just ignored me. I was an Asian man in a smart three-piece suit. I think they couldn't work out which category to put me in.

The whole city was far edgier then than it is these days. There was a lot of crime, violence, racial tension and poverty. I began to see this side of New York more and more clearly. One day when I was walking up Broadway I saw a massive guy hit an innocent woman in the eye. She lay on the pavement screaming for help but nobody came. I could not understand it.

I rushed to her side and asked people in the street why they were not helping. They told me that if I got involved, the police would question me for hours. I felt that my better instincts, like everyone else's, were shrivelling up. We were all – black, white, Asian, Latino – prisoners of this mentality in which compassion had been sacrificed to self-interest. We were only half alive.

I had spent years living among the elites around Manhattan, Long Island, Washington, Boulder and Los Angeles. For a long time I'd believed in the idea of America as an optimistic and equitable place, built on aspirations for a better life. Now I felt that my eyes had been opened to the poverty of this materialistic viewpoint. For millions of people life was tough in the heart of the Western world. Even among the white middle classes whom I met at our centre and Trungpa's, I saw how unhappy people were. They were so attached to everything they had acquired, but on some level they knew it was worthless. I was lost, and I was waking up to the fact that almost everyone around me was lost too.

There was an obvious exception in those who had stepped onto a spiritual path. Many of them were my Tibetan companions, others were new to Buddhism, but all were sincere and humble. I had never been either of those things, especially not in my relationship with Dharma, but sitting in Central Park I felt my mind settle down. Its waters were clearing and I began to think I could make out my next step.

His Holiness the Karmapa arrived in New York and as usual I was his official driver. Jamgön Kongtrül, one of his four Heart Sons, was travelling with His Holiness. One day when just the two of us were in the car, Jamgön Kongtrül said to me, 'You don't realize how well His Holiness treats you. Not even other high lamas are treated like you. But you have no gratitude. You just take it all for granted.' This really affected me. It touched my heart. I reflected that I was no longer young and I was just wasting my life. I made a decision. It was time to renounce my old ways.

Within days of this conversation I'd resolved to ask the Karmapa to ordain me as a Buddhist monk. I didn't want to take *getsul*, or novice ordination, which is the traditional provisional step on the path to taking full vows. I was determined to move straight to *gelong*, or life ordination, which entails taking more than 250 precepts that date back to the time of the historical Buddha. I knew with absolute certainty that I needed to become a monk, to go into long retreat and give myself over to contemplation and meditation, in order to tame my mind so that I might eventually be able to help others. This certainty flowered in me over the course of a few days. It was as if this joyful commitment had been waiting only for the auspicious moment to burst into full bloom.

I went to His Holiness and asked him to bestow upon me full ordination. I promised that if he gave me these vows I would not break them. He was overjoyed. He looked at me with that radiant expression of his that seemed to encompass the whole world.

I felt a tremendous relief when His Holiness accepted my request. Once I had decided that I wanted to be ordained, I never wavered. I had a serene conviction that none of my time had been wasted. Those years spent drifting in a cloud of muddled thinking and rancour had allowed me to accumulate the life experiences I needed, in just the right balance, so that I would be fully prepared for this moment.

Many people at the time were sceptical. Some in the Tibetan community, including Akong, were horrified. He said to me, 'How do you expect to keep the vows when both Trungpa and

I (who are recognized tulkus) could not keep our monastic vows in the West? If you break this vow you will go straight to the hell realm in your next life.'

It didn't upset me, because I knew I had earned this reaction. I had never shown any serious interest in or sincere devotion to the Three Jewels of the Buddha, the Dharma and the Sangha. True, I was absolutely devoted to His Holiness the Karmapa and I respected Trungpa greatly, but I think many observers attributed that to the fact that the two of them had always been supportive of me personally. While that was certainly the case, I had learned so much from Trungpa and been profoundly touched by the Karmapa. They had been readying me, almost without my knowing. When I realized I needed to abandon the life I was living there was only one place for me to go.

Still, the transition from selfish waster to monk was quite extreme and I can understand that it might look to some people as if it all happened mysteriously quickly. Even now, when I'm telling my story and I come to this part some people look at me quizzically, as if to say, 'How did you change so fast? What was the process?'

I think there are a number of explanations. One is that I had in fact been preparing for this moment all my life. It was a question of the timing needing to be right. Secondly, I am a person of extremes. In this I am typical of Khampas, people from my native region of Kham, who tend to have the mindset that if you're going to do something you should do it in a big way or not at all! So, for example, I never drank alcohol again after that morning in Boulder, Colorado. Moderation is simply not my way. I'm an all-or-nothing kind of person. That's why I never took drugs. I feared I would be a junkie if I went down that route. I am simply grateful that I had sufficient self-knowledge to recognize this about myself and eventually, after years of false starts, to put it to good use.

The third explanation is that such transformations are ultimately a bit mysterious. Can any of us truly say that we know why we do what we do? Why do we fall in love? Why do we choose the person we marry? In each case there will be many reasons but there is also mystery. What I can say is that my decision to become a monk felt both easy and absolutely right. That is not to say that it was easy to learn to live as a monk, or to purify my mind. That process was arduous; in fact it was the hardest thing I have ever done. I am fortunate, though, that despite the challenges I have never wavered in my commitment. At the time the fact that His Holiness the Karmapa supported me was the ultimate confirmation that I was doing the right thing. I was terribly in awe of His Holiness. I felt he could see into my mind. If he was happy to ordain me, it must be the correct decision. Gradually everyone else came to see it in the same way: His Holiness had agreed, and his was the ultimate stamp of approval.

By far the most significant voice of support was my brother's. From the moment His Holiness agreed to my request, Akong was supportive. He came to the States to be at my ordination ceremony, and I felt that the dynamic between us was different. The old mistrust and resentment had softened. I think he was still a little sceptical, and I had not yet spent years in retreat purifying my negative thoughts, so they lingered, but we were glad to see each other after more than five years apart.

My ordination ceremony was just one small part of a much bigger concern: the Karmapa's visit to see his newly finished seat at KTD. I have never felt prouder than on the day I stood with Akong, Trungpa, Khenpo Karthar Rinpoche, who was abbot of KTD, and so many other revered masters of Tibetan Buddhism as His Holiness blessed the centre that I had been instrumental in helping to establish. I was leaving behind that layperson's role and stepping into a different, sacred space. My plan was to go into solitary retreat for five years as soon as His Holiness's visit came to a close. His Holiness had advised me to spend twenty years in retreat, but I thought that was a bit of a tall order! I was a novice Buddhist practitioner about to embark on many years of solitary practice. Sometimes I think I must have been a little crazy. But I had the feeling, shortly to be proved correct, that I needed to spend time in retreat before I would be ready to live as a monk in the world.

The ordination ceremony took place in the centre's main shrine room, which had been the ballroom in the original house. It had been painted and fitted out with thangkas (religious paintings), statues and other beautiful artworks. There were two of us taking ordination: me and another man, a European. I wasn't nervous at all. The ceremony took all day and required ten masters of the Kagyu lineage to officiate, but I was guided through the words and I felt a deep feeling of peace and rightness. The warmth of the community was wonderful. I felt the total support of everybody who was there. Above all I was immensely grateful to His Holiness. I felt deeply privileged. After the ceremony I was no longer Jamdrak, Akong's little brother, scoundrel and waster. I was now Yeshe Losal. This filled me with happiness.

I spent the night after the ceremony in a tent in the grounds of KTD. I had offered my bungalow, where I was planning to live in retreat, to Akong, so that he would be comfortable. Just as I was preparing to go to sleep I heard someone unzipping my tent. A very attractive woman from the community popped her head through the opening and clambered in. She had been flirting with me for days but I couldn't believe she had come to pay me a visit.

'What are you doing?' I asked her and for answer she tried to kiss me. I was totally shocked. I was a monk now. I was a different person. But apparently not that different, because I felt the familiar pull of desire.

I didn't hesitate. I scrambled out of the tent and ran away from her as fast as I could. It is difficult to become a different person overnight, or, in this case, during just one day, even if it is the day of one's ordination! I had spent years indulging myself with no thought for the consequences. Those habits had not yet been purified by vigilant practice.

I did not blame the woman. I regarded her actions as an expression of *mara*, which is the Sanskrit word for 'obstacle'. Buddhism teaches that when we embark on something positive we attract negative opposing forces, which can take a variety of forms. This is not to say that attractive women are maras in themselves; it refers more to the context – if you are a man with a strong sexual drive who has renounced sexual activity and then an attractive woman pursues you then this is a mara. The teachings suggest that it is best to avoid any situation that might give rise to maras, as much as we can, until we have enough inner strength and stability not to be affected by them. Then we can adopt them onto the path, which means working with them by not avoiding or indulging them. This incident simply confirmed to me that I must enter retreat as soon as possible, otherwise I was at risk of breaking my vow of celibacy. I was not prepared to let that happen. In fact I had taken a personal vow that if I broke my ordination vows I would kill myself. I was still the same old creature of extremes!

The Karmapa was going on a visit to Washington DC before he returned to India and he asked me to accompany him, along with Trungpa and a number of other monks. The time I spent with His Holiness on this trip was infinitely precious to me, as it was already apparent that he was not in good health. It was probable that once he returned to India and I went into retreat, I would not see him again in his current incarnation.

This trip also provided my introduction to participating in Buddhist rituals as a monastic, for which I was woefully unprepared. On one occasion His Holiness was conducting a puja, a ritual of chanting, mantras and visualizations that invokes a tantric deity. The idea is that we learn to see reality through the eyes of the deity, leaving behind our mundane dualistic way of looking at things. Instead of believing that we are an individual who is separate from other people and external objects, we see everything and all beings as interconnected and sacred. It is a way of getting in touch with our own innate Buddha Nature.

There I was in the front row, chanting in Tibetan, doing various hand gestures – *mudras* – and invoking elaborate visualizations as many hundreds of people watched, when I suddenly realized how little I knew about the daily activities of a monk. For as long as I could remember I had been rebelling against the monastic lifestyle. I had no idea what I was doing! Jamgön Kongtrül even had to turn the pages of the text for me because I could not follow them. I had everything to learn.

After the Washington DC trip ended, His Holiness went on to Trungpa's centre in Vermont. As we said goodbye he told me, 'Now go back to Woodstock and start your retreat.' I admitted that I did not think I was capable of simply sitting in meditation for years as he had previously recommended. He suggested I do the *Karma Pakshi* practice, which combines Guru Yoga, protector and deity practice all in one. Guru Yoga opens our heart to the grace of our teacher and his lineage, through fervent prayer. Protector practice invokes the blessing of a Dharma protector, which helps clear obstacles to our spiritual practice. Deity practice awakens our innate potential, our Buddha Nature. His Holiness knew that I was not that well versed in all the elaborate Tibetan practices, and felt this one would cover all bases.

On my return to Woodstock I set about building a small extension to my bungalow. Akong and I worked together for almost a week, passing tools from one to another, chatting about practicalities or labouring in companionable silence. I was deeply grateful for his help. I found the task very calming and I think this period helped to prepare my mind to relinquish the old resentment I felt towards him. Then I said goodbye to him and to a small group that had gathered to wish me well, and I went inside the cabin that would be my home for the next five years.

It was very basic. In the extension was a shrine and my meditation box, which was where I slept in a seated position, as was traditional for those on retreat in Tibet. The box was half bed, half meditation seat, with a ledge for prayer texts. It was beautifully decorated and one of my most valued possessions. The cabin's main room was a simple square with a small kitchen, a toilet and a bathtub as well as an attic space. It was cold in winter, but it was light and bright and looked out onto the woods. There was a Western nun on retreat not far away and Khenpo Karthar Rinpoche's cabin was also close by, though since I had opted for solitary retreat I would see nobody except those masters who came to give me instruction. Khenpo Karthar Rinpoche checked in on me once a month and I had a substantial meal delivered once a day, though I had no interaction with the person who brought it to me. So I was very much alone apart from the badger and the snakes that lived beneath the cabin, the squirrels in the wall cavities and the deer that appeared outside my window looking for the scraps of food I sometimes tossed out.

I had swapped my comfortable and highly social life for one of confinement and solitude. Instead of travel, flirtation, rich food, meeting new people in meditation centres and in night-clubs, and general gadding about, I was going to spend years in this small space with little company but my own thoughts. I was not exactly worried but I knew that I needed to be disci-plined in my approach. I did try to follow His Holiness's injunction to do *Karma Pakshi* practice, but I quickly realized that although my body was content to be contained within my cabin, my mind wanted to be anywhere else in the world but there! It was jumping about like a wild monkey. I spoke to Khenpo Karthar about this and he advised me to do thou-sands of prostrations every day. I was back to doing prostration practice, as I had in Rumtek, but this time I threw every ounce of my being into it.

Prostration practice is physically arduous and very rigorous. It involves doing full-length prostrations while reciting a devo-tional prayer and imagining taking refuge in all the masters of our spiritual lineage. You can't really daydream or ruminate while you're doing prostration practice, because it engages your body, your speech and your mind so fully. I found it exhausting but effective. Gradually, over weeks and months, it helped tame my mind and bring me into the present moment. Even so my mind still jumped around a lot. So Khenpo Karthar then instructed me to do shinay, or calm-abiding meditation, as well as prostrations. Modern mindfulness meditation derives from shinay meditation. The idea is to tether the mind to a focal support in the present moment such as breathing or a mantra, and each time the mind wanders we bring it back to the focal support, again and again and again.

In the beginning of my retreat I slept a lot. I think this was a form of avoidance. But you cannot sleep for five years, so I had no option but to find a way to deal with my unworkable mind. I persisted with the prostrations and the shinay as best I could, alternating between them day after day. I was absolutely unwavering. Even when my knees were lacerated from throwing myself on to my prostration board, I continued. After a while I no longer needed to use a mala and pebbles to keep track of how many I had done. I just counted in my head. I lost a lot of weight because I was only eating one full meal a day and a small breakfast, and the prostration practice was vigorous and energy-consuming. It was all very tough-going, but the physical discomfort was the least of my problems. I had spent my whole life running away from any boring or unpleasant situation, and refusing to face myself. Now I had an uphill battle overcoming these powerful habits.

To make matters even more challenging, about six months or so after I went into retreat, work started on building the centre's temple. The site was right next to my cabin. Every day when I began a particular prayer the cement mixers would whirr into action. The noise of drilling and workmen shouting was constant and I grew so annoyed that eventually I spoke to Khenpo Karthar about it. I was convinced that the workmen were deliberately sabotaging my meditation practice! KK replied that the workers had noticed that I kept very regular hours. There was a particular series of loud and vigorous chants that accompanied yogic jumps called *beps*, in which I leaped up and then landed in full lotus on a mat. The labourers took them as their cue to fire up the cement mixers.

As well as the noise, I had been cut off from both electricity and running water. I didn't actually mind this too much. I decided to use rainwater to wash my clothes and flush my toilet. For drinking I relied on a small quantity of water brought from the main centre with my food. The Western nun in the next cabin was in the same predicament and she demanded that people drag large containers of fresh water up for all her needs. She also wrote and received a lot of letters. I decided to write none. I could see how the Western lifestyle made it hard to find simplicity and renunciation.

Throughout my first year in retreat I was haunted by images of my escape from Tibet. I thought obsessively about the loss of my family. The nightmares I had suffered for years came with even more frequency and I spent my waking hours tormented by painful memories and imaginings of what might have become of my loved ones. I was grieving. I was processing the loss and the trauma that I had spent years evading. This is typical of what happens when we sit down to do meditation, especially as we go deeper into our practice. Prolonged meditation can unearth deeply buried thoughts and emotions. This is precisely what happened to me.

I knew I needed to address this problem, because if I did not it would become a big obstacle to my progress. So I cultivated the thought that those Chinese soldiers who had shot at us and still chased me in my dreams were not the enemy. They were not responsible for my suffering. In fact they too had suffered through that event. The only ones who were truly responsible were the leaders of the People's Republic of China, Mao and Zhou Enlai. But they too were sentient beings and were labouring under the spell of ignorance and confusion. It occurred to me that by going to the root of my hatred and fear, I might be able to purify those feelings. So I decided to incorporate both Mao and Chou into my prostration practice. Typically we do prostrations while visualizing our father and all male sentient beings on our right-hand side and our mother and all female sentient beings on our left-hand side. I visualized Mao and Chou standing very close to me and imagined that they were doing the practice with me. I did this over and over again.

Then one night I had a very auspicious dream. I dreamed that I had opened up a grocery shop in New York. (So I had gone from a clothes boutique in Dumfries to a food store in New York!) Mao and Chou were my assistants. In my dream they bustled about with aprons on, stocking shelves and serving customers. After that I had no more nightmares and I found it much easier to turn my waking thoughts away from disturbing memories and imaginings. My mind began to settle and I felt more at peace.

I often tell this story to my students when they come to me with feelings of despondency about their practice. It is not unusual to run into obstacles once we get beyond the initial honeymoon phase of meditation. Some people lose heart and want to give up. I advise them to persevere, to be patient and to hold faith with their practice, because even our most deepseated obstacles can hold the key to freedom. This is what I discovered with the story of Mao and Chou.

So good things were happening to me but it was still tough. Some days I felt like giving up. Then, in 1981, an opportunity presented itself for me to escape from retreat and I very nearly took it. Akong wrote to me with the news that the Chinese had relaxed their restrictions on visiting Tibet. He had managed to go back for the first time since our escape and discovered that our parents were still living in our homeland. I could do the same.

I was overjoyed to hear that they were still alive and immediately hatched a plan to see them. I had some money in the bank. I was determined to go. It seemed perfectly justifiable to me because there was no knowing how much longer they would live, and in Buddhism it is important to revere and respect one's parents. Though I had to admit to myself that part of my motivation, a large part in fact, was to get out of retreat since it was so much tougher than I possibly could have imagined.

I told Khenpo Karthar my intention the next time he visited me. I thought he would agree that I could pop over to Tibet and then come back and just carry on. Instead he looked at me with a very stern expression and said quite calmly, 'If you try to leave this retreat cabin I will break both your legs.' I just stared at him in shock. He didn't so much as blink.

That was the moment I realized that KK was as uncompromising as the great Tibetan masters of old. His words put a stop to any thought of escape and I resolved never to bring the issue up again. Not that he gave me the opportunity. He didn't visit me for six months after that conversation. He just left me to stew in my own juices!

I felt terribly ashamed after this because it was clear to me that, though I did of course long to see my family, the visit would have been a pretext to run away from retreat, as I had run away from every challenge I'd ever faced. I had pandered to my mind's whims all my life and this was the source of my difficulties. Being in retreat was not the problem. The problem was that I had not yet tamed my mind. This realization was a great blessing because things then became very clear. There was a direct link between how I related to my mind and how much happiness or unhappiness I experienced. If I went along with my old habits – if I had left the retreat, for example – it would be gratifying in the short term but over the long term I would not be happy and I would not find any authentic meaning in my life.

This was a hugely significant moment for me. I felt I had understood the cause of my unhappiness for the first time. Even more crucially I could see the way out. This was the realization that the Buddha came to when he left his life of luxury as a prince and wandered alone into the wilderness to meditate. Once he attained Enlightenment his profound realization was encapsulated in his very first teaching, called the Four Noble Truths. He described the first truth as the truth of suffering. The second is the truth of the cause of suffering. The third is the truth of the end of suffering. And the fourth is the truth of the path that leads to the end of suffering. To put this teaching simply, painful events are unavoidable in life. We fall ill, fall out of love, are hurt, hurt others and eventually die. The suffering we experience as a result of these events is typically compounded by our mind's treatment of these events. It is always painful to be betrayed in love, say, but once the initial shock has passed, our reaction to the event is what determines how much we suffer. Our mind is the true source of our suffering, and if we can turn to face it, and observe how it is enslaved to habits of attachment and aversion, we have the opportunity to free ourselves from suffering. This is not the work of an instant for any of us but it is perfectly possible. We accomplish it by perfecting the essentials of Buddhist training: ethical conduct, meditation practice and wisdom, all of which are contained in the early Buddhist teaching the *Noble Eightfold Path*.

Buddha's core teaching landed like a blow in my heart. I felt profoundly touched and my commitment to retreat was redoubled. Now was the time to take things seriously and make proper use of this precious human life. I asked Akong to pass on my heartfelt message to our parents, and then returned all my focus to my practice. There was no more time to mess around. Even today, I still feel infinitely grateful to Khenpo

Karthar for his intervention and for all the instruction he subsequently gave me. My first long retreat was the making of me. I have no doubt that my life would have turned out very differently if I had left it early.

At about this time His Holiness the Sixteenth Karmapa returned to the United States to receive treatment for the cancer that had spread throughout his body. As a gesture of renunciation I sent him $15,000, which was all the money in my bank account; the money that I'd planned to spend on the trip to Tibet. I also sent him some valuable silver offering bowls and a big thangka (painting), which were some of my most prized possessions. When he received the money and the gifts he did not thank me. The message he sent back read, 'If you are so intent on giving up all your wealth and possessions then why have you not sent me your fancy bed?'

I was stunned. How could His Holiness have known that the only object of value I had retained was the traditional meditation box that doubled as my bed? His powers of clairvoyance were legendary and always served to increase my faith in him.

His Holiness died shortly afterwards. I was briefly saddened but my overwhelming feeling was of gratitude for having known this remarkable man, and for the benevolence he always showed me. I never lost my feeling that he looks over me. Of course, I have in any case been privileged to meet him again, in his next incarnation as His Holiness the Seventeenth Gyalwa Karmapa, whose discovery and enthronement were two of the most joyful moments of my life.

During the months after my realization of the nature of suffering I continued to struggle. Kalu Rinpoche, the revered meditation master who had been one of the Sixteenth Karmapa's foremost students, came to KTD and visited me in my retreat cabin. I had met him before in Samye Ling. He used to say of me during the Samye Ling years that I was the worst Tibetan he had ever met! Now he was immensely helpful to me. Once, when I complained about the noise of the construction site outside my window, Kalu Rinpoche said briskly, 'That is not a problem. Just make the noise part of your practice.' He said that I should be prepared to die in retreat if need be. That was the kind of attitude I needed to overcome the obstacles in my path.

After two years or so I had finally settled my mind sufficiently to feel that I was ready for more advanced practices. I was fortunate to receive teachings from the many great masters who visited KTD. I would get up at 3 a.m. and do 1,000 prostrations before a small breakfast, then carry on until it was time to eat lunch. In the afternoons I did various tantric practices, including Powa, White Tara (which Jamgön Kongtrül taught me), Six Yogas of Naropa and Vajrayogini. Like many of the deities, Vajrayogini is concerned with cutting through ego-fixation and awakening the wisdom energy of emotions that are normally tied up in afflictions or mind poisons. I also went back to the Four Foundations and practised them again. I spent a whole year just on Dorje Sempa, the purification practice, which I think of as like a solvent for the glue of grasping and clinging. I needed to practise it a great deal. It is a preliminary practice but also very profound and very important. Then in the evening I would do more prostrations, and when I grew tired I switched to calm-abiding meditation, which was a good way of calming my mind and readying myself for sleep. I would go to bed at 8 p.m.

I found the Six Yogas of Naropa particularly powerful. It is a very deep and profound practice that entails purifying the energies in one's subtle energy body. It involves breathing exercises, intense visualization and strong yogic movements. My brother Akong asked Lama Ganga to teach it to me after they met at Samye Ling. Lama Ganga was a specialist retreat master and empowered to pass on ancient tantric practices to students in long retreats. He promised Akong that he would visit me and I was delighted to receive him. I found great inspiration in Dream Yoga, which is related to the practice of Lucid Dreaming, but far more advanced.

During Dream Yoga we train to maintain conscious awareness of our dreams. This enables us to see that the dream state is an illusion, even though it feels utterly real while we're asleep. The idea is to apply this same awareness to daytime activity and so understand that waking life is just as illusory. During daily life we usually feel as if we are actively engaged with 'reality', but in fact we are sleepwalking through a world of our own mind's creation. If we can hold this awareness we can gradually train ourselves to feel less attachment to events and emotions. I've heard people express the worry that this might make our experience feel empty or alarmingly unreal, but in my experience the opposite is true. Life feels more vital and vivid.

When we become accomplished in this practice we can direct our dreams in order to travel to places both earthly and heavenly. The modern secular term for this is astral travelling. I practised dream yoga very diligently, and one day I chose to go to the pure land, or spiritual abode, of the deity Vajrayogini. When I came into the presence of Vajrayogini she appeared in the form of a large black woman who hugged me so hard that she almost crushed the life out of me. On another occasion when I travelled in my dreams to meet her she sliced my head off with her curved dagger and told me that I had too much ego! After that I was not so keen to go back.

One of the most memorable Dream Yoga experiences I ever had turned out to be deeply prescient, though I didn't work out why until much later. During this particular dream, which I had towards the end of my retreat, I flew somewhere I had never been before. It was an island off an island and I arrived there in the evening time. I vividly recall that there was a bay on the larger island that was lit up by the lights of houses and bars and restaurants. Across from this bay was a small island, shaped like a lion whose mighty paws came down to the sea. It was sparsely inhabited and there were very few lights. I recall landing there and looking across to the lighted bay. I had no clue where I had ended up and shortly afterwards I awoke to find myself back in my meditation box in my cabin in Woodstock. At the time of the dream it felt very auspicious and it certainly proved to be so later when I visited Holy Isle, off the Isle of Arran, in my flesh-and-blood body. I recognized it immediately as the place I had visited in my dreams all those years before. At the time, when I mentioned the dream to Khenpo Karthar he told me that I should give it no importance and forget about it. This is the traditional way for retreat masters to guide their retreatants, to ensure that they do not get too attached to what they might mistakenly regard as their own accomplishments.

I am for ever indebted to the many great masters who taught me so well. Those five years of my first long retreat allowed me to embed the changes that have slowly brought about the transformation of my mind. I owe a particular debt to Kalu Rinpoche, who on one of his visits told me to read the life of Milarepa, the great Tibetan saint from the eleventh century. He felt that I needed radical inspiration, and I found it in Milarepa's story. From that day to this I have never concerned myself with any of the mundane pleasures of life. I was able to engage with the Dharma from the very bottom of my heart.

Milarepa is a beloved figure in Tibet, so I was already familiar with the outlines of his life story. He was born into a prosperous family and had an idyllic childhood until the death of his father, after which his uncle and aunt assumed responsibility for the family and took control of their wealth. Milarepa, his mother and siblings were all forced to work like slaves, but they pinned their hopes on everything being returned to Milarepa when he came of age. When that day came the uncle and aunt refused to honour their agreement and left the family destitute, whereupon Milarepa's mother demanded that her son seek revenge. She urged him to visit a famous teacher of black magic, learn everything he could and then come back and destroy the uncle, aunt and all their children. This is exactly what happened. But Milarepa didn't stop there. He caused the death of thirty-five people, and when the villagers threatened to kill his family in return, he summoned up a hailstorm to destroy all the crops except those in his mother's field. The teacher of the magic was saddened by this and went to Milarepa to insist that he learn the ways of Dharma in order to mitigate all the bad karma he had generated for both of them. So Milarepa approached a teacher whose methods were said to guarantee liberation from samsara in one lifetime. But he didn't even practise them. He was too lazy. This teacher told him he could not help, because Milarepa's sins were too great and his efforts too small. 'Only Marpa the Translator can help you,' he told Milarepa. When Milarepa heard this name his heart was full of joy. But it was to take him many years of effort and self-sacrifice before eventually, after he had performed many trials, including building and tearing down three tall towers, Marpa agreed to give him the teachings that would allow him to purify his negative deeds. Marpa sent Milarepa off to meditate for years in a cave in the mountains and from then on, Milarepa was committed to the path of Enlightenment. When he ran out of food he ate nettles. He grew as thin as a skeleton and his body turned green from this diet, but he was not afraid of death and he eventually attained Enlightenment, within one lifetime.

Even though I had been told this story many times, when I read it for myself in retreat I connected with it in a profound way. It reminded me so forcefully of many incidents in my own life. Thankfully I had not killed thirty-five people, but I had been lazy, proud, resentful and self-indulgent. I had blamed others for my problems and made no effort to let go of rancour, fear and grievance. I now saw that big change is always possible, even if you have generated a great deal of bad karma, but you cannot be lazy and you cannot indulge in self-pity. It was plain to me that until I had made a commitment to sincere practice, I would never have attained real happiness or fulfilment. But, of course, for the first half of my life I was stuck in a vicious cycle of my own making. I could not commit, because my mind's innate Buddha wisdom was obscured by negativity. Once the intention to shift from negative thoughts and emotions into positive ones had flowered in my heart, that downward spiral was reversed. It was very difficult to turn things around, but, once I had, my life began to flow in an upward spiral. We can all do this. I have seen it happen over and over again. Significant effort is required at the beginning, but the process becomes easier and the rewards are enormous.

It took me five years, but having established myself on the path to fulfilment I wished for nothing but to stay in retreat for the rest of my life. That was not to be. I was about to be wrenched into a new phase of life. As on so many previous occasions, the agent of this change was my brother, Akong.

11.   *Teacher*

When the second possibility of leaving retreat arose, in 1985, I was completely certain that I didn't want to go. What a change in me, from the days back in 1981 when I had leaped at Akong's suggestion that I travel to Tibet with him to visit our parents.

Once again it was the possibility of seeing family that prompted Akong to write to me. He wanted me to return to Scotland to meet with our older brother, Palden, and our younger sister Zimey. He had been back to the Tibet Autonomous Region for the first time in 1983 and discovered that, since 1981, our parents had both died. This was a blow. The opportunity to see them again in this lifetime had gone. But he also found out that our brother and two sisters were still alive, and began to make the complicated arrangements for Palden Drakpa and Zimey to travel. Yangchen Lhamo declined the offer to come to England.

My first thought, as I scanned the letter, was that it would suit me much better if they came to the USA. But, as Akong explained, they were travelling on Chinese passports and at that time the US did not routinely admit Chinese passport-holders. If I wanted to see them, I would have to go back to Scotland.

I was really torn over this matter. I was forty-two years old and I had finally found my life's purpose. I very much wanted to continue in retreat as I felt I was progressing on my path towards fuller realization. There was so much more to do. I did not consider that I was ready for the next stage in my life;

in fact I could not yet see what that should be. On the other hand I was sad at the prospect of missing out on another family reunion, especially since the letter confirmed that I would not see my parents again. This might be my only chance to see my siblings, and the possibility to reconnect with my past tugged at my heart.

I spent days in meditation, seeking clarity. I then spoke with Khenpo Karthar. I told him that I was contemplating a trip to Scotland. If I went I would be there for just three weeks and then return to KTD to continue in retreat. I considered that my meditation practice was now solid enough to accommodate this short period away, but what did he think?

This time there were no threats to break my legs. Much to my relief he gave me his blessing, so I made arrangements to travel. I left my shrine, my meditation cushion and my bed all neat and tidy for my return. I envisaged that this would be no more than a brief pause, as if I had stepped out into the forest for a stroll.

I felt calm throughout the journey. I had wondered whether I would remember the ways of the world after years of having so little interaction with it, but, though the airports were noisy and hurried, my mind was well able to handle the onslaught of stimulation. I chatted and smiled with those I met in the queues and on the planes.

Once again I was greeted at Glasgow airport by Akong, who looked exactly as he had the last time I'd seen him, five years before. He was as healthy and robust as ever. If he was taken aback by my appearance, he didn't show it. My curly black hair was long gone since it had been shaved off when I became a monk, and I was wearing a monastic's deep red robes rather than the fancy fashions I'd always loved. This he had of course seen in the States. But I was now thin from years of vigorous practice and a sparse diet. Above all, I felt so different in my mind.

We drove to Samye Ling. I was astounded by what I found. The last time I'd been there, ten years previously, it had been just one building and a few huts. Now there was a huge and beautiful temple under construction behind Johnstone House and a new block of guest accommodation next door. A nearby property had been acquired and turned into a retreat centre where a group of Westerners – nine women and seven men – were one and a half years into a four-year retreat under the guidance of Lama Ganga, who had taught me the Six Yogas of Naropa practice.

Akong had told me about these changes but I was still amazed to see them for myself. I felt so moved by this flowering of faith in the Dharma, and very proud of Akong. He had motivated a team of fundraisers and volunteers to build the temple and had worked tirelessly himself on the project. The site had been consecrated in 1979 by Lama Gendun, a revered master who presided over His Holiness the Karmapa's seat in France. Sherab Palden, whom I was delighted to see again, had created a series of beautiful paintings and artworks for the main shrine room in collaboration with many volunteers and Tibetan craftsmen. Samye Ling was no longer a hangout for hippies. It was on its way to being a monastic complex and cultural centre of huge significance.

My meeting with my other brother, Palden Drakpa, and my sister Zimey was joyous but also heartbreaking. I could scarcely believe that I was able to embrace them and to speak with them again after thirty years of separation. Zimey, with whom I had paddled in the shallows of the river in Darak, was by this time a very capable, mature woman. She was married and the mother of six children. A whole lifetime's worth of experience had left its traces on her face, as they had on mine, but her smile was just the same.

I had few memories of Palden from before. We had only been together in Darak for a few months after he returned from the village where he grew up, to assume his role as the family's heir. I left for Dolma Lhakang shortly after his arrival. He had been in Darak with the rest of our family when the surrounding area was taken by the Communists. Now he looked much older than his nearly fifty years. He was haggard and subdued. The story he told was devastating. My brother had been tortured repeatedly and was mentally very unwell. He recounted how, after our escape, the Chinese rounded up the family and exacted revenge for the fact that their son, a tulku, had escaped. They were all forced to participate in indoctrination sessions. My father was tortured every evening for fifteen years in what were called 'struggle sessions'. This involved public humiliation, verbal and physical abuse as he was paraded around the village with a list of his supposed crimes written out on a sheet of paper tied around his neck. In addition to being the father of a tulku, my father, who was relatively wealthy and successful, was accused of being an enemy of the proletariat. Palden felt it was his responsibility, as the family's successor, to take our father's place every second evening so that he would be beaten less frequently. After that my brother was sent away to do forced labour on a road-building programme. The labourers weren't even given adequate food. Palden had to kill many animals just to survive. He was truly a broken man.

I listened to his story with immense compassion. I felt glad that I had been able to stabilize my mind before I heard it, because, otherwise, I have no doubt that it would have stirred up feelings of anger and hatred towards the Chinese. As it was,

I felt deeply saddened for all my family and for the soldiers and officials who had tormented them. Everyone involved had suffered terribly. This was also another turning point in my long journey to stop blaming Akong for my life's losses. I had mostly let go of that resentment during my years in retreat, but now I was receiving another important lesson. If I had stayed in Darak rather than going to Dolma Lhakang, I too would have been tortured and sent to do forced labour. I would almost certainly have ended up as broken as my poor brother, if not more. I felt immensely grateful to Akong for having been the agent of my escaping this fate and instead being able to embark on a spiritual path.

Sadly my oldest brother's story did not end well. He and my sister both lived at Akong's house in Dumfries for a number of months, but Palden was unable to adjust to the local way of life. He would lie on the neighbours' lawns and roll around, and refuse to move when he was asked to. He could speak no English and he used to talk wildly in Tibetan. One day the neighbours called the police. Akong smoothed the situation over, but it made him realize that Palden was so unwell that life would always be difficult for him in Britain and he would surely be happier in Tibet. So Zimey stayed in Dumfries but Palden returned and was cared for by our other sister, Yangchen Lhamo, with support from Akong.

I was about to be offered another chance to practise the discipline of mental training that I had cultivated over the previous five years. Within days of my arrival at Samye Ling, Akong announced that he would not permit me to return to Woodstock. I was shocked. In fact I have to admit that I was furious. I had made it absolutely plain when I agreed to come back for a visit that it would be short. My initial response was to refuse to stay. I had promised Khenpo Karthar that I would return. But Akong was absolutely insistent. He explained that he had been terribly worried about me because I had neither answered nor written to him any letters during my years in retreat. It was true that I saw letters as a distraction, but I had sent a message to Akong and our parents via Khenpo Karthar back in 1981. I knew that Akong and Khenpo Rinpoche were in touch with one another, so he would receive news of me.

I had to bring all my powers of forbearance and equanimity to bear on this matter in order to root out my resentment. It was a big challenge. Akong eventually won me over by promising that I could continue my retreat. He would not expect me to work in the team running Samye Ling. This promise, combined with my newfound gratitude towards him, meant that I was able to resign myself to the situation. I informed Khenpo Rinpoche that I would be continuing my solitary retreat at Purelands, the new retreat centre at Samye Ling.

For the next few weeks I settled myself into my new home. I had my own accommodation separate from the larger retreat houses in which the men's and women's retreats were going on. The house was simple but comfortable, with a small kitchen and bathroom and a living space with my meditation box and shrine. My days were exactly as they had been in Woodstock, though the view out of my window was once again of green rolling hills rather than the woods of New York State.

In April 1987, by which time I was more than a year and a half into my solitary retreat, I had a vivid dream about Trungpa, whom I hadn't seen since 1980. He was telling me to come to visit him in Karma Choling, his first US centre in Vermont. Some days later I heard the news that he had passed away, at Karma Choling on 4 April. I had felt very good about that dream, and even more so after I heard the news of his passing. I believed then and still believe that our connection is very strong, that Trungpa and I have been together for many lifetimes.

Over the next year I did a lot of inner-heat practice (known as *tummo*), the main purpose of which is to transform mind poisons. These are called *kleshas* in Sanskrit and refer to the emotional afflictions of anger, desire, jealousy, pride and ignorance. There are different ways of working with mind poisons. One option is to try to avoid falling prey to them in the first place by practising various skilful means that have mindfulness as their basis – paying close attention to our mind and not indulging in negative emotions. Another way is to take the negative emotions as our path, so not avoiding them but transforming their energy as they arise. This is an advanced practice and is done by working with the subtle energies that move through our energy body via different channels and chakras. We purify them at their source by working skilfully with posture, breathing and visualization. This is the method of tummo. As a byproduct of this energy work our body can become very warm, which is useful if one lives in a cold climate such as that of Scotland or Tibet!

I was single-mindedly focused on my practice and I felt that I managed to generate some warmth. When I told Lama Ganga about this he said that my achievement was not a big deal; many practitioners of old in Tibet were able to melt snow as they meditated outdoors in the freezing winters. I felt as if he'd thrown cold water over my inspiration. For a second I was discouraged and thought that I might as well just switch on the central heating if I wanted to get warm!

This was typical of Lama Ganga, who was a complete traditionalist and very tough on everybody, regardless of their circumstances. He was a great master but he had little understanding of how the Western retreatants in his care had a very different mindset from his own, and how that might affect their practice. It was my observation that he did not grasp how complicated and how fragile Western people are in comparison with Tibetans, who have a much simpler and tougher approach to life and don't get so absorbed in self-preoccupation. Lama Ganga did not believe in talking about personal issues, for example, so he was not prepared for the amount of distress that arose in his retreatants' minds as they went deeper into their practice. Neither did he take account of the fact that, unlike Tibetans, who are born into a culture of Buddhism, it is hard for many Westerners to really trust in the power of the teachings and the masters who pass them on. When the Western retreatants had questions or fears, they did not have faith to fall back on, at least initially. This made them vulnerable. Lama Ganga didn't seem ready to make any allowances for all these differences. He instilled a very harsh regime, and though some people flourished, many others became troubled.

Lama Ganga was not permanently based at Samye Ling. He was the representative of His Holiness the Karmapa at various centres in the States, had a centre in California and also taught at the Samye Dzongs (branches of Samye Ling), so he was often away. After a while I found myself getting more and more involved in helping out with the retreatants, who were by then nearing the end of their retreat. Though I was dedicated to my own practice, I did not want to be selfish about it. I felt increasingly ready and motivated to help others, so I thought I should engage with them. After all, they might find my perspective useful since, unlike Lama Ganga, I had not been trained in a traditional way, I had spent a long time immersed in Western culture and could speak fluent English.

I felt really sorry for them. They were very responsive to the way I spoke about my own experience and theirs, and I found myself going over to see them more and more frequently. I tried to make their time lighter. I asked them how they were finding things, what was worrying them. I made jokes and we would all end up laughing.

I remember talking to one female retreatant who went on to become ordained. She was having a very tough time. She had been doing thousands of prostrations, far too many, and developed a hiatus hernia in her chest. I told her to take it easy and give herself six weeks off prostrations so she could heal. She looked doubtful, but I said to her, 'You are not going to get enlightened in a big hurry, so take a more relaxed approach.' She also had an important question about her practice, and I arranged for Lama Ganga to come over so that I could translate both her question and his answer.

This unofficial helping role was not exactly what I'd had in mind when I'd agreed to stay on in Samye Ling, but I felt pleased to be able to support the retreatants. My hunch that they might find it helpful to talk with someone who hadn't found it easy to purify their mind's afflictions and commit to a spiritual path turned out to be correct. When I laughed about my mistakes I felt them relax about their own struggles. It was wonderful to see them realize that vulnerability and laughter were just as helpful as study and analysis and far more helpful than self-castigation.

In the spring of 1988 the retreat finished. Nobody apart from Lama Ganga and me had been into the retreat house and none of the retreatants had left it since they had all been ceremonially sealed in, four years previously. Akong came to formally open the boundaries and welcome the retreatants back into the world. They looked a bit overwhelmed as I waved them off on their way down to Samye Ling to celebrate with friends and family. I remained up at Purelands and settled down to focus on my own practice. Life felt peaceful for all of about a week and then the builders moved in. Once again I was having to meditate in the middle of a construction site. I should have been used to it after my time at Woodstock but, at least to begin with, it didn't feel any easier. Plans were already being made for the next four-year retreat, which would begin in March the following year. This time there would be forty-four people participating, and therefore more accommodation was required. The team of volunteer builders who had been working so hard to finish the temple now turned their attention to pulling down one retreat house and building a much bigger one. There were seventy-five people, working seven days a week to get the project finished, right outside my front door. As well as the noise there was the small matter of the dust. They stored their bags of cement on the porch of my house and I could feel my one lung struggling. Then, to cap it all, my water supply was cut off.

I was so annoyed. Hadn't I lived through this precise experience once already? Must I really go through it again? But then I resolved to change my way of thinking. Everything in life comes down to mind, I knew this already, and that made it easier to decide that all I had to do was simply meditate, in whatever conditions presented themselves. I focused on the joyful fact that all this work was happening because so many people wanted to go on retreat. I rejoiced in that. When I was able to cultivate the right view of events – these people are working so hard to enable others to do retreat, not to annoy me – I saved myself many months of suffering caused by getting angry over something I could not change. I have been a strong believer in the benefit of holding the right view and having the right motivation ever since.

On 8 August 1988 our beautiful new temple was inaugurated. On this auspicious date more than 1,500 people gathered to witness the ceremony. It was presided over by Tai Situpa Rinpoche, usually known as Situ Rinpoche, one of the four Heart Sons of the Sixteenth Karmapa. When His Holiness died, back in 1981, the Heart Sons had become regents and were charged with acting on his behalf until the Seventeenth Karmapa was found. Once they'd unveiled a marble plaque on the temple wall there were displays of traditional religious dancing and then there was a cake-cutting ceremony and tea for everyone. Akong was serene and modest, looking splendid in a yellow silk *chuba*, the traditional feast-day robe. I was thrilled for him. It was his project, through and through. It had taken nine years and been achieved through his quiet determination and his extraordinary ability to inspire people to give the best of themselves. In the end a building that would have cost approximately £1,500,000 to construct at market rates was built for less than a quarter of that, thanks to the sheer hard work and devotion of everyone involved.

I took a day away from retreat to participate in the temple's inauguration and then I returned to Purelands. I expected to spend the next few months closing my ears to the sound of cement mixers and my mind to its irritations, with nothing further to trouble my practice. But events were about to overtake me.

In the October of 1988 Lama Ganga, who had been expected to continue to lead the four-year retreat, was taken ill in Tibet and died suddenly. It fell to Lama Thubten, a revered master from Palpung monastery in Kham who now had a centre in Birmingham, to be the retreat master for the second long retreat. The paint was scarcely dry on the new retreat houses when he officiated over the closing-in ceremony in March 1989. There were forty-four Western participants, including nine who had done the first retreat and wished to continue. Lama Thubten gave the initial instructions even though, as Akong discovered, he was already gravely unwell. He too died, some months later. Kalu Rinpoche, who had been so instrumental in my own retreat, died around the same time. Suddenly there was nobody to lead this retreat, which was already underway and taking place literally on my doorstep. Akong came to me and asked me to step in. There was nobody else, he said.

I freely admit that I didn't want to. It was one thing to help out but quite another to be the retreat master, with primary responsibility. I would very much have preferred to continue my own practice. I felt that the most beneficial thing I could do for other practitioners was to deepen my own realization. Compared to Lama Ganga or Lama Thubten, both of whom had acquired profound knowledge of the Buddhist teachings and vast experience of retreat rituals, I was very much a novice. But I could not refuse Akong. It was impossible to leave these people without any of the guidance they required. The whole situation was comical, really. I only got the job because literally all the other candidates had died.

I decided that if I were going to do this, I would make some changes. I felt that it was crucial to accommodate the fact that almost all of our retreatants did not speak any Tibetan and for the most part had not undertaken serious study of Buddhism. Many of them were virtual beginners, so asking them to do so many pujas (prayer rituals involving chanting, mantras and visualizations) and read scripts in Tibetan was just too discouraging. I suggested to some of the participants that it was fine to simply meditate. I tried to tailor the programme to individuals' requirements and strengths, which might sound like an obvious idea but was unprecedented within the Tibetan tradition. I wanted people to feel joyful and enthusiastic as well as committed to facing the rigours that lay ahead of them in retreat. It seemed to me that they must be hopeful about their practice, not fearful that they were not up to the task. Meditation practice is not like school. There is no final examination to swot for and we are not in competition with anybody else. Many of the Western people who come to Buddhism are fascinated by its esoteric side, and it is true that there is a vast and sophisticated philosophical system that could occupy our analytical mind for many lifetimes. But I always encourage people to see Buddhism as an everyday practice, first and foremost. An open heart and a positive mindset will benefit us more than any capacity for intellectual analysis.

Since I was still carrying out my own practice just next door to the retreatants, I was able to give interviews and advice whenever someone had a problem. But I refused to play games. I didn't indulge people and wouldn't see them if they became too demanding. During some parts of the retreat, when complete silence was required, and towards the end when I expected participants to be more mature, I would not give personal interviews. I wanted people to become self-reliant, which is very important.

Though I had been a reluctant retreat master, I came to love it very quickly. Far from undermining my own practice, as I had feared, it proved to be complementary. I learned so much about the mind by working with other people to overturn their mental blocks. Everything confirmed my conviction that my own obstacles and digressions had developed my ability to be a bridge between the Tibetan and Western mindset. The fact that I was not a tulku like Akong, Trungpa and so many of the great Tibetan lamas was not a problem but an advantage in helping others. This seemed to me a perfect illustration of the necessity of bringing our obstacles on to our path. In my experience, obstacles *are* the path.

My experience as retreat master between March 1989 and March 1993, and then again between November 1993 and January 1997, allowed me to deepen my understanding of how to spread the Dharma in contemporary Western society. It was like a laboratory for me to understand what helped people, what reached them and what didn't.

I quickly realized that it was essential to warn participants about what lay ahead, not to alarm them, merely to prepare them. Retreat is certainly not for everyone, but I believe that all of us can benefit from a period of seclusion, whether it's four years or four days. It is important to set aside hope for a desired outcome as well as fear of not getting what we want, and instead open ourselves up to the unexpected inner journey that unfolds on retreat. But it helps to accept that some of this may be a struggle. In retreat there is no escape from your mind, its negativities and habits. Most of us spend our lives refusing to face our mind, using any method of distraction at hand, whether that's alcohol, long hours in the office or bingeing on box sets. So when we come to a sustained period of meditation (or even quite a short one, when we start out) we are alarmed to see what comes up when we actually pay attention. Old fears, anxieties and resentments. Endless mind chatter of the most banal kind. It can feel very noisy in there when we start to meditate and it is understandable to want to drown the noise out. Understandable but not very wise because, of course, it doesn't go away if we can't hear it.

Over and over again retreatants would come to me feeling bad about themselves and their past: traumatized, unable to let go, upset with themselves for not being able to do meditation 'properly'. Many people told me that they were particularly challenged by anger. They were unable to stop digging into past hurts and insults and unable to forgive those who had caused them pain. Often they were angry with their parents. Sometimes with partners or ex-partners. A huge number of them were also angry with themselves. When I suggested that they might find it healing to forgive, they would again list everything they had to be angry about and wait for my nod of understanding. They were completely identified with their negative emotions and struggled to see them as mere phantoms of the mind. Letting go of attachment to trauma rather than continuing to focus on how we got wounded is so important because, if we cannot let go, that trauma will dictate our whole life and distort all our thinking. Identifying with past hurts entrenches a lack of forgiveness, of others and of ourselves. The problem is, without compassion for every living being, we can never be at peace. Any joy we experience is short-lived.

I'm not saying that this is easy. All of us carry painful feelings, because it is inevitable that difficult things happen in this life. For years I was burdened with memories and dreams of my escape from Tibet and the loss of my family, homeland and way of life. But gradually I learned not to make them solid and real by believing that they were me and that I *was* my trauma. I chose to align myself with a deeper reality – Buddha Nature, that core wisdom, kindness and goodness. My faith in this part of myself, along with the blessing of my teachers and their lineage, opened the door to profound change. Over time and with sustained practice, I was able to walk through it. I became free.

I also observed that many people who came to see me had low self-esteem, even when (especially when) they appeared to have vastly inflated self-confidence. They had been told at a young age either that they were a genius or the opposite: that they were not good enough. In each case, they ended up believing it, which caused them difficulties. In retreat, when things didn't go well, these people punished themselves for being a failure. They forgot that the main purpose of retreat is to overcome obstacles by seeing their lack of solidity. I would urge people to focus on the fact that whatever had provoked their suffering was not happening in this very moment except in their own mind as they relived it. It was not a real thing but a story, a creation of their mind from memories of the past. With determined practice, they could begin to see through these stories and take refuge in the simplicity of the present moment. But this is hard. It takes persistent effort. Rather than plug away with their practice, many people would go back to feeling sorry for themselves, or punishing themselves for their inability to overcome their obstacles as fast as they felt they 'should' be able to. I would do whatever I could to help disentangle them from these patterns. I affirmed and reaffirmed their Buddha Nature to them until, finally, they could believe in it for themselves, at which point wonderful changes would begin to happen. It was always such a joy to see these flashes of opening and release.

The learning was a two-way street. One of the key things I wanted to teach was that, according to the Dharma, there is never any need to feel inadequate, or low, because our true nature is pure, whole and free. But this is hard to grasp if you have no direct experience of it and lack the faith to accept your teacher's assurances that it really is your true nature. In addition, I began to realize that Western people have a very different relationship with their emotions from Tibetans and other Asian practitioners of Buddhism. In Tibet we learned that emotions, like thoughts, are not real and not necessarily useful. Buddhism holds that anger, desire, pride, jealousy and ignorance (the five mind poisons) are not sins as they were in traditional Christian thinking, but afflictions of the mind that make it harder for us to see our true nature. In contemporary Western culture, on the other hand, it is emotion that is king, not mind. The way you feel about something is of supreme importance. People in the West typically identify with their emotions, both good and bad, and find it hard just to observe them. This leads to trouble because they get caught up in reactivity and inner conflict. And to make matters even more difficult, in the West there are two additional mind poisons that we did not have in Tibet when I was growing up – guilt and shame. I realized that I needed to find ways to help people detach from their emotions in general, and these ones in particular.

I tried to do this by suggesting that they identify with a *yidam* instead, since the yidam is flawless and free and endowed with an abundance of qualities. 'Yidams' can be roughly translated as 'deities'. They are radiant expressions of our Buddha Nature, and are charged with blessings. There are many different deities, such as Green Tara and Chenrezig, and each deity practice has its own specific image, liturgy and mantra. When we do deity practice we meditate on our body being an image of light, like a rainbow, and filled with qualities such as love, compassion and wisdom rather than flesh and blood that is filled with issues and problems. Yidam practices were a big part of the long retreat programme. I hoped they would help retreatants to loosen their tight identification with painful memories, emotional afflictions and the illusion of the solid sense of 'me'.

Sometimes it worked but sometimes it ended up being counterproductive. Some people used the practices to inflame the mind poisons. For example, people who had a lot of sexual feeling misunderstood yidams and used their deity practice to indulge in sexual fantasy. Others got lost in daydreams. This led to boredom, distraction and a retreat into fantasy.

So the retreats were very much a learning experience for all of us, but I have no doubt that they were hugely beneficial to many people. I would include myself in that group. I, like many others, learned a lot about the mind. We might not have achieved the pinnacle of the Buddhist path – Enlightenment – but we got a sense of the immensity of the task, we became more mature and realistic, and we learned invaluable practices that would serve us for the rest of our lives.

In September 1992, six months before the second retreat finished, I left Purelands to attend an occasion that was absolutely momentous for me on every level. I was going back to Tibet for the first time since I had escaped thirty-three years before. I would be travelling with Akong to Tsurphu monastery, near Lhasa, for the enthronement of His Holiness the Seventeenth Karmapa.

The Seventeenth Karmapa was then a seven-year-old boy, who had been officially recognized as the reincarnation of the Sixteenth Karmapa by His Holiness the Dalai Lama, the Kagyu lineage regents and the Chinese Communist authorities earlier in the year. This was highly significant as it was the first time that a reincarnate high lama had been recognized by the Communists. The practice of Buddhism in Tibet had been virtually outlawed since the Cultural Revolution of 1966–76, but politics had shifted since then and the leadership in Beijing was now keen to be seen to allow freedom of worship in Tibet.

On the day that I received the news that the Seventeenth Karmapa had been found, I was ecstatic. I couldn't wait to meet my old master in his new body and continue our relationship. So it was with a mixture of excitement and bubbling joy that I set off to travel to Tibet for his enthronement, some months later. The prospect of going back to my homeland could not have been any happier now that I was going to see the Karmapa and to witness this most spiritually significant moment for our Kagyu lineage. There was an additional excitement and sense of pride for me because it had fallen to my brother to be asked to join one of the two search parties who were charged with finding the young boy. I couldn't wait to talk to Akong, and to hear his story of finding His Holiness.

12. *Mystic*

On the day of the enthronement I felt I was participating in an outpouring of spiritual energy. The atmosphere was electric. Akong and I were privileged to have a place in the front row of the shrine room of Tsurphu monastery, the principal seat of the Karmapas, which was packed to bursting. Outside the doors of the temple there were thousands of people pushing to get in. Even some very high lamas were unable to gain entry. The mood was ecstatic but undercut with desperation. The Tibetan people had finally been allowed to practise their faith after decades of repression and now their devotion was overflowing.

As I stood in the throng of people within the shrine room, I realized that it was becoming dangerous. If the crowd did not fall back there was going to be a surge, a crush and people might be hurt or even killed. Tens of thousands of Tibetans had travelled from far and wide to witness this most significant event for our Kagyu lineage. The Chinese authorities were unprepared. They had closed roads leading to Tsurphu but that hadn't deterred people, and now the soldiers stationed at the doors to the temple had lost control of the situation.

Then I saw Akong striding through the crowd, which fell aside for him. I couldn't see what happened outside but I heard later that he had stood on a platform at the temple gates, spoken to the people and beaten some of them back with a bullwhip, preventing them from surging into the hall. To my mind, he was manifesting as Mahakala, the protector deity of the Kagyu lineage. However he managed it, it worked. The crowd became quiet, the danger passed and the ceremony began.

His Holiness the Seventeenth Karmapa was still a little boy, but the grace and patience he exhibited astounded everyone who saw him. The ritual took several hours. Once it had finished he sat for many more hours as tens of thousands of devotees filed past him, seeking his blessing. He was undaunted and calm as he blessed each one. When it was my turn to speak to him, I asked him if I might be permitted to return to retreat now. This was a significant question for me as his predecessor had told me that if I spent twenty years in retreat and practised well I would attain a high level of realization. He smiled, gave me a swift kick to the head and, in the same old tones he had always used with me, said, 'Go back and help your brother!' It was just like being back with His Holiness the Sixteenth Karmapa again. From that day forward I accepted unquestioningly that I should serve Akong in whatever capacity he decided.

Akong had given me his account of finding His Holiness the Seventeenth Karmapa, who up until his enthronement was known as Apo Gaga, or 'the one who makes us very happy'. The boy was the child of nomads from Bagor in Kham. His birthplace and the names of his parents had been predicted by His Holiness the Sixteenth Karmapa in a letter he concealed in a protective amulet that he gave to Tai Situpa Rinpoche, one of his four Heart Sons, shortly before he died. It is customary among the Karmapas to write and conceal a prediction letter with details of where the next reincarnation will be found, but a number of years passed and nothing was discovered. It then occurred to Tai Situpa to check the amulet His Holiness had given him more closely, and he was delighted to find the letter hidden inside.

Once the letter had been authenticated, a search party of three monks was sent out from Tsurphu monastery to look for the child. On 21 May 1992, they found him. Having been directed by the steward at the local monastery, they arrived at Apo Gaga's family tent. The family already knew they were coming. Their eldest son, Yeshe Rabsel, had been staying at the local monastery when the search party arrived. The monks were careful not to divulge the real reason for their presence. The word 'Karmapa' was not mentioned. They announced that they were looking for a local woman called Loga, for whom they had a letter from India. The steward correctly deduced that this Loga was the mother of Yeshe Rabsel and called him in to talk to the visitors. When they discovered that Yeshe Rabsel did indeed have a seven-year-old brother and that his father was named Karma Dondrub, they could not contain their excitement. The child's parents' names tallied with those in His Holiness the Karmapa's prediction letter, as did the location of his birth. The monks told Yeshe Rabsel that they were looking for the reincarnation of a tulku from their monastery, and arrangements were made to visit the family two days later.

When Yeshe Rabsel arrived home that evening to inform his parents of the exciting news, his little brother began to dance for joy. That morning Apo Gaga had packed his things into a bundle, ready to take with him, and told his mother that it was time for him to go to his monastery.

Once the distinguished guests were settled on the sheepskins that had been placed on the floor of the family's tent, and food had been served, they began to question Loga and Karma Dondrub. Apo Gaga hung back, looking serious, as his parents recounted his life story with all its omens and auspicious events. Three days after the birth, the seventy or so families of their community had heard the sound of conch shells, which are associated with the Buddha, but could find no source for the music. Then the air was also full of cymbals and reed horns. Loga's other children searched all round the tent but nobody could identify where the music was coming from. And then the baby boy, just three days old, stopped feeding, looked up at her and addressed her as 'Ama', the Tibetan word for 'mother'. He quickly confirmed himself to be a highly unusual infant. From the time he was three months old, the baby emanated light. After nightfall, his older sisters would sit close to their sleeping brother and use the glow from his face to finish their domestic tasks. There were many, many such stories. The group from Tsurphu were in no doubt. Apo Gaga was pronounced the genuine reincarnation.

Things moved very quickly from there. It had been intended that Jamgön Kongtrül would head a second search party representing the four Heart Sons, but tragically he had been killed in a car accident in April a month earlier. So the surviving regents then asked Akong and another lama to take on the task of going to the child and conducting further tests on their behalf.

Akong had a very personal test to carry out, concerning an event that only he knew about. When His Holiness the Sixteenth Karmapa was dying, Akong had visited him in hospital in Chicago. This was not long after my ordination, when I had just entered retreat. His Holiness knew he would die soon and asked to see his closest disciples in order to make arrangements. He sent Akong off on a mission. As my brother left, Akong made a request. Could he have one of His Holiness's teeth, after his body had been cremated, as a personal relic? His Holiness the Karmapa immediately agreed, but since Akong was away when the cremation took place, he was not present to collect the tooth.

Eleven years later, Akong arrived at the tent of Apo Gaga's family. Having greeted everybody, he turned to the rosy-cheeked little boy and asked if he had anything to give him. The child immediately reached under the rug he was sitting on and pulled something out. When he opened his fist he revealed one of his milk teeth. Akong was overjoyed and gathered His Holiness the Seventeenth Karmapa in his arms for a hug. The Karmapa grinned at my brother and ruffled his hair as if they had known each other for ever. You can imagine how my heart thrilled to this story when I heard it.

Akong also told me of the extraordinary experience of travelling with Apo Gaga and his family to Tsurphu monastery, along roads lined by thousands of joyful people who had come out to greet the new Karmapa. Once they arrived, the child began a series of preparations for his enthronement. Many of these were highly elaborate and had been performed for hundreds of years, but some were the stuff of everyday family life. It fell to Akong to give Apo Gaga his first ever bath, for example. The little boy was not at all keen on the idea and protested, just like any other seven-year-old. Akong was of course a father and had seen all this before with his own children.

My return to Tibet was quite brief and was focused on meeting His Holiness the Seventeenth Karmapa, which for me was the experience of a lifetime. The day of his ordination was one I had never expected to see. Officials from the People's Republic of China sat on one side of the shrine room, across from the lamas and tulkus, as the clamour of thousands of Tibetans trying to get into the room filled the air. At the centre of all this was His Holiness the Seventeenth Karmapa, the living embodiment of the continuity of our Kagyu lineage. The wave of destruction that I had believed had swept away my world more than thirty years before had not in fact erased it completely. Tsurphu monastery was still here. The twelfth-century buildings may have been torn down during the Cultural Revolution, but the shrine room had been rebuilt and was being used to celebrate the happiest occasion. The valley was still beautiful. This place was still sacred.

I did not feel any need to dwell on my own past. I did not travel back to Darak. My parents had passed on by this time so there was nobody there to visit, since my sisters Zimey and Yangchen Lhamo both now lived in Lhasa with their families. I wanted to devote myself to activities that would nourish my current life rather than take me backwards, so after a brief stop to see my sisters I went to India on pilgrimage with a group of twenty of the Sangha from Samye Ling. We were heading for Bodhgaya, the birthplace of the Buddha, where I performed 100,000 prostrations at the Bodhi Tree under which the Buddha sat for forty-nine days in silent meditation until he attained Enlightenment. It was such a moving experience for me to be at this special place. I was full of devotion and gratitude. So I threw myself into prostration practice. Literally. Once again I ended up with torn and tattered knees. I failed to follow my own advice and take things at a sustainable pace. This was a problem because the next stop on my trip would be the most challenging spiritual practice I had ever undertaken, and I was not in the best physical shape for it.

I was heading for Nepal to receive instruction from the renowned master Tulku Urgyen, who had spent two decades in retreat in his mountaintop hermitage and was one of the few remaining practitioners in the world who held the lineage of dark retreats. It was Akong who suggested that I was ready for this teaching and I leaped at the chance to receive it. Dark retreat is regarded as one of the most advanced of all

From a Mountain in Tibet

meditation practices. The retreatant spends forty-nine days in the pitch blackness and silence of total sensory deprivation, in preparation for the bardo, or the interval between death and rebirth.

The bardo state is characterized by hallucinatory experiences. Buddhists believe that when someone dies, their consciousness continues into the after-death state but is still linked to the body of their last life. Often, beings in this state do not realize they have died, so it can be a very frightening experience for them. As the moment for rebirth draws closer, the being starts to have premonitions of the life to come. Dark retreat trains a participant to become familiar with the bardo hallucinations and so avoid being overpowered by them when the time comes. The aim is to be able to see that the hallucinations are not real but a powerful spell. Through meditation we can break this spell, and the enlightened state that was always there can shine through. This releases us from the cycle of death and rebirth. We also gain an ability to see daily events in our current lifetime as like the intangible events of a dream state rather than solid 'reality'. This can help us to approach life in a lighter way and spend less of our emotional energy clinging on to or avoiding things.

I was excited when I met Tulku Urgyen at the temple complex of Swayambhunath outside Kathmandu. My enthusiasm was a bit dampened when he took one look at me and pronounced that he would not allow me to begin the retreat until I'd been to hospital for a check-up. I had seriously damaged my knees doing prostrations and I was quite unwell. He knew better than anyone that dark retreat is an intense experience for which the participant must be in the best physical and mental condition. Even highly experienced meditators find dark retreat challenging and as Tulku Urgyen warned me, for most people it is extremely dangerous. An extended period of total sensory deprivation is virtually guaranteed to send a normal person mad. When it is imposed on people, it is a form of torture.

The dark retreat hut was a single small room within a larger primitive construction made of concrete with no windows. It had been built on the hilltop of Nagi Gompa by a Norwegian student of Tulku Urgyen who was desperate to do dark retreat. There was a pipe to bring oxygen into the retreat room. This primitive ventilation system made a rasping noise when the wind blew that reminded me of *radongs*, the Tibetan horns used in pujas. The hut had a dirt floor and not a single chink to allow in even a gleam of light. There was no way to tell what time of day or night it was. You could see nothing at all, not even your hand in front of your nose. The silence was complete, apart from this haunting noise of the ventilation pipe, which alone would have been enough to unhinge most people. The poor Norwegian only lasted a few days before fleeing. Tulku Urgyen had prepared him carefully, but even so it had all been too much. Tulku Urgyen vowed to be more careful about who he allowed to attempt the practice from then on. I was the first candidate he had approved since those events. So I followed his advice, got myself checked out by the doctors, rested, received the instructions and agreed that only when he judged that I was ready would I begin.

An Italian pupil of mine called Renato Mazzonetto, who was one of the people from Samye Ling who had been on pilgrimage with me, stayed on to act as my attendant. He and I cleaned out the hut and then, when Tulku Urgyen agreed, we made our final preparations. We went to a supermarket in Kathmandu to buy supplies. I felt the strangeness of stocking up on food in the brightly lit store, knowing I was heading for total darkness. It would be Renato's job to bring me my meal once a day and pass it to me via a tiny hatch like that in a medieval dungeon. Renato would also pass me a bucket and a plastic bag for me to perform my necessities. Can you imagine the trickiness of having to relieve yourself into a single plastic bag in total darkness? It was quite a challenge! I would pass the bag and bucket back the following day for Renato to dispose of.

After the retreat finished he told me that he had thrown the bags into the forest. Some Nepalese street people seem to have assumed that there might be something of value in them, given that it was a Westerner who was throwing them away, so they went foraging for the bags. They must have been terribly disappointed when they found nothing but stinking excrement! That story gave me a good laugh at the end of the retreat.

I went into the retreat house gradually. Over a period of three days, I spent more and more time in total darkness in order to accustom both my mind and my eyes to the experience. Normally the instructing lama visits the retreatant to talk them through the visualization for each day of the retreat. Both the visualizations themselves and the daily contact help to keep the retreatant's mind stable. Tulku Urgyen informed me that he was not going to do that with me. He gave me the most advanced instruction, which is simply to maintain present-moment awareness and to regard all thoughts, feelings and experiences that arise as empty. So, no visualizations, no mantras, just sitting meditation.

As I've said, I am not a worrier but I did feel some trepidation as the complete darkness closed around me and I prepared to face my mind without any distraction whatsoever. I trusted Tulku Urgyen completely and I felt that my faith was strong. Even so, I knew that I would experience hallucinations. Akong had told me that even the most experienced meditator will inevitably hallucinate, because the inner winds, or energies, are very difficult to control. That's why it's important to eat foods that help to rebalance the subtle energies. Meat is said to be good for this but my diet was very simple and vegetarian.

As I rapidly discovered for myself, sensory deprivation stimulates mental activity. There is nothing to interrupt it, no one to talk to, nothing to look at except your own mind. So if you start to see something and to think it is really happening, there's nothing to show you that it's not real. There are stories of people who are convinced there is a tiger in the room with them or that part of their own body is meat to eat. If you have any hidden fear then it will manifest itself and you will be confronted with it again and again.

I reminded myself that I was not a prisoner, even though the door was locked. Renato was coming once a day. We were forbidden to speak or to see each other, but if I were truly losing my mind I could of course ask him for help. I didn't think it would come to that but it was a necessary safety precaution. I just had to hope that I would be able to see through the hallucinations. I was careful to listen out for his arrival with my food and the bucket. Aside from the practicalities, it was my only marker of the passage of time. Before long, I lost track of how many days I had been there.

The first few days, while I could still count them, passed without incident. I felt I was able to maintain present-moment awareness. I slept, though I suspect not for long. Then the imaginings began. I began to think that there were spiders crawling over my body. I was prepared for this. As soon as the fears arose I would look directly at them and recognize them as the product of my mind rather than reality. It was essential not to indulge them even for a second.

More and more I had the feeling of being surrounded by

moonlight. When I put out my hand in front of me I still could not see it, yet the whole room was bathed in soft light. My sense was that it was the inner light of the mind manifesting all around me. It was an odd sensation but I welcomed it.

At some point I realized that I could see through the walls. This was truly strange. I could see the stars in the night sky above my ceiling, just as if I were outside looking directly at them. I wondered whether I was hallucinating, but after I finished retreat I was outside one night when I spotted the same constellation. When I mentioned this to Tulku Urgyen, he told me that the sacred texts say that if your retreat goes well then you can see through walls to the stars.

By the end of my experience I felt a deep calm. I had become accustomed to these otherworldly experiences and recognized that they too were simply the products of my mind. I think Renato actually had more of a hard time than I did. He worried about me a great deal and was not used to the living conditions in Nepal, so he struggled with that. He was a kind person but definitely the worrying type!

My retreat finished abruptly. The ideal is to emerge slowly, over three days, so as to give the mind and body time to readjust to normal life. Daylight is painful on your eyes after forty-nine days in total darkness and disorientation is inevitable. But Tibetan New Year was beginning, so I just came straight out. Thrangu Rinpoche, whom I had known since my days at Rumtek, where he taught me the Four Foundations, sent a car to get me and take me to the celebrations at Thrangu Tashi Choling, his monastery near Kathmandu. Somebody offered me a cold Coke and I drank it all down. It tasted so good. Not for long. My body was overwhelmed by its instantaneous return to modern life and I vomited it all straight back up!

I returned to Samye Ling at the beginning of March 1993 feeling mentally invigorated but physically drained by my experiences. In a photo taken to celebrate the end of the second long retreat, which finished on 6 March, I am surrounded by retreatants in the shrine room, swaddled in heavy clothing and a fur hat. I could not shake the cold that had taken hold of me.

1993 was a year of change. I felt different after witnessing His Holiness the Seventeenth Karmapa's enthronement and completing the dark retreat. My faith was now unshakeably strong. In May we welcomed His Holiness the Dalai Lama to Samye Ling, for his second visit. This was a huge event for our community, not least because nearly 5,000 people came to attend His Holiness's public talk. Many of them were moved to tears and I was buoyed up by this flowering of devotion.

There were changes in the everyday world too. In September I celebrated my fiftieth birthday. By the time the third long retreat started in November that year I was virtually running Samye Ling as well as acting as retreat master. You probably won't be surprised to hear that I was still ambivalent about this, despite my commitment to doing as His Holiness the Seventeenth Karmapa had directed, and helping my brother. But I knew it was time for me to step up. Akong had been spending more and more time in Tibet overseeing humanitarian projects there via Rokpa, the charitable organization he and a woman called Lea Wyler had established in 1981. He could see that I had grown in faith and devotion, and gradually he drew me into the day-to-day activity of running Samye Ling. He wanted me to gain in confidence so that I could do what he needed me to do. He had always been tireless in his compassionate work, but now he too was broadening his scope. His projects with Rokpa provided food aid and healthcare to hundreds of people not just in Tibet but also in Nepal, South Africa and all over the globe. It was finally time for me to find a way to be a monk in the world rather than in retreat.

My increased responsibilities meant that I was less involved in the third long retreat, which ran from November 1993 to November 1997, though I continued to give talks and some interviews. I still loved to help, but I confess that I found the admin side of my duties more onerous. I felt very strongly that I would need to ensure that my busy outer life was balanced by deep commitment to my own spiritual path.

Sometimes, fortuitously, it felt as if there were no conflict between the spiritual path and my role as a leader of the community. I began to feel that, through the force of my own activity, certain things were drawn to me without my desiring them or trying to make them happen. It was as if I were witnessing the laws of karma in real time. It is like planting seeds in a garden. If you plant tomato seeds then tomatoes grow, not pumpkins. If you plant the seeds of anger and resentment in the mind then hatred grows. If you plant the seeds of loving kindness and tolerance, compassion grows. We set in motion certain causes, create the right conditions and then results inevitably follow. That's precisely the way I feel about the Holy Isle project, which has been one of the most rewarding of my whole life.

Back in 1990, when I was in retreat in Purelands, I had received a message from a woman called Catherine Morris. She urgently wanted to talk to me about her proposition that I, or, more precisely, Samye Ling, should buy the island she and her husband owned, which was a small outcrop off the Isle of Arran. I was baffled. Buying a Scottish island was not exactly in my plans. I really wanted to carry on in retreat. But the next bit of the message got my attention. She wanted me to know that this idea had come to her in a vision. Catherine was a devout Catholic and had been visited in a dream by Mary, the mother of Christ, who had instructed her to pass the island on to a 'Lama Yeshe'. When she awoke she had a very clear recollection of the name, but it meant nothing to her. Once she began to look, though, it didn't take her long to find me.

I rang her back and we talked. Catherine explained to me that she and her family had been living on the island for a number of years, but it was such a spiritually powerful place that, in her own words, she 'couldn't handle it'. She could not afford to give it to me, but she was open to negotiating a fair price. She felt strongly that the island, which had been a place of Christian pilgrimage for more than a thousand years, must find an owner who would be able to work with its spiritual energy.

I was very intrigued, so I agreed to go and visit her. It was December by now, the middle of winter. The weather and the seas were stormy and fierce. I didn't relish the prospect of having to take two boats, firstly the ferry to Arran, and then a tiny boat from Arran to Holy Isle. I'd never quite got over my horror of water, ever since the Brahmaputra River crossing. I had no clue what I was going to see, but I set off with two others from Samye Ling.

Catherine's son came and collected us from Lamlash on Arran and took us in his boat over to Holy Isle. Here I was, somebody who had no love for crossing water, on my way to an island so remote it was located off another island, in Scotland, in December. Who would have thought I would end up here? And yet there was something about the place that felt familiar. Holy Isle's imposing, central mountain looked to me like a reclining lion and I felt excitement building. We walked down to the south end, over the top of the lion-mountain, and then as darkness fell we went to the north end and found the farmhouse where we were to stay overnight.

In the evening something extraordinary happened. I went outside and looked up at the immense sky. The sun was setting and the only sound was the booming of the waves on the shore. As I looked across the bay, back towards Lamlash, the twinkling lights of the town were coming on. I suddenly recognized that view. This was the island that I had visited years ago while doing Dream Yoga in my retreat in New York. At the time Khenpo Karthar had advised me not to give the dream any significance, but now I was certain that I was revisiting the place I had seen in my visionary dream. All the details of the island I was standing on, the bay and the view of Lamlash were exactly as I had dreamed them. The feeling of excitement, which had been bubbling in me ever since we left Arran, was flowering into joy. What an amazing omen, especially since Catherine Morris had also had a vision in a dream, instructing her to seek me out and pass the island to me.

I said nothing about this to the people I was with at the time, but this moment was the seed of my determination to buy Holy Isle and establish a retreat centre for people of all faiths or none. The problem was, I had no money. Akong suggested we mortgage Samye Ling, but I didn't want to do that. Catherine and I settled on a price of £350,000 and I was quite open about not yet having the money, but she agreed to wait and in fact turned down a higher offer. I didn't know where the funds would come from, but I trusted that they would arrive. I felt an unshakeable faith that this was the right thing to do. I also had a very clear vision of what we should do on the island. On the south end we would build a long-term Tibetan Buddhist retreat with retreat pods built into the mountainside, and on the north end an interfaith centre where anyone – whatever their religious beliefs, identity or life problems – could come for a short retreat. I wanted to honour Holy Isle's Christian heritage and also to establish the rest of the island as a nature reserve where the bird colonies and the group of wild ponies who lived there would be undisturbed.

Many people thought I was crazy. They said it was just a piece of rock in the ocean and was not worth the money I'd agreed to pay for it, which I didn't even have. I kept to my own faith and vision. And then the money came so easily. Within four months we managed to raise the entire sum from individual donors. There was one very big donation from a Buddhist student in Belgium who later became a nun.

On 21 April 1992 we held an inaugural interfaith meeting on the island to celebrate its purchase by Samye Ling. My first priority was to renovate the lighthouse cottages on the south end of the island and convert them into retreat accommodation. My plan was to shift the long-term retreats from Purelands at Samye Ling to Holy Isle and the Isle of Arran for the women's and men's retreats respectively. The renovation was carried out by volunteers. It took several years, but when it was complete it was a beautiful testament to so much faith and hard work. I loved the symbolism of the lighthouse, which was like a manifestation of our shining Buddha Nature. We took on a professional fundraiser, held a competition for architects to design retreat pods and began a tree-planting programme to reforest the island. The Holy Isle project began to draw attention from media all over the world.

The next stage was the interfaith centre for world peace at the north end of the island, which we built as an extension of the original farmhouse. This was a huge challenge, because everything had to be shipped out and not many contractors wanted to quote for working on an island off an island! The workers for this phase were professionals, as it was such a big project, and they refused to stay on Holy Isle. I think they wanted to eat meat and drink alcohol, and, of course, these things were not part of our ethos. So we had to lay on a boat to transport them to and from Lamlash every day. It cost us millions of pounds, and once again I just had to trust that the money would come.

Throughout this time I had the joyous feeling that everything was in flow, that my faith was attracting what I needed in order to realize the visions that Catherine and I had experienced. People told me it would be impossible to raise the money and impossible to build a big building on such a remote island, but we achieved both objectives. The Centre for World Peace and Health was officially opened on 31 May 2003 at a ceremony attended by Buddhist, Christian, Muslim, Hindu and Sikh leaders from different communities in Scotland.

I remember taking the group to see St Molaise's cave. St Molaise was a sixth-century monk and mystic and an important figure in the spread of Christianity from Ireland via the Celtic Church, and eventually throughout the British Isles. He had a hermitage on Holy Isle in the late sixth century, believed to have been in the cave we were setting off to visit. Naturally I felt a deep connection to the idea of monks in silent retreat in caves. I was thrilled to find this similarity between the mystical traditions of my homeland and my current home.

As we were walking along the coast to the cave I paused to catch my breath and a robin came and perched on my foot. The bird followed me all the way to our destination. I interpreted this as a visit from a local deity. Tibetan Buddhism respects local deities, which are like nature spirits linked to particular areas that guard and protect the integrity of the land. Bringing them onside is seen as important if you want your venture to work out.

The robin and I respectfully acknowledged each other. I felt I'd been officially welcomed to Holy Isle by its resident deities, just as I myself had given an official welcome to our visitors. Everything about the Holy Isle project confirmed my belief that when our actions are in harmony with an unselfish vision we are touched by grace and receive whatever we need, while obstacles are easy to clear from our path.

When we were building the original retreat centre on Holy Isle back in the mid-nineties, a generous donation meant that I was fortunate to be able to construct a room in which I could carry out another dark retreat. I had found my first experience in Nepal so beneficial that I was keen to repeat it, though with better hygiene! I felt deeply at home on Holy Isle and I thought it would be a wonderful setting for a second dark retreat. In 1997 the space was ready. Once again Renato came to attend on me. We joked that compared to conditions in Nepal, this was like being at a holiday camp. He brought me cooked food every day and I had the use of a toilet, because there was a small bathroom within the dark cabin.

I had a wonderful time during this second experience. I had learned a few practical things about how to make it comfortable, and I was careful to go in and come out gradually to avoid shocking my body or my mind. I did not experience many hallucinations or have any negative thoughts the entire time I was in retreat. Once again I felt that the space was bathed in soft light, even though I could still not see my own body. This illumination seemed, as before, to be the light of my own mind. I felt that I hardly slept at all and was never hungry. It was a supremely positive experience and restored balance to my life, in which my own spiritual practice had been taking something of a back seat to a great deal of 'public' life and duties.

When I came out I was convinced that it would be beneficial to the people we hoped would come to Holy Isle to make it a condition of their visit that they observe Buddhism's five precepts for ethical conduct. These are to respect life and refrain from killing; to respect other people's property and refrain from stealing; to speak the truth and refrain from lying; to encourage health and refrain from intoxicants (including alcohol, cigarettes and drugs); and to respect others and refrain from sexual misconduct. I felt that this would establish a foundation for people's spiritual development. These are the Five Golden Rules we ask anybody coming to Holy Isle or Samye Ling to observe. I think this has been a great success and is appreciated by our volunteers, visitors and the many people with addiction and mental health problems who have found peace on Holy Isle. True, it sent our costs soaring when we were building the Centre for World Peace. The labourers refused to stay on an island where there was no alcohol so we had to ferry them back and forth from Lamlash twice a day. They might not have been fully on board with our vision, but I still think it was worth it!

Some people are very intrigued when I talk to them about the more mystical elements of the spiritual life that I have experienced. Some, of course, are sceptical. Others become anxious to have intense mystical experiences themselves. I have come to realize over the years that some of these people do not necessarily have the right motivation. They are like experience junkies, excited by the idea of pushing themselves to extremes. There is an element of ego involved, and a lack of self-knowledge. This always ends badly. One student of mine endangered his mental health by insisting that he would do a dark retreat, even though he did not approach me for teachings or guidance. I was away from Samye Ling at the time and regret I was unable to give him the advice he needed. He lasted two weeks. Sadly he has been unwell ever since and has renounced Buddhism.

I always say that the mind is the most powerful thing in the world and once we learn how to pay attention to its wanderings, to train it and nurture it, it will reward us a thousand-fold. There is no need to force things. All we have to do, in order to bring about positive change, is to allow its innate wisdom to illuminate our lives. I was fortunate to be able to use the deep focus I attained in dark retreats to fuel a radiant outward-looking focus in my work at Samye Ling and on Holy Isle. Balancing the inner work of meditation with the outer focus of living in the world is very important for all of us. Without this balance we cannot fulfil our potential or live at peace with others. But there's no need for exotic locations or punishing regimes. Daily meditation practice can purify the mind poisons, deepen our compassion for ourselves and for every living being, and set us on a path to a new positive way of life.

13.   *Rinpoche*

In 1995 I was formally appointed abbot of Samye Ling by my brother Akong and Tai Situ Rinpoche. I was honoured and slightly amazed to find myself in this position. If you'd told me back in 1980, as I awaited the blessing of ordination from His Holiness the Sixteenth Karmapa, that within fifteen years I would be head of Samye Ling, I would have scoffed. I was a novice, just starting out on my spiritual path. And yet, in the intervening years, a total transformation had taken place in my mind and my heart.

From now on Akong was free to focus on his international humanitarian work and I turned my attention back to the task of helping the many people who arrived at Samye Ling looking for guidance. There was a constant stream of lost and directionless folk arriving at our door. Many of them were suffering with addiction and mental health problems. In some cases we really were the last refuge after their friends and families had withdrawn support. They would come to do some volunteering and be so moved by what they experienced that they wanted to stay on, to stabilize their minds. Often they would ask for an interview and I would sit and listen as they poured their heart out to me.

I had always felt a deep connection with these 'lost' people. They reminded me of my younger self. I knew from experience that looking for fulfilment outside of ourselves, via our career, partner, family, social status or hedonism, can suck us into a vortex of dissatisfaction and destructiveness. It is a source of great freedom to find peace, wisdom and fulfilment within ourselves. Meditation had been my medicine and I had no doubt that it could help countless others. I began to think that an extended period of reflection and discipline would be beneficial for many of the people I talked with. The trouble was that ordination as a monk or nun did not feel like a realistic prospect. It was just too daunting.

I already knew from my years as the Samye Ling retreat master that most Western people, however sincere, will struggle with going straight from being a curious beginner to doing a three- or four-year secluded retreat. They are full of enthusiasm but have yet to develop either the experience of extended meditation or the faith that sustains it. Some of our long-term retreatants had gone on to commit to lifelong ordination, but many had become discouraged and abandoned the path, either before or after ordination. This led to feelings of failure, frustration, depression and resentment. Surely there was a better way for all these people?

The problem was that there was no tradition of what I began to think of as temporary ordination within Tibetan Buddhism. In Tibet lifelong ordination is a way of life, and a significant chunk of the population are monks and nuns, but, of course, that is not the case in modern Europe. What if I could offer people a sort of beginner's ordination for a year? At the end of the year people could either give their robes back, with no sense of failure attached, or commit to another two or three years.

I became really excited at this prospect. I also knew that I would have to act alone to make it happen. Anyone who was a tulku or a high lama would be unable to endorse such an unprecedented step since they would need approval from His Holiness the Dalai Lama and others. But I was a nobody, and I really wanted to help. I had a certain amount of leverage and I ran my own ship at Samye Ling. So I made the decision to try, and from the mid-nineties onwards I began to offer temporary ordination to men and women.

The initial group was almost a hundred people, who all took vows: first for a year and then longer if this worked out. Those were crazy times. I was always on the go, listening and advising, trying to help so many troubled minds to settle down so that they could help themselves. I became a bit of a father figure to many people. I encouraged them to face their negative habits and not kid themselves: to look at their issues honestly and begin to purify them using Buddhist practices. Once their minds became less wild and more malleable, I would reflect back to them that nothing was intrinsically wrong with them. All their negative self-beliefs were simply untrue. In essence, each one of them was unflawed and whole. I then taught them how to practise compassion towards themselves and towards all those they blamed for their troubles, and eventually towards every single living being. And to my absolute joy, in many cases it worked. In this very secure and safe context that we had created people grew more stable. There was less shouting and more laughter, less grievance and more understanding.

The other goal for me, aside from finding a framework for offering ongoing support, was to build up the Sangha, which is the ordained Buddhist community. Most Buddhist practitioners worldwide are laypeople and their role is very important, but in Buddhism the Sangha are regarded as one of the Three Jewels, one of the sources of inspiration and refuge. They are the ones who keep the spirit of the Buddha's teachings, the Dharma, alive. So it's terribly important to have a stable and flourishing Sangha.

It was a great joy for me that Samye Ling was soon full of monks and nuns who lived, volunteered, studied and above all practised in our community. Many of them decided at the end of a year or two or three that they wished to return to mainstream society. They went back out into the world as more positive and mature people. Having found their own inner stability and peace they were now able to offer some loving kindness and compassion to others. Some people did decide that they wanted to take lifelong ordination with a high lama like Tai Situpa or Thrangu Rinpoche, and this too filled me with delight. Many of them have gone on to become stalwarts of the Samye Ling community. Gelong Thubten, for example, who became personal secretary to Akong, initially took one-year ordination in one of the first groups.

Temporary ordination has now been adopted by many Tibetan Buddhist lamas all over the world. When His Holiness the Seventeenth Karmapa later endorsed it, my innovation received the highest blessing and is now part of our lineage in the West. The idea came out of my own lived experience of being miserable and directionless, tempted by superficial and external pleasures. My lack of status as a tulku allowed me first to have these experiences and then to try to create something new from them. I was a nobody in the hierarchy of Tibetan Buddhism, and this gave me an enormous amount of freedom to try things out. Many tulkus have told me that they envied me my opportunities. They admitted that they lacked experience of what ordinary people went through, because they lived a life of privilege and status. I recognize that I have been very fortunate in this regard. To my mind there could be no clearer example of the obstacles being turned into the path.

Having seen what happened when we established temporary ordination, I felt emboldened to take on another issue, namely the lack of full ordination for women within the Tibetan Buddhist tradition. More and more Western women were dedicating their lives to practising the Dharma at Samye Ling, and they felt understandably frustrated and overlooked, because they, unlike their male counterparts, were not able to take full lifelong ordination.

There are three steps in the process of ordination in our Tibetan tradition: the first is *genyen*, which consists of observing lay precepts for varying lengths of time and is a precursor to the second step of getsul, which is novice life ordination, and finally gelong, which is full lifelong ordination, and only available for men. So, for example, most of the Samye Ling Sangha, men and women alike, took genyen vows for one to three years and then moved on to taking getsul vows. After that, men could take full gelong vows but women could not take the equivalent *gelongma* vows because, for some reason unknown to me, the full ordination of women was not preserved as a tradition in Tibet. Either it was lost or it never reached Tibet from India, though it flourished in some other Buddhist traditions; in China, for example.

Whatever the history, I was very aware that equality of opportunity for women was extremely important in our day and age. I suspect that we never did have gelongma (female) ordination in Tibet, because Tibet was a patriarchal society that was unusually closed off from the influence of outside cultures. Tibetan Buddhism had simply reflected the norms of this society. But one thing about Buddhism is that it has always been adaptable and has taken on the flavour of the society it finds itself in. I believed it was time for Tibetan Buddhism to adapt to the contemporary world.

The problem, as with temporary ordination, was that it was impossible for a high lama to take the step of offering something that had no precedent within our tradition. Unbroken lineage is the cornerstone of the Dharma and it is the duty of high lamas to uphold it. Neither His Holiness the Karmapa nor His Holiness the Dalai Lama could promote a system of higher ordination for women, but perhaps I could. Maybe gelongma ordination would gain wider acceptance once it was up and running, as had happened with temporary ordination.

So, once again, I made a decision. I channelled the power of being a nobody and began to explore whether we could establish gelongma ordination in Tibetan Buddhism. I made a connection with the Venerable Master Hsing Yun, a Mahayana teacher in Taiwan who held this lineage of full ordination for women. He and another high lama from Hong Kong were arranging a *bhikkhuni* ordination in Bodhgaya, India, which took place in February 1998. ('Bhikkhuni' is the Sanskrit word for what we call 'gelongma' in Tibetan: a woman who has taken full ordination.) They invited me to be one of twenty-seven preceptors for the ceremony. I was the first Tibetan lama ever to participate in the ordination of women. More than a hundred women and fifty men received full ordination over the course of the ceremony, including eleven nuns from Samye Ling.

His Holiness the Dalai Lama did not attend but he sent a witness. He had been unable to get backing from all his high lamas, some of whom were concerned that they could not know for sure if the Mahayana tradition was a pure, unbroken lineage. They were reluctant to throw their trust behind the move since it departed so significantly from our own tradition. I was neither surprised nor concerned. I understood their reasoning and trusted that this would be a gradual process of change.

I was so proud to participate in the ordination. Preparations took place over nine long and rigorous days and one overnight session. The third and final part of the ceremony, when the Bodhisattva vow is taken, was conducted under the Bodhi Tree where the Buddha attained Enlightenment. This felt hugely profound and significant to me.

In the years since then the changes have become embedded at Samye Ling. There are now more nuns than monks in our community, and there is no hierarchy according to gender anywhere in the organization. Gelongma nuns do not have to sit 'below' gelong monks in the shrine room. Of the four individuals who have been empowered with the title 'lama' since I became abbot (the title recognizes someone who has proved themselves to be a stable and mature practitioner over many years in retreat), three are women. Lama Zangmo, for example, is a Danish woman who was appointed the head of Samye Dzong London, Samye Ling's outpost in the capital, and is one of the most senior people in our organization.

Even more importantly, the innovation has created ripples in the wider world of Tibetan Buddhism, as I hoped. His Holiness the Seventeenth Karmapa has now indicated that he accepts gelongma ordination, receiving all Gelongmas as absolute equals to their male counterparts. He is now working to introduce gelongma ordination throughout the Kagyu lineage. I am so happy to have played a part in creating this opportunity for the many devoted and committed women whose merits are now being properly recognized.

My great aim has always been to give people the conditions they need in order to meditate and mature their minds. This applies just as much to laypeople as it does to monks and nuns. I try to provide a framework that is flexible enough to accommodate people's needs but also gives them clear boundaries.

From the mid-1990s I began to suggest to people who did not wish to take ordination that they might benefit from taking precepts as a layperson, either on a temporary basis or for life. The idea behind precepts is to create an ethical container that holds our spiritual practice. I gave people the opportunity to abide by one or more of the Five Golden Rules. Many people chose to take the precept of not consuming intoxicants, or not engaging in harmful or destructive sexual relationships. If they'd got into the habit of using drugs, including alcohol, or having thoughtless sexual relationships, I would encourage them to swear off these activities for a year. They would take the vow in my presence and I would check in with them regularly to see how they were getting on. I tried to be firm but fair. I would give people three chances before I said, enough. A lot of people benefited from this framework for breaking bad habits, and from our relationship of trust and communication.

Not that I am claiming to be any kind of miracle-worker. Misery is a powerful spell in the mind, which many people find it hard to break free from. It is difficult to stop reinforcing the thoughts that give rise to our misery. I have found that people need a lot of time, a lot of kindness and a lot of patience if they are to change the habits of a lifetime. I was always very sympathetic to people because I had been just like them. I too needed years to build my faith and resolve, and I could not have done it without the unshakeable support of His Holiness the Karmapa and the constant care of my brother Akong. There are few things I love more than welcoming people back, years after the last time I saw them, and listening to their stories of how, in the end, they were able to turn their lives around.

One man who took temporary ordination with me had a terrible time wrestling with his drug addiction. I pretty much locked him up on Holy Isle, which was the ideal location to help people with substance abuse issues, because it was just too hard to get off the island to go looking for supplies! He stayed for a while and then left, came back and had another go, but eventually began using drugs again and disappeared for good. I worried about him but hoped that he had gained enough stability to eventually find his way back to sobriety and a life of peace. Some years later he came to Samye Ling to see me. He had been clean for many years and had married a Nepalese woman, and they were expecting their first child. He looked so well and happy in his life. He very generously thanked me for helping him at a critical time in his life. Being a monk was not for him in the long term, but his time with us gave him the clarity to know that he needed to seek professional help to deal with his addiction. I was so happy for him. He was a changed man from the one I met.

I have learned not to be rigid in my thinking about what change looks like, or how and when it will pan out. It doesn't matter to me whether someone is a monk, a nun or a layperson. All that matters is that they are kind to themselves and others, and tame their own mind. This is the teaching of the Buddha in a nutshell. My whole approach has been built on flexibility, because reality is not as solid as it appears, so it helps to approach it with as few fixed ideas as possible. I always say that our minds should be as flexible as a willow tree – the trunk is solid and rooted but the wind can blow the branches in different directions. When our minds are like this we ourselves are healthy and we can help anyone we meet, because we do not insist on the correctness of any single philosophy or piece of advice. My attempts to help people have always been grounded in trying to identify what it is they need, rather than imposing my ideas on them.

In 2003 I turned sixty. We were coming to the end of the second phase of building work at Samye Ling, to add an accommodation wing for visiting dignitaries as well as resident monks and, downstairs, a large refectory capable of accommodating the many hundreds of people who came to Samye Ling for our bigger events. I could hardly believe it when I walked into my birthday party and saw that the refectory was full of friends and well-wishers who had come from all over the world. I couldn't stop smiling that day, as I listened to music and speeches and watched a beautiful traditional dakini dance performed by a group of nuns. His Holiness the Seventeenth Karmapa had honoured me by writing a long-life prayer, which Akong read out. And at the end of his speech Akong astounded me by announcing that from now on people could address me as Rinpoche, if they wanted.

It is hard to convey to those unfamiliar with the term, which means 'Precious One', exactly why this moved me so much. I do not care for prestige and am not swayed by titles, but, coming from my revered elder brother, this was a lovely gesture. In his speech Akong stressed that the title could be used for teachers who had gained accomplishment through navigating the hard trials of life, as well as the tulkus who were born into such accomplishment. It was a beautiful birthday present.

14.   The great test

On 8 October 2013 I was on Holy Isle, working in the office of our Centre for World Peace, when the phone rang. It was Thubten, Akong's personal secretary, and he was in tears. 'Akong Rinpoche has been killed,' he said.

I froze, struggling to take in what I was hearing. Thubten, who had just taken a call from China, told me that Akong had been attacked by three men in his house in Chengdu, in the Sichuan province of China, where he was staying on his annual trip back to China and the Tibet Autonomous Region. He and Loga, our nephew with whom he had been travelling, as well as an attendant lama from Dolma Lhakang, had all been murdered.

I finished the call in a state of numbness. For a moment, as I sat and contemplated the fact that the world no longer contained my living, breathing brother, I felt nothing at all. I was briefly frightened that the news would overwhelm me, but seconds later I knew that it would not. I felt my mind relax.

I walked out of the building. I needed to be outside, and alone. When I looked up I saw a massive pillar of rainbow-coloured light, coming out of the sea and reaching into the sky above me. It is usual for such natural phenomena to occur when a Bodhisattva is born and when he dies, so I took the pillar of light as an auspicious sign. It gave me comfort and focus as I exerted all my ability to remain absolutely calm and in this present moment. My brother had left this life. Over the course of my lifetime he had been like a mother, father, teacher, sponsor, protector and latterly best friend. He was the central pillar of my life, the person I relied on and loved most in the whole world. Now he was gone. Had I learned enough from him to manage without him?

I remember thinking straight away that I could not falter, because there was going to be an enormous amount to do. Akong Rinpoche was beloved by so many people around the world whose lives he had touched. He had been a key figure in the spread of Tibetan Buddhism throughout the West and lately had become famous for his exceptional contribution to spiritual life and charitable work. There would be an immense outpouring of grief. I was absolutely determined that I would do everything in my power to contain that grief, to support people and to set about honouring the legacy of my brother.

But, of course, I was myself in shock. My initial thought was to tell nobody what had happened until I got back to Samye Ling and had some time to think. I returned to the office, told people that I needed to leave but didn't explain why, and then called Ani Lhamo, my personal assistant of many years' standing. I asked her to drive up from the monastery and pick me up from the ferry terminal in Ardrossan Harbour. When we met she suggested we go for lunch before driving back and, feeling distracted, I agreed. I found I had no appetite, which is most unlike me. In the car I could no longer contain the shocking news. Poor Ani Lhamo was absolutely stunned when I told her and the shock of it hit me again. My brother and two other innocent people had been murdered. How had this unthinkable act occurred?

It took a while for us to piece together the full story, but what seems to have happened is that a man called Thubten

Kunsal, a monk and master craftsman who had spent five years at Samye Ling creating statues and other fine works, had come to see Akong several times in Chengdu about a grievance over money. He claimed that he had not received adequate payment for the work he had carried out, which was absolutely not the case. Knowing that Akong had brought money with him for various Rokpa projects, he demanded an additional large sum.

The first time Thubten Kunsal came, Akong heard him out and then gave him almost £1,000 for urgent medical treatment, because Thubten Kunsal looked so distressed. Akong explained that this was his own money and that the rest of the funds belonged to Rokpa, so there was no way he could hand them over since they were not his to give. Thubten Kunsal came back the next day with two relatives and made another demand, which Akong refused.

On 8 October the three men came back again, armed with knives. There were four people staying in the flat that day: Akong, Loga, the attendant from Dolma Lhakang and a woman, whom Akong told to leave as soon as the three agitated men arrived. A row broke out and Thubten Kunsal and one of his relatives began to attack Akong, who seems to have offered no resistance. Loga and the other monk threw themselves in front of my brother and were themselves fatally attacked. My brother received more than forty stab wounds. The three assailants then ransacked the room looking for valuables and ran off when they were disturbed. The police were called and they found and detained the attackers very quickly. All three confessed to their part in the crime.

On the day I found out he was dead I knew nothing of all this, but I knew that a great test had come and that I needed to rise to the challenge. By the time Ani Lhamo and I arrived back at Samye Ling I had decided to call a meeting of the entire community later that afternoon. I spoke with Akong's wife, Yangchen, who had heard the news via a relative in China. She preferred to stay at home in Dumfries with the children. Ani Lhamo and I rang as many people as we could, told them what had happened and asked them to come. So by early evening Samye Ling was full of people milling around as if in a dream, struggling to fathom what had happened. Many of them were in tears. Others could not speak. For those of us who believe in karma and reincarnation there is the great comfort of knowing that death does not mean the end of an individual consciousness, but that doesn't mean we are immune to shock, sadness and grief at a loved one's passing.

I felt that my first responsibility was to help people to apply everything they had learned through their practice in order to manage their reaction to this event. Given its extremity, this would not be easy. A Buddhist monk, a man many of us had known and liked, had broken the most universal of all precepts: that against killing a fellow human being. How could we respond to this? Many people struggled to believe that it was possible. At this point all I could hang on to was the great example that Akong had left us, so when I stood up to speak, I focused on that. We were standing in the place that represented Akong's extraordinary vision, I said. This building and all of us were here because of him. He had now left us for a while but he would return.

As I was speaking, in that very moment, I had a strong sense that when he did return he would not be wandering around in old clothes, pitching in on the building site and clearing drains. He would be a monk, highly educated and an even greater teacher. This prospect made my heart joyful.

We must make sure that this next incarnation of Akong Tulku Rinpoche finds Samye Ling thriving, as positive as ever, I told everyone. This should be the focus of every single one of us.

I then sat down, tired out by the emotion of speaking but feeling calm and purposeful.

Over the following weeks and months condolences poured in for Akong's wife, children, family and friends from all over the world. Many people simply turned up at our door, needing to be back at the place where they had known him and to be among others who felt the same way about him. There was considerable media interest. Ani Lhamo and others helped me to field our response to all the enquiries and requests, to put out statements and liaise with the authorities in China to arrange for Akong's body to be taken to Dolma Lhakang for cremation. It was, as I had anticipated on Holy Isle as I gazed at the rainbow pillar in the sky, a terribly busy time. As anyone who has been bereaved will know, the death of a loved one is a strange combination of devastating emotion, surreal normality, and lots and lots of admin.

I didn't want the normal routines of the monastery to be entirely disrupted so we carried on with our daily schedule of pujas and teaching. We also said special prayers, every day for forty-nine days, for Akong's easy passage through the period of bardo, the interval between death and rebirth. I asked Tai Situ Rinpoche for guidance on this and he was very supportive. I think it helped people to process their grief. It certainly helped me. Once the deep shock and initial sadness had passed, I felt confident that we would be able to move forwards as Akong would have wished. I knew that some people back in Tibet were already calling for revenge, but I never felt one moment's anger or bitterness towards

Thubten Kunsal. I had known him. He had trusted me. I could not repay this trust with hatred; it would have been the worst possible way to react, for him but also for me. In fact I was really sorry for him. He and the other killers had done a terrible thing, and would suffer for it. Akong, on the other hand, was free and would continue to be so. So I concentrated on consoling others, bringing people together and encouraging them to support one another, and on repaying my enormous debt to my brother by not allowing his death to derail his work.

On the forty-ninth day of prayers I gave a talk to mark their end. I wanted to publicly affirm my absolute commitment to Samye Ling and the Rokpa organization. Before Akong's death I had been considering retiring from the day-to-day running of Samye Ling, going back into retreat and handing responsibility to my nephew, Lama Katen, who is one of my sister Zimey's sons. All that would have to wait. It was not the time for stepping back but for continuity and determination. So I told the community that though I knew I was not half the man that Akong Rinpoche had been, I promised there and then to do everything in my power to build on his legacy.

Throughout this period I continued to meditate for six hours a day, and in late November I decided to go into retreat for three months as I always did at the end of the year. While meditating I recalled something interesting about the events leading up to Akong's departure for China.

In the May before he died we had celebrated my seventieth birthday with a day of festivities at Samye Ling. To my surprise, Akong took charge of the ceremony himself. He installed a throne on the stage of the lecture hall and created a shrine behind it. He then invited me to sit on the throne and he himself stood below me, on the floor, all of which was completely unexpected and in breach of the usual protocol. During the gift-giving, Akong handed me the various gifts from individuals and groups. Samye Dzong in London had arranged for His Holiness the Seventeenth Karmapa to paint a beautiful White Tara thangka for me. White Tara is one of the twenty-one manifestations of Tara, the female Bodhisattva, and is particularly associated with healing and long life, so is a very popular focus for meditation.

I immediately offered the painting to Akong, but he said to me quietly that it would be useless to him once he was dead, and gave it back to me. He then turned to the crowd and announced that from now on Samye Ling would no longer celebrate his birthday, only mine. At the time we had no idea that he would never see another birthday, of course, but the more I reflected, the more convinced I was that Akong had known he was going to die.

There were other incidents. Before Akong left for Tibet he had assembled us, saying, 'Let's all go to Dumfries [to the family home] and take a family photo.' He then asked Kami, his daughter, to look after her mum when he was gone. Normally he took many sacred objects with him to Tibet when he travelled, but on this occasion he left his protection amulets behind. And when I came out of retreat in January 2014 I went straight to my personal shrine to check something. Akong had given me a package before he left on his travels. To my astonishment, when I unwrapped it I found one of his most precious possessions, a sacred Guru Rinpoche *phurba*, which is a ritual dagger that has exceptional protective powers. He had left it behind for me. I was certain that Akong's clairvoyant powers had shown him that his time to die was approaching, so he would have no need of the phurba.

I sat in front of the shrine with the dagger in my hand and felt the blessing of my brother's care for me, which had never faltered. I was full of love, gratitude and admiration. A Bodhisattva uses his death to benefit other human beings. I knew that Akong bore no grudges and wanted only to liberate those who had harmed him. If he could do it, how much more could I?

A year after Akong died the three attackers came to trial. All were convicted and two were given death sentences. Akong's immediate family and all of us at Samye Ling urged the judge not to apply the death penalty, though I do not know whether he did or not. A group of five observers from Samye Ling went to the trial and reported back to us, but once we had made our position plain to the authorities, neither I nor Akong's wife or children felt any engagement with the outcome. We had forgiven Thubten Kunsal and his relatives and it was important to us that they knew this. Beyond that, we wished only to get on with our lives.

There has been a great deal of interest in the question of Akong's reincarnation, and several people in Tibet have presented their children as the third Akong Tulku, but as yet he has not been identified. My brother spoke to me briefly about this and said that only His Holiness the Karmapa or Tai Situ Rinpoche would be able to identify his reincarnation. I have made a vow not to bring the wrong child to Samye Ling but to wait patiently until the authentic incarnation appears and is identified. I very much hope that I will meet my brother again in my current lifetime.

Since Akong died I have felt no attachment to any personal preference. I have come to a place of acceptance and surrender and appreciation. I owe this to Akong. When he was alive I still had the feeling that I should be spending more time in retreat, but when he died I let go of that desire. I see this in terms of karma. Sometimes it is good karma, like Holy Isle, which just landed in my lap. At other times it is more difficult karma, but in either case there is no choice but to accept it. When you believe in karma, as I do, it makes it easier to work with whatever life throws at you.

Readiness is crucial, though, and must be worked for. We need to train for the bad times by never wasting any of the opportunities for learning that our human life affords us. Unlike animals, much less the hungry ghosts and other unfortunate beings in any of the other realms, human beings have an amazing capacity for self-awareness, insight, and changing how we think and behave. The ultimate fruition of this is Enlightenment, which is the complete flowering of our innate capacity for wisdom and compassion. It is such a tragedy that so many of us squander the opportunities of this lifetime. For myself, I have no doubt that were it not for my many years of devoted practice to the wisdom of the Buddha and the ways of Dharma, the death of my brother would have been a blow from which I would not have recovered. If he had been murdered when I was thirty-five, full of pride and deluded self-belief, and stuck in deep confusion, I suspect I would have been submerged by grief and anger. I would have been trapped in rumination about that hideous day and unable to move away from my own pain. As it was, my mind was able to absorb the emotional impact and recover itself.

I say this not to praise myself as some sort of exceptional being, only to reiterate that our minds are in fact capable of extraordinary feats. All of our minds. Yours as well as mine. But this positive outcome was possible only thanks to years of training in meditation and the practice of compassion. It was made possible by my devotion to the path of Dharma. In fact, it was made possible by my brother, who taught me and supported me. He knew, all his life, that we must be ready for whatever change may come. Since he embodied this awareness, I have no doubt that he was ready for the end.

15. More work to do . . .

I did not expect that my life would turn out as it has. At no stage, as I moved from Tibet to India to Scotland to the States and back to Scotland again, could I have predicted what was coming next. I certainly did not imagine, in Dolma Lhakang or in the refugee camps of India, that it would be so happy, so peaceful and joyful. I feel lucky. Being grateful is the basis of much of my happiness. Seeing things flexibly is another important element. Letting go of the conviction that life must be a certain way and accepting the way it actually is, in the here and now, has helped me. Learning to relinquish my attachments to outcomes, to let go of my desires and purify my negative mind states, has all been beneficial. The engine for all this change has been my practice of meditation and it has served me well. It has enabled me to help others to move towards a state of peace, calm and joy.

Not long ago I turned seventy-five. People at Samye Ling were kind enough to organize a party. To show their appreciation of my commitment to them and their commitment to me, they offered me several sets of monks' robes. These I offered to others. Some people also said very generous things about my role in the ongoing success of Samye Ling. I do not want to claim credit for anything, since without the devoted efforts of so many hundreds of people, especially Akong, we would not have enjoyed the successes we have had. I believe that any positive impact in the world is the result of devotion, hard work and the right motivation, and it makes me so happy to see that

Samye Ling and the wider Rokpa organization of which it is a part are moving in a profoundly positive direction.

I'm still amazed sometimes, as I walk in the Peace Gardens or spot the beautiful golden spire of the Victory Stupa radiating positive energy far and wide, to think that all this has been brought into existence in this unlikely place, for the benefit of every sentient being. It's a long time since I sulked in Johnstone House, furious with the drab cold world I found myself in, railing against the smelly hippies and my brother Akong for bringing me here. Now Samye Ling is known around the world as a place of retreat, learning and faith.

My part in this great team effort has been small but I hope it's been useful. I've always tried to understand what people need, to listen to what they tell me and think flexibly in order to find ways for them to access the unparalleled wisdom of the Dharma. This has often meant being something of a father figure, a giver of advice and setter of boundaries. The word 'guru' is a very loaded term in English, and it doesn't sit that comfortably with me, because it carries connotations of someone who is high and mighty. I prefer a more straightforward approach. I see myself as someone who has been through a lot in his life, and I can offer people the wisdom that comes directly from my own experience. Part of my job as a teacher has been to point out the issues and flaws within my students which they cannot see or do not want to see. Some of my students used to call me a 'truth doctor' because I wanted to tell them the truth and not beat around the bush. But another very important part of being a teacher is to point out the hidden jewel of our wisdom to us – our Buddha Nature – which many people are unwilling to own, because they see themselves as limited and small. This has been a crucial part of my role: to empower people. Our teacher is the person who believes in us when we can't yet believe in ourselves. In my own life this has above all been His Holiness the Sixteenth Karmapa. I aspire to be for others as he has been to me, despite the fact I lack so many of his great qualities.

I was asked a couple of years ago to write some words for a friend's wedding. I started to write a tongue-in-cheek take on Christianity's Ten Commandments, calling it the Ten Commandments for a Happy Marriage. I was pleased to find that it raised a smile. Admittedly I've never been married and all my romantic relationships back in the day were built around the needs of my ego, so I might seem an unlikely person to give relationship advice. But I've spent many years in the lab of the mind, talking to people from every walk of life, and I have observed a great deal and learned a little. Now I'm turning the Ten Commandments into a guide for my married students. My first precept is to stop looking for faults in the other person. The second is to be mindful of the other's good qualities. Love is nourished by focusing on the positive and not dwelling on the negative, especially resentment. The third is to refrain from imposing your own ideas on the other. The fourth is to respect them at all times. The fifth is to live by the Five Golden Rules, the sixth is to always bring awareness to how you think, what you say and what you do, and make sure it is not hurtful, harmful or selfish. Number seven is to look beyond your partnership and engage in your community. Number eight is to always take refuge in Buddha, Dharma and Sangha. Number nine is to make these principles an active part of your life through meditating on them. They're no use if you don't apply them. And, finally, number ten is to truly engage in the practice of unconditional compassion, loving kindness and forgiveness. If both people in the partnership do this, then they will have a fulfilling life together.

As I grow older I come to see more clearly the things that are within my power to offer to others, as well as those tasks left for me to tackle. I have been privileged to represent Samye Ling and a wider British Buddhist community at a number of interfaith events over the years, for example. I visited the Vatican in 1989 as part of a convention to increase dialogue between Buddhism and Catholicism. I attended two meetings on religion and environmentalism organized by the World Wide Fund for Nature at Windsor Castle, as well as an event run by the Scottish Interfaith Council, which was set up after the terrorist attacks of 11 September 2001 to do more work to break down barriers between religious groups.

I think this has all come about because of karma. It reflects the fact that I have been in the UK for so long now that I've learned how to really communicate with people. I don't just mean the language, though that helps. I mean years of living here as a layperson and even more years as a monk, meeting people from every walk of life. Being able to imagine the viewpoint of others underlies all attempts to boost understanding. Buddhism has much to say about the principle of breaking down the difference between self and other, increasing empathy and turning it into active compassion. I am always delighted when I'm able to talk about these ideas, whether with the Archbishop of Canterbury or somebody struggling in one of our retreats.

The practice of meditation is still the cornerstone of my life. Lately Lama Katen, my nephew, has been stepping up to take over the day-to-day running of Samye Ling, which makes me very happy. Finally I get to sit in my little house at Purelands and meditate all day! I am constantly inspired by Nelson Mandela's words about the value of meditation. Mandela meditated in his prison cell every day for many years. He found meditation a useful tool to bring about the internal changes that are the true markers of our development as a human being. In 1975, when he was nearly twelve years into his imprisonment, he wrote a letter to his wife, Winnie, who at the time was also in jail. He suggested to her that a cell was 'an ideal place to learn to know yourself, to search realistically and regularly the process of your own mind and feelings . . . to overcome the bad and develop whatever is good in you'. This, he assured her, would lead to more important benefits than any marker of worldly success such as wealth, social position, popularity or education. He identified 'Honesty, sincerity, simplicity, humility, pure generosity, absence of vanity, readiness to serve others – qualities which are within easy reach of every soul – [as] the foundation of one's spiritual life'. He also gave very clear and simple guidance on how to cultivate these good qualities. 'Regular meditation, say about fifteen minutes a day before you turn in, can be very fruitful . . . You may find it difficult at first to pinpoint the negative features in your life but the tenth attempt may yield rich rewards. Never forget that a saint is a sinner who keeps trying.'

I suspect I may never do another dark retreat, though I will never say never. I did my third one back in June 2009, in a purpose-built cabin at Purelands. Life was particularly busy at that time so I pretty much ran from the office straight to the retreat house. It was the beginning of summer, but I realized quite quickly (though only once I was locked in with shutters down and the power off) that I didn't have enough clothes with me. Summer is no guarantee of good weather in Scotland and that year was very wet and cold. I was so cold that I hardly slept. Now what was I going to do? I remembered that Milarepa had said he didn't need to sleep, so I just decided to rejoice in the lack of sleep. When I got tired I sat in the bamboo chair that was the only furniture apart from my meditation box.

Perhaps it was the almost total lack of sleep, but I found myself disorientated at various points despite my two previous experiences of dark retreat. I felt unsure of the space as I groped round to the bathroom, clinging on to the handrail. I could not tell my left from my right. I must have banged my head on the wall every single time I stood up from the toilet! I also lost track of time. One day Tsering Tashi, who was my attendant throughout this retreat, brought me lunch as usual but I didn't notice it. The following day I was confused to find two trays. I had missed a whole twenty-four hours.

I also experienced a very unpleasant hallucination. I looked down at my body and saw that one leg and one arm were absolutely crawling with maggots. It felt as if my arm was actually coming away from my body. Fortunately I was prepared for this sort of thing. I was able to touch my arm and experience that it didn't feel bad and wasn't coming off, even though what I could see seemed absolutely real.

I think this was the best of my three dark-retreat experiences, because I completely lost all sense of day and night, had no need of sleep and managed to see through the unpleasant hallucination. Once again I completed forty-nine days in total darkness and silence without the daily support of a mentor. I am the only person in the world (as far as I know!) who has accomplished this and am proud that my brother Akong asked me to carry the dark-retreat lineage on his behalf, which means that I can pass on the teaching to others.

As I've said previously, dark retreat is certainly not for everyone, but for those who have truly stabilized their mind it offers unparalleled opportunities to experience selflessness and the illusory nature of reality. Interestingly neuroscience is increasingly demonstrating the neural basis for the way our brain creates our own subjective reality. The brain perpetually filters the information it receives from our sense organs and uses it to build a coherent understanding of the world 'out there' beyond us, as well as an interior sense of self. This is an enormous job, so to make things easier the brain makes assumptions about what the sense organs are perceiving. It filters the information through a set of beliefs about the world based on what it (or rather, the eyes) has seen before, for example. The latest research suggests that what we experience as objective reality, as well as our subjective self, is in fact the unique products of our brain's attempt to impose order on this blizzard of incoming signals. Each one of us will come up with a slightly different model of what we perceive. I recently read an interesting piece of writing by Anil Seth, Professor of Cognitive Neuroscience at the University of Sussex, which explored this. His conclusion was that we don't observe the world so much as generate it. Reality is the product of a conscious hallucination. This is not to say it doesn't have meaning, only that it isn't solid as we tend to assume but fluid, and very much shaped by the projections of our own minds.

I find this description of how we create our own reality absolutely compelling. It feels like what I experienced first hand in dark retreat. My only niggle is with the insistence on the brain rather than mind. For us Buddhists the brain and the mind are not synonymous. But that's a whole other topic!

In June 2017 I welcomed His Holiness the Seventeenth Karmapa to Samye Dzong London, our centre in the capital city. It was his first visit to the UK. He was much more grown up but just as gracious, relaxed and generous with his wisdom as he had been on the day I met him, back in 1992.

As always, he was accompanied by representatives of the

Indian government, and his movements were tightly controlled. On a previous visit to see him in India I was frustrated at the lack of time alone with His Holiness, in which I could talk to him freely. I missed the complete ease of my interactions with His Holiness's predecessor. We were able to speak a little more intimately over lunch and His Holiness told me that he felt very trapped by the restrictions of his lifestyle. He once refused the gift of a caged bird, presented to him by a follower who knew how much his predecessor had loved them, saying poignantly that he would never keep caged birds since he himself knew what it was like to live in a cage.

I could not contain my joy at seeing him in my adopted home country. I felt the unbroken connection with his predecessor, who had changed my relationship with mind and enabled me to change my way of life. My heart was full of gratitude. I've noticed that in all the photos taken that day I am beaming from ear to ear as I sat at His Holiness's feet.

When I think about His Holiness the Karmapa I feel hopeful about the future. He is a high lama who is very much a product of our times and for that reason I am certain that he will exert a huge influence. He speaks fluent Mandarin and English. He is the first lama of his status to accept nuns on an equal footing to monks and has been working to restore full ordination for women within our Tibetan tradition since 2013. His Holiness has begun to invite Chinese nuns to the Monlam, the annual Kagyu prayer festival in Bodhgaya in India, so they can pass the lineage to Tibetan Buddhist nuns. This gesture is typical of his non-sectarian approach. He is actively seeking to unite the various schools of Buddhism.

He is also an environmentalist. He himself is vegetarian and in 2007 insisted that the kitchens in all Kagyu monastic institutions worldwide refrain from cooking meat. He has also encouraged all lay supporters to eat less meat. This obviously derives in part from the Buddhist prohibition against killing any living being, but His Holiness the Karmapa also emphasizes the value of a diet that puts less pressure on the environment. He has requested that every Kagyu monastery make environmental concerns a top priority, with a particular focus on tree-planting programmes and on switching to clean energy sources and minimizing energy consumption. All of this seems to me to be absolutely right. Buddhism teaches that every creature is profoundly interconnected with every other. Modern life has encouraged us to think that we humans are separate and superior from the rest of the natural world, but, of course, this is a dangerous, ego-driven illusion. Ever since the early days of the Holy Isle project I have felt that Buddhism has a useful perspective to offer on the climate and biodiversity crises because of its profound sense of the sacredness of all life. As His Holiness said in an interview with *Yale Environment 360* in 2015, 'The environmental emergency that we face is not just a scientific issue, nor is it just a political issue, it is also a moral issue. [A]ll of us . . . have to pick up our share of the responsibility to find and implement solutions.'

I feel fortunate to have known two incarnations of His Holiness the Gyalwa Karmapa and to witness their impact on the world. I have learned so much from them, and am very grateful. I certainly needed all the guidance they and Akong could give me. I was not born a highly realized being like my brother, or Trungpa, much less His Holiness the Karmapa. Any scrap of insight I've attained has been the result of efforts I have made in this lifetime with the support of my gurus.

During my early life I was exposed to amazing Buddhist teachers, but I could not appreciate them or get any genuine feeling for them. The first thirty-seven years of my life were spent floundering. I needed to go through many difficulties to arrive at the point where I could see clearly enough to penetrate the overwhelming stupidity of my mind! This process required patience but allowed me to develop a better understanding of the difficulties people face. Ultimately it has meant that I've been in a good position to help them.

When I began to lead the retreats at Samye Ling I realized the potential of all that I had gone through. The transformation of my own mind, even though it was long and arduous and could not have happened without the help of my teachers, had equipped me to support others to bring about their own changes. This realization made me proud to be a nobody and very appreciative of the lack of constraints that high lamas operate within. It became my mission to bring the Buddha's wisdom within everyone's reach, and I regard this book as the latest step in that process.

I have always tried to make the Buddha's teachings accessible and to present them in simple language that anyone can understand. I want the Dharma to touch people's hearts, not to get stuck in their complicated heads! I've observed that some Western people struggle to appreciate this approach. Either they are very identified with their intelligence, so they feel they are already knowledgeable and find the Dharma too simplistic, or they have a soft heart but they don't realize the essence of mind. Compassion has been awakened, but there is not yet enough wisdom to support it.

There is also the fact that many Westerners are suspicious of religion in general and make the mistake of thinking of Buddhism as a religion that worships the Buddha like a god. This could not be further from the case. 'Buddha' is really nothing more than a metaphor for a state of awareness we can realize in ourselves.

Mine is a deeply practical approach to Buddhism. We take refuge in the Buddha because we are grateful to him for showing us the path to freedom, but we recognize that Buddha is within each one of us as a potential. We take refuge in the Dharma because we need methods and practices to awaken that potential within us. Finally, we take refuge in the Sangha because we need the support and guidance of those who possess the Buddha's knowledge, to guide us on the path towards that potential.

I always say to my students that they don't need to identify with the label of being a Buddhist. It is better to work directly with their own mind than to 'be a Buddhist'. Practise meditation, cultivate positivity and live according to the Five Golden Rules. Resolve to become a loving and compassionate person. All Buddhist practice boils down to uprooting the poisons of aversion, attachment and ignorance. When you are truly looking inwards and trying to transform yourself rather than looking at the faults of others then you are a good human being. Only then can you be a Buddhist.

I am not a psychologist and have never aspired to be a therapist, but I absolutely believe, and this is borne out by decades of working with countless people, that positive change is possible for every one of us. It is all about working with our mind. The mind is the source of both our happiness and our confusion. The key question to ask ourselves in order to move away from confusion and towards happiness is, 'What am I feeding? Am I feeding the negative habits or the positive tendencies?' We can be digging a hole in the garden or bathing our children at night; doing the end of year accounts or chanting mantras; but, whatever it is, we must ask ourselves this question. It is much better to dig a hole mindfully, taking pleasure in the physical exertion and the turning of the soil, than to chant mantras in a distracted way, stewing over some past grievance. The right motivation is a habit of mind. So are awareness and compassion. If we put in the hard work, if we have willpower and determination, we can do anything. Dharma is tried and tested and has never failed in 2,600 years, since the time of the Buddha. I invite you to discover its merits and benefits for yourself and to patiently work through the obstacles that will inevitably arise on this profound path to the complete ripening of your potential as a human being.

Glossary

baa	a tepee-style tent made from yak hair
bardo	the forty-nine-day period after death and before rebirth, when a being's consciousness is in a suspended state
bep	a jumping movement performed during the practice of the Six Yogas of Naropa, in which the practitioner leaps up and lands in full lotus
bhikkhuni	Sanskrit word for full-life ordination for women
Bodhicitta	the deep aspiration to attain Enlightenment so that we may bring all other sentient beings to Enlightenment
Bodhisattva	a person who has taken a vow to work for the Enlightenment of all sentient beings
Bon	(adj. **Bönpo**) an ancient pantheistic religion that reflected Tibetan people's reverence for the natural world
chakras	psychic-energy centres in the body
chang	mild barley beer, brewed and drunk by Tibetans
chuba	an ankle-length robe for a layperson, tied at the waist with a sash
dakini	a female expression of wisdom energy, similar to the Christian angel
Dharma	the teachings of the Buddha
dogpa	a traditional expulsion ritual, to ward off malign forces
Dorje Sempa	a purification practice that involves reciting a 100-syllable mantra 100,000 times

dri   a female yak

drog-khyi   or nomad dog, which is known in the West as a Tibetan mastiff

dukkha   suffering

dzo   a male yak–ox crossbreed

dzomo   female yak–cow crossbreed

gelong   full life ordination for men

gelongma   full life ordination for women

genyen   beginner-level vows taken by a layperson as the first step towards ordination

getsul   novice life ordination for both men and women

Green Tara   a female Bodhisattva strongly associated with compassion, healing and protection

guru   literally, the Sanskrit word for 'teacher'; esteemed teacher

Kangyur   the sacred texts made up of the words of the Buddha

karma   this key doctrine says that all of our thoughts, speech and actions as well as the emotions that drive them, shape both this life and our lives to come

Karma Kagyu   the particular school of Tibetan Buddhism, or lineage (one of four) to which LYR belongs

Karma Pakshi   Second Karmapa

Khampa   person from Kham, in east Tibet

khenpo   the equivalent in the West would be a PhD-level scholar; someone who has completed a long programme of specialist study within a religious institution

klesha   mind poison; emotional affliction; the three root kleshas of ignorance, attachment and aversion give rise to all the others, such as anger, fear, jealousy and pride

Glossary

krapse   deep-fried biscuits, eaten at the Tibetan New Year

labrang   the institution set up to preserve the wealth and religious artefacts of a spiritual teacher in the time after his death and before the next incarnation is recognized; the building where a particular teacher lives during his lifetime alongside the treasures and sacred texts that are part of his line of transmission

lama   the nearest translation would be 'priest'; a person of authority in the hierarchy of monks or nuns; an esteemed teacher

Losar   the Tibetan New Year, which typically falls in late February in the Western calendar

mala   a string of (usually 108) beads, similar to a rosary

Mandala Offering   a practice concerned with accumulating merit and wisdom

mantra   a sound, word, or series of words repeated over and over again in order to focus our mind and invoke blessings

mara   the Sanskrit word for 'obstacle'

momo   steamed dumplings, a Tibetan delicacy

mudras   hand gestures

Ngöndro   the Four Foundation practices, the core preliminary practices of Tibetan Buddhism

Padmasambhava   the eighth-century Indian Buddhist master who brought Buddhism to Tibet; in Tibet he is known as Guru Rinpoche and is regarded almost as a second Buddha

phurba   a ritual dagger with protective powers

pujas   prayer rituals, like a service in a church, involving chanting, mantras and visualizations

radong   a musical instrument, a very long horn, a little like a trumpet, used in pujas

Rinpoche   an honorific title, literally meaning 'Precious One'; a mark of deep respect and devotion to an outstanding teacher

samsara   the endless cycle of birth, death and rebirth that can only be broken by attaining Enlightenment

sang   fragrant smoke offerings made to welcome guests

Sangha   the ordained community of Buddhist monks and nuns

shinay   calm-abiding meditation; this is similar to the modern practice of mindfulness, in which we bring our attention repeatedly back to a focal point such as our breath, in order to calm our mind and bring awareness to our thoughts

stupa   a shrine containing relics and sacred texts, particularly relics of the Buddha; typically shaped like a tower with a dome and then a spire on top; the stupa radiates positive energy throughout the world and is a focus for devotion

sutras   written records of the oral teachings of the Buddha

tantra   a later development of Buddhism and one of the hallmarks of the Tibetan tradition

thangka   a religious painting, usually on silk or fine cotton, typically depicting a particular deity, saint or mandala, such as Green Tara

tra   a mirror divination, invoking the help of protective deities

tsampa   the staple foodstuff for Tibetans, a mix of roasted wheat or barley flour and salty butter tea, rolled up into balls

tulku   a reincarnate lama

tummo   inner-heat practice; a purification practice that generates heat in the body

Glossary

Vajrayana   the third of the three historical phases in the development of Buddhist teaching and practice

Vajrayogini   one of the main tantric deities of the Kagyu lineage, red-coloured, female and wrathful

wangkur   rite of empowerment conducted by a master to initiate practitioners in to particular tantric practice

yidam   an expression of our innate Buddha Nature; a deity

Reading list

Books on Buddhism and Buddhist practice:

Chödrön, Pema; *When Things Fall Apart*, Boulder, Colo.: Shambhala Publications, Inc., 1997

Dalai Lama, The, *An Introduction to Buddhism*, Boulder, Colo.: Shambhala Publications, Inc., 2004

Nairn, Rob, Choden, and Heather Regan-Addis, *From Mindfulness to Insight*, Boulder, Colo.: Shambhala Publications, Inc., 2019

Rinpoche, Chöje Lama Yeshe Losal, *Living Dharma*, Karma Samye Ling Monastery: Dzalendara Publishing, 2008

Thubten, Gelong, *A Monk's Guide to Happiness*, London: Hodder & Stoughton, 2019

Trungpa, Chögyam, *Cutting Through Spiritual Materialism*, Boston, Mass.: Shambhala Publications, Inc., 1973

Trungpa, Chögyam, *Shambhala: The Sacred Path of the Warrior*, Boston, Mass.: Shambhala Publications, Inc., 1984

Biographies and memoirs of people mentioned in this book:

Brown, Mick, *The Dance of 17 Lives: The Incredible True Story of Tibet's 17th Karmapa*, London: Bloomsbury, 2004

Drodül, Lama Karma, *Amrita of Eloquence: A Biography of Khenpo Karthar Rinpoche*, Woodstock, NY: KTD Publications, 2009

Levine, Norma (ed.), *The Miraculous 16th Karmapa: Incredible Encounters with the Black Crown Buddha*, Merigar, Italy: Shang Shung Publications, 2013

Reading list

Lhalungpa, Lobsang P. (trans.), *The Life of Milarepa*, Kathmandu: Pilgrims Book House, 1997

Mackenzie, Vicki, *The Revolutionary Life of Freda Bedi: British Feminist, Indian Nationalist, Buddhist Nun*, Boulder, Colo.: Shambhala Publications, Inc., 2017

MacLean, Grant, *From Lion's Jaws: Chögyam Trungpa's Epic Escape to the West*, Mountain, 2016

Mukpo, Diana J., *Dragon Thunder: My Life with Chögyam Trungpa*, Boston, Mass.: Shambhala Publications, Inc., 2006

Naher, Gaby, *Wrestling the Dragon: In Search of the Boy Lama Who Defied China*, Melbourne, Vic.: Random House Australia, 2004

Trungpa, Chögyam, *Born in Tibet*, London: Allen & Unwin, 1966

Whitehead, Andrew, *The Lives of Freda: The Political, Spiritual and Personal Journeys of Freda Bedi*, New Delhi: Speaking Tiger Publishing, 2019

Acknowledgements

Many people have helped make this book happen and I would particularly like to thank two of them. Helen has been the most wonderful person to collaborate with; she was easy and sympathetic and a joy to work with. And Torey, who started the writing, with her confidence and experience, put together the initial section so perfectly that only success could follow! I offer my heartfelt thanks to both of them.